T0341864

Secret Witness

SECRET WITNESS

The Untold Story of the 1967 Bombing in Marshall, Michigan

BLAINE L. PARDOE

The University of Michigan Press
Ann Arbor

Copyright © by the University of Michigan 2012
All rights reserved

This book may not be reproduced, in whole or in part, including illustrations, in any form
(beyond that copying permitted by Sections 107 and 108 of the U.S. Copyright Law and
except by reviewers for the public press), without written permission from the publisher.

Published in the United States of America by
The University of Michigan Press
Printed and bound by CPI Group (UK) Ltd, Croydon, CR0 4YY

2015   2014   2013   2012   4   3   2   1

A CIP catalog record for this book is available from the British Library.

ISBN 978-0-472-11823-6 (cloth : alk. paper)
ISBN 978-0-472-03502-1 (pbk. : alk. paper)
ISBN 978-0-472-02846-7 (e-book)

This book is dedicated to my family still back in Michigan—
   Dave and Rose Pardoe
   Jim and Marlene Pardoe
   Chris and Don Miller
   Sarah Miller
   Kari Pardoe

—and to Win Schuler's, the Hi-Lite, Roma's Cafe, and Louie's Bakery in Marshall. Some of my best memories are stirred with the flavors of these establishments.

A part of me is always there . . .

Preface

In writing this book, I relied heavily on the investigation files from the crime and augmented my research with supporting interviews. Where possible, I have employed a technique to change the names of individuals to avoid embarrassment to families. The names that have been changed are marked with an asterisk (*) in the list of characters in the back of the book and at their first occurrences in the text. Marshall is a very small and closed Michigan community, and revealing the names, especially those associated with adulterous acts, might prove embarrassing for some families. Names that I could not alter include those of families directly tied to the crime, such as the Puyears and Chisms. This was one of the most celebrated and notorious murders to take place in Calhoun County, and the names of those tied directly to the case are known and are presented here.

Memories often are corrupted over time, weathered and worn. Those associated with the case are bound to see things they might not remember specifically. Any errors are unintentional, and I assume the blame for them as the author.

Finally, I encourage anyone reading this book to go to Marshall for yourself. Walk its streets. Meet its people. See the places I have written about. You won't be disappointed.

Acknowledgments

A large number of people were instrumental in helping make this book a reality. This list is far from inclusive. Any omissions are purely my fault and not intentional.

Jean Armstrong, my friend and a dedicated researcher, who postulated some of the more entertaining theories

Ellen McCarthy, acquisitions editor at the University of Michigan Press, who always understood that this story was more than what it appeared

John Jereck

Bert Schulz

Ronald DeGraw

Fred Ritchie

John Lohrstorfer

Don Damon

Herold Reuss

Lewis Shellenberger

My uncle Jim Pardoe, who seemed to field more tips than I managed

Marshall Public Library staff, particularly Beth Dowson

Marshall Ad-Visor & Chronicle staff, especially Donna Daines, who penned an article about this book and generated a number of wonderful leads

Wendy Draper at the Calhoun County Sheriff's Department

Toni A. Fritz, chief deputy clerk of the Thirty-Seventh Circuit Court of Michigan

Willard Library staff, Battle Creek, Michigan, particularly George Livingston and Ed Groff

Kelly Fenwick and Greg Kenney

Cecilia Beck

Contents

Author's Note

Every small town has a moment when it changes—when the real world abruptly intrudes on it and shatters its notions of itself and its people. For the citizens of Marshall, Michigan, that moment came on the hot morning of August 18, 1967, at 9:03 a.m. The event that turned people's view of Marshall was hideously violent and savage, a drama that played out on the main street of the town and behind the closed bedroom doors of its citizens. It was not just a murder but a seemingly random bombing of a well-known and loved local woman. And it led to police prying open the seamy private lives of some of the citizens in search of a devious killer.

In researching this book, I heard a common theme in my interviews about the change that came about in the Calhoun County community. Until the murder on August 18, there had never been a reason for citizens to lock their doors or look at mailed packages as potential threats. That changed overnight. There was a killer in their town. The citizens instinctively knew that and reacted to that grim realization. They started to look at their neighbors and scrutinized their actions out of fear—fear that one of them was a violent murderer. A normally open and quiet community was forced to open its dirty little secrets and was appalled at what it saw.

Even today, Marshall appears, at first glance, to be the set for a 1950s TV sitcom. If you were to ask me what town it resembled, I'd say the closest would be Andy Griffith's Mayberry. For visitors, Marshall appears trapped in a time, like an antique sepia image from another era. It is an image that the citizens strive to maintain. The people who live there thrive on small-town life and are deeply protective of the illusion of timelessness.

Marshall's immaculate main street, Michigan Avenue, is bounded by a magnificent white pillared Brooks fountain and driving circle to the west. The east end of town is marked by the red-bricked GAR building, with its distinctive Civil War cannon and pile of cannonballs. Between these landmarks is the kind of small city featured on postcards to show off quaint streets and pristine businesses.

Marshall is a small place where homecoming is celebrated by the whole town and where you can tell where you stand on Michigan Avenue by the power of the smell of fresh bread from Louie's Bakery. Magnificent elms, maples, and oaks—some nearly a century old—line the side streets, as if they crept out of a Norman Rockwell painting. The black squirrels flirt with traffic on the shaded streets during the spring and summer. With only five thousand people in the city limits, it is difficult to walk down the street without someone recognizing and calling out to you. Over the years, all that really has seemed to change about the city is the style of cars. Most things don't seem to have changed with the passage of time. Instead, they have become more quaint.

The people of Marshall are warm, friendly, and very protective of the reputation of their small town. Marshallites covet the town's appearances and the way it still clings to the 1950s imagery. You are often identified by your last name: "Which member of your family are you related to?" Strangers stand out, and that is considered acceptable. Your ability to fit in is often governed by who you know and how you know them. Like many small towns, it is a closed community. Newcomers are welcome . . . over time . . . eventually.

The brutal bombing/murder that took place in 1967 shattered some of that idyllic illusion in which the little city wallowed. Marshall was no longer able to cling to its peaceful past but was violently thrown into modern times. Before that autumn, innocence reigned. After it, things would never quite be the same. Marshall's prized innocence was lost, and like the proverbial genie, it couldn't be put back in the bottle.

I was in Marshall, Michigan, on August 18, 1967, when the murder took place. Though I was only four years old at the time, I remember it vaguely, because it was the first time in my life that I saw adults afraid. We lived ten miles away from Marshall, but it was my hometown, and the bloody terror that was unleashed there reached every home in the surrounding communities. My own memories are not entirely clear. I never heard the explosion, but I remember the police coming and trying

A postcard of Marshall's Michigan Avenue in the year of the explosion. (*From the author's personal collection.*)

to relay information to the concerned mothers in Ketchum Park that day. I remember the sirens and the crowds that were drawn into the heart of town to see the scene of the crime.

I had to do this book if only because it was history—a history that people wanted to forget—and because it subtly altered this small town. When I began to speak to people, I got their jumbled memories of real events. But what I got more often than not were the rumors that circulated both about the victim and the murderer. The rumors had a life of their own but were not as tantalizing as the truth. These inconsistent memories of citizens intrigued me to begin to look into the facts of the case. The collective memory of the community was tainted and remembered events often in a very different light than reality.

The crime itself was hideously violent—a bombing that disemboweled the victim. Anyone wanting to kill someone would be hard pressed to find a more vicious manner than blowing the person up. Such a brutal act seemed to demand it being a crime of passion. The fact that it took place on the main street was blatant and defiant.

The investigation into this murder was incredible, because it was good old-fashioned police work. In an era before the technology-laden *CSI Miami,* a team of investigators from multiple jurisdictions came together and worked to solve the crime. What they uncovered about pastoral Marshall and its citizens was stunning and embarrassing. The sexual escapades of the mild-mannered citizens of the community were horribly laid bare during the investigation, as the team attempted to find the killer. These tawdry sexcapades were swept under the proverbial rug discreetly, to ensure that they did not come out at trial. Marshall's dirty side, a side the general public never saw, was carefully protected.

The killer was, in many respects, brilliant but diabolically twisted and violent. As I researched this crime, what dumbfounded me was the motive he had—or, better yet, lacked. The motive was so disproportionate to the staggering viciousness of the murder that it was hard for me to comprehend. Then it hit me: for the first time, I got a clear glimpse into madness and true evil. Pure evil requires no motive, only an opportunity.

While I was raised in the area, I have since moved away, returning to where I was born, in Virginia. Distance, in this case, offers perspective and a certain degree of objectivity in writing about the case. Many of the parties involved still live in the area. Relatives of the victim and the murderer still live in Marshall. If I still lived in Michigan, my interpretation of the events related to the case might have been tainted.

The events of the autumn of 1967 go beyond Marshall, Michigan. They could mirror *any* small town in America. The events in this book tell the story of what happens when any community goes from being one of open trust to one of fear-filled terror and mutual suspicion. Marshall is the home of my youth, but it could just as easily be your hometown anywhere in America.

To fully understand this crime and its impact on the town, you have to go back in time and onto the main street of Marshall on that fateful day . . .

Prologue

Delivery of Death

My own memory of that day is that the center of town was like a magnet, drawing every person to the scene of the crime. Looking back, I realize that an odd mix of morbid curiosity and terror took hold of the people. The fear in the air was like electricity, but as a four-year-old, I didn't understand why. I could tell something was wrong. I was in Marshall a great deal as a child, and the sounds of sirens and the gathering crowd told me that something new and unique had happened.

In an era before mobile devices, Facebook updates, and Twitter tweets, the word spread like a brush fire through town. All the people who spread a rumor or passed the word on added their own spins, their own thoughts or suspicions. Most of these would live on and be treated as gospel, since real information was hard to come by.

Marshall postman Donald Damon, who had taken Thursday off, leaving his rounds to another carrier, was back on duty that Friday morning. The day was hot and humid, typical for mid-Michigan summer. As Don walked his rounds from business to business, he was greeted with a chorus of hello's and salutations. In a town the size of Marshall, the postman was often a fixture, a friendly face that everyone knew by name. Everyone greeted him on his route, with friendly nods, cordial waves, smiles. The morning pavement was already starting to get hot in the sun, and in two hours, he would feel the heat through the soles of his shoes, as if he were walking across a hot grill. The postman did not wear shorts but was decked out in long blue pants and a tieless blue uniform shirt.

Damon was highly patterned in his rounds. He was the kind of postman against whom you could set your watch. Always charming, always friendly, he was proud of the fact that he was in the same place at the same time every day. People relied on such patterns in their life.

The buzz around town was about the fair, which started in a few days. The Calhoun County Fair was the oldest such fair in Michigan and was the focal point for Marshall. The fairgrounds were only a few blocks outside of town, and the *Marshall Evening Chronicle* covered the repainting of the fair pavilions as front-page news. The fair brought a lot of business into town and was the social event of the year. Kids speculated about what rides would be offered this year—the word was that an eighty-foot Ferris wheel was going to be arriving.[1] The local citizens and surrounding farmers competed in everything ranging from harness racing to quilting to livestock. Fair week was a time for the common men and women to shine in the community. Winning a ribbon at the fair for your prize pig or an apple pie was something that would be talked about (and bragged about) for months. Competition between children, farmers, and blue-haired old ladies was fierce and contentious. But the fair was more than a social event, more than competition. It marked the end of the summer.

Marshall was quiet, stable, pleasant. The new Elvis Presley movie, *Double Trouble,* was starting that night at the Bogar Theatre. The Bogar was only open on the weekends—there simply weren't the crowds to merit keeping it open during the week. People could either go to the Bogar for air-conditioned entertainment or go to the Battle Creek Drive-in Theatre six miles down the road. Of course, once the fair came into town, no one would be going to the movies.

An entire world away, on the West Coast, it was called the "Summer of Love." Large numbers of hippies were converging on the Haight-Ashbury district of San Francisco. Other gatherings of long-haired hippies took place in other major cities. The Mamas and the Papas sang songs about the events changing the culture of America. *Rolling Stone* magazine was about to debut in two months. Those things happened outside of Marshall, seemingly in another world. The most popular haircuts for men in town ranged from the crew cut to the more stylish "Princeton." Long sideburns and long stringy hair, beads, and other trappings of hippie lifestyles simply were not accepted in town.

As Don made his rounds through the streets of Marshall, he didn't know that he had assumed the role of murderer that day. Marshall had a stalking murderer on the loose, a killer who had carefully and meticulously planned the death of someone on Don's route. The longtime post-man did not know that he was carrying the implement of death in his bag on his shoulder. He never realized with each bump of the heavy canvas bag against his hip that he was tempting fate and risking his own life.

He stepped into the Tasty Cafe at 209 East Michigan Avenue as he had hundreds of times before. The little restaurant was one of several on Michigan Avenue. It was painted white on the outside. Out front hung a bright yellow sign advertising Vernors ginger ale. An L-shaped counter extended to the rear of the restaurant. There was a series of tables and booths—their vinyl seats buckled from use—along with a jukebox. At the rear of the restaurant were a large refrigerator and a small office area. The rear door was a double screen door, perfect for hot, humid Michigan summers. Air-conditioning outside of a movie theater was an unheard of luxury in little Marshall. On the counter was a display case for cold food, usually stocked with donuts from Louie's Bakery down the street.[2] The Tasty was only a block away from the high school and was a favorite place to dine for students attempting to dodge the cafeteria meal or the one their mothers packed.

The air inside the cafe wafted with the smell of eggs and a hint of bacon—someone's breakfast. In the Tasty were three customers, all dressed as workingmen. None seemed to pay attention to the postman, and Don gave them little thought that morning; there were always customers in the little diner. He was more interested in the warm greeting he got from the Puyears, Nola and Paul, who owned the cafe.

Paul was sixty-two years old, wore horn-rimmed glasses, and appeared more like a white-haired church elder than a short-order cook. Nola was ten years younger and had dark curly hair. She was known to be bright, energetic, and outgoing, whereas Paul was content to serve quietly as a cook at the Tasty. Nola was a plump, churchgoing woman who was warm and friendly with anyone who crossed her path. She and her husband had been raised in Arkansas. Nola brought her southern hospitality to the Tasty Cafe that she and her husband owned. On that Friday, she wore a plain dress, grandmotherly glasses, and an apron splattered with the remains of meals past. She had never fully shaken her southern drawl, a hint of which was always in her voice.

From the depths of his postal bag, Don pulled out a package for Nola.

It was wrapped in plain brown paper and was roughly the size of a book. He later estimated the dimensions at two and a half inches thick, seven inches long, and five inches wide.[3] The package bore the word "BOOKS" printed in large red block letters. It weighed about two pounds and had two twenty-cent stamps on it.[4] It was addressed to the Puyears' home at 857 East Michigan Avenue, specifically to Mrs. Paul Puyear. From what Don knew, it was supposed to have been delivered the day before but had been put on the wrong truck, leaving it for him to deliver. The Marshall Post Office allowed postmen to deliver personal packages to the owners of businesses at their place of work. It was the kind of gesture that happened in small towns where people knew each other, a casual convenience that people expected.

The addressing stood out to Damon. It had been addressed in red ink or an indelible pencil. The handwriting was a distinct scrawled jumble of letters and numbers. There was no return address.[5] At the time, he didn't give it a second thought. He didn't realize that the murderer had taken the step to make it stand out. At the moment, Don didn't know that he was being used as an instrument of death and destruction. Only later did he realize just how close he had come to being killed himself— the victim of the same killer who was stalking unsuspecting Nola.

Donald Damon handed the day's mail, including the package, to Paul Puyear. Paul shook the package and heard a "clunk clunk" noise, like books inside of a pasteboard box. Nola was standing next to him and asked, "What is it?" Paul replied, "I don't know." She took the box from him, saying, "Let me take it."[6] Don heard her say something about the package possibly being from her son, John.[7] John Puyear was in the Air Force, stationed in California. He and Damon knew each other—but then everyone knew each other in Marshall.

Damon left the cafe and started up Madison Avenue to continue his route. He knew that at 9:00 a.m., the church bells tolled the hour for everyone in town to hear.[8] Damon's role in the murder of Nola Puyear was over. He had beaten fate that morning. Don had done the gruesome work that the murderer had been too cowardly to do personally.

The law firm of Schroeder, DeGraw, and Mathews was next door to the Tasty Cafe. Attorney Ronald DeGraw had two appointments that morning, both concerning divorces. His eight o'clock client finished up, and DeGraw walked him to the lobby. DeGraw suggested that his client go next door and get a cup of coffee; then they could walk together down Michigan Avenue to the court. The only wrinkle was that his 8:15 a.m. client didn't show. So Ron spent a few minutes in the lobby with his first client, talking and killing time.[9]

At the counter of the Tasty Cafe, nineteen-year-old Ed Bowman sat nursing a cup of coffee while waiting for his breakfast, which Paul Puyear was just finishing on the grill. Ed watched Nola take the package and head to the back of the cafe, standing at the counter between the refrigerator and the metal case that held bakery goods. "She picked up the package and walked by me past the counter, and started to open the package on a small table under the counter. It was 9:03 a.m. Nola turned her back to the patrons to open the package at a small workspace next to the refrigerator. 'This is a big surprise,' she said."[10] No one was sure if she was surprised to receive a package from her son or if the package coming at all was a surprise. As she tore the paper, Bowman heard her say, "Oh—"[11] Perhaps in that last moment of her life, she realized something was horribly wrong with the package in her hands. Perhaps Nola realized that her life was about to end.

The package exploded with a fury and force that tore apart the rear of the Tasty Cafe and Nola with it. The explosion instantly destroyed the refrigerator and work area along with Nola. Her body shielded much of the force of the blast from hitting the two patrons nearby. The force of the explosion was so great that it bowed the eating counter outward and flipped it over. A hole was blasted in the drop ceiling, tossing the grease-splattered ceiling tiles about like a deck of cards left to the wind. Apartments above the cafe, on the building's second and third floors, were rocked hard by the explosion. The large front windows of the cafe were blown out, turned into thousands of pieces of jagged shrapnel, littering the sidewalk and Michigan Avenue.[12] The rear of the cafe was a jumbled wreck from the blast, and the shattered remains of the counter were in the dining area. A bluish gray smoke tinged with the smell of gunpowder or exploded firecrackers filled the restaurant, smothering the smell of eggs that had hung in the air only a few seconds earlier.

The explosion had mercilessly destroyed most of Nola Puyear in a millisecond. Gore, blood, and thousands of bits of shrapnel covered the interior of the once quaint little diner. From her head down to her navel had been ripped open by the explosion. Her left arm was missing just below the elbow, the right arm just above. Her nose had been torn from her face. Her thighs rested on the upturned shelves of the counter. The right lens from her eyeglasses was found fifteen feet away, lying on the floor between two booths—the only part of her glasses that would ever be found. There were parts of human flesh, blood, and torn shards of clothing everywhere, fanning out from the epicenter of the explosion. Nola Puyear's remains, savaged by the detonation, draped over the counter. She was on her back, her face turned to one side.[13] On the floor, near one of the booths, lay her rings, spotted with blood, gnarled and twisted by the force of the blast.

Young Ed Bowman was knocked off his counter stool by the concussion of the blast and tossed hard onto the floor of the Tasty. Donald Page, a truck driver with the Michigan Transportation Company of Dearborn who had stopped for a cup of coffee, had been sitting at the front window when the explosion had gone off. The occupants of the diner were temporarily deafened by the blast. To them, the world around them had been a silent, chaotic, and confusing place of death. Bowman was knocked down by the concussive force of the explosion but was otherwise uninjured. As he staggered to his feet, he was surprised to see that somehow his cup of coffee had been eerily undisturbed by the blast.[14] It was on the counter, forever unfinished. The eggs that Paul Puyear had been making on the dingy grill for Bowman were also oddly unaffected by the force of the explosion. The survivors tumbled out to the safety of Michigan Avenue.

Donald Page kept focused on Paul Puyear. As he headed toward the door, Paul cried out to Page, "My God, Nola!" Don said, "Who's that?" Puyear responded, "My wife's inside!" Page followed him into the smoking restaurant. Paul made it halfway into the restaurant when he saw Nola's remains and began to scream. Page tried to comfort him, getting him out of the restaurant and onto the sidewalk. Paul muttered, "My God, she's dead. She was opening the box she got in the mail and it killed her." As Page stood with him, Paul looked up at him for answers, asking, "Who would do such a thing? Why? Why?" Don saw someone in uniform—probably a policeman—and guided Paul over to him.[15]

Next door, attorney Ron DeGraw was rocked by the explosion. His early-morning client asked if it was a sonic boom, but DeGraw felt otherwise. The telephone mounted on his wall was knocked down by whatever it was. Rushing out, he saw the glass tinkling from the shattered windows of the Tasty Cafe. He approached Paul, who was in a daze. "Who did it?" he asked. DeGraw noticed something on Paul's shoulder, gray and fleshlike. "Where's Nola?" he asked. Paul coughed and pointed back at the restaurant. "Inside," he said.

The Tasty was filled with smoke. "It smelled like the Fourth of July," DeGraw recalled later, "the smell of firecrackers after they had been set off." The air was filled with a dense grayish smoke. DeGraw was worried. If this was a gas leak, he was standing there with his lit pipe in his mouth. He paused for a moment and realized he had to go in. "I wouldn't have been able to live with my conscience," he later explained, "if I didn't go check on Nola."

What he found was a shambles; the counter had been flipped into the middle of the dining area. The refrigerator had a hole blown into it. What remained of Nola stunned him. She had been blown apart, thrown back over the shambles of the counter. Her flesh was gray, except for a hint of color near her hairline and down at her socks. The rest of her body looked as if the flesh had been scraped off—replaced with a gray visage. DeGraw left quickly. There was nothing that could be done for Nola now.[16]

Postman Don Damon had just reached the Consumers Power building a half block away. He had just handed Cliff Wise a package when he heard the blast. He knew that something was wrong. Leaving Consumers, he retraced his steps back to Michigan Avenue. As he rounded the corner, he saw the carnage at the Tasty Cafe—the patrons spilling onto the street and smoke rolling out of the front of the restaurant. He heard the siren of a fire truck within a minute of the explosion but quickly realized that it was speeding away. The manager from the Citco gas station across the street was rushing over. Don saw Paul Puyear standing outside. He assumed that there had been a gas explosion.

Damon wanted to stay but could not be distracted from his rounds. People counted on him delivering his mail at the same time every day. Turning around, he continued on his rounds. Whatever it was that was causing all of the commotion, he was sure he would get the details later. After all, the Marshall Post Office was right across the street.[17]

Nola's murderer had succeeded brilliantly. His grisly work had been completed by an innocent, unsuspecting postman. His intended victim was not just dead but savagely disemboweled. Her murderer had managed to kill without dirtying his own hands with the horrific crime. The terror that was going to grip Marshall in that hot autumn of 1967 was just beginning.

1

A Blast in the Heart of a Small Town

Bombings are exceedingly violent crimes. Their violence is starkly contrasted by their impersonal execution. When I pored over the police reports and discussed this with my editor, we arrived at the same conclusion. The murderer could have killed countless other people in addition to the intended target—Nola Puyear. What kind of mind would or could contemplate such a vicious plot?

Marshall is nestled along the ribbon of highway between Detroit and Chicago. Originally, it had been formed on what was called the "Territorial Road," which roughly followed the course of the Kalamazoo River across the state. The town had been named after Justice John Marshall and had broken with tradition by taking his name before he had died, becoming the first town so named in the country. The conjunction of Rice Creek and the Kalamazoo River provided fertile soil and sources of water power, vital for the early community. The early town founders had believed that Marshall would be a perfect capital for the state of Michigan, but the town lost in the balloting to the crossroads town of Lansing. Local legend proudly brags that the voting was close, but in reality, Marshall had been edged out by a majority in one of the early rounds of voting.[1]

In its early days, Marshall was a stopping point along the Territorial Road, with inns and hotels to support stagecoach travelers. Most of Marshall's settlers came from New York, and they brought with them the home designs with which they were most familiar. Marshall's streets took on names that originated from New York. Many of the original settlers were farmers, and the town was simply a hub for social activity and much-needed supplies—especially after the Michigan Central Railroad ran through the community.

It is often said that if you want to understand a community, you need to follow the money. Marshall's money came from a number of sources

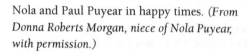

Nola and Paul Puyear in happy times. (*From Donna Roberts Morgan, niece of Nola Puyear, with permission.*)

throughout its history. At the turn of the twentieth century, the patent medicine industry took root in the community. These unlicensed businesses produced pills and serums that could cure, according to their advertising, almost anything. One local man, C. E. Brooks, created a new "appliance" (truss) for hernia patients, so revolutionary that it was in demand around the world. The Brooks family's wealth became renowned in Marshall folklore. During World War II, a number of businesses helped feed Michigan's burgeoning auto industry. The largest of the local employers was Eaton Corporation, which produced hydraulic pumps used in the war industry. Marshall became a mix of old money and new— trapped somewhere between a rural community and a small industrial one.[2]

In the mid-twentieth century, Marshall was a place that epitomized small-town living. Saturday nights were characterized by teenagers "cruising the gut" on Michigan Avenue. Teenagers' cars filled the parking spaces on the main drag, and a steady stream of autos looped around the white pillars of the Brooks fountain that marked the unofficial western edge of town. The far eastern turnaround was anchored at the Hi-Lite drive-in restaurant. On a typical Saturday night, kids were there to be seen and to watch others. While kids enjoyed simply hanging out on Saturday nights, the adult population enjoyed dinner at Win Schuler's— considered one of the best restaurants in the state.

Friday nights in the cool Michigan autumn were marked by bundling up and watching the high school team, the Redskins, slug it out with the big-city kids from nearby Battle Creek or with teams from the other small towns dotting Calhoun County. At Halloween, small children struggled with wearing winter coats under their costumes. Christmas was not celebrated in Marshall until the annual Christmas parade took place. While the decorations went up earlier, the holiday lights were not turned on until Santa made his way down Michigan Avenue. Summers were spent swimming or fishing, providing you could find a friend with a pond or lake. If you couldn't, there was always a chance of pulling a catfish out of the lazy stretch of the Kalamazoo River that meandered through the county.

Marshall was the kind of town where your kids could play outside at night. Fathers took their kids in the back of their trucks to the Dairy Queen, where they could order *both* flavors of ice cream—vanilla and chocolate. The ornate gingerbread architecture of the quaint old buildings gave Marshall a warm comfortable feeling—like a familiar blanket on a cold night. Time was measured in town by the ringing of the church bells. Crimes were minor, petty. Most—such as domestic disputes—were swept politely under the rug and never discussed openly. Felonies were rare events that made the newspaper.

Marshall's police department numbered six officers and two patrol cars in 1967. The crimes that they dealt with daily involved traffic enforcement. The job paid so little that most officers had side jobs to help augment their pay. Yet their traffic work was integral to the community, because the tickets generated a meager revenue stream. People in Marshall in 1967 didn't fight traffic tickets; they just paid them. Respect for the law was something that had been ingrained in the people there—it was part of their culture. There was the occasional petty larceny, a polite phrase for shoplifting. The biggest criminal demographic in town was teenagers. In the autumn, there was always the occasional garden theft in town, with someone complaining that their prize tomatoes or watermelons had been heisted. It was hard to commit crimes in a small town where everyone knew each other and where even a minor infraction would be mentioned to your parents.

That changed on August 18, 1967. Marshall's innocence was torn away. Things would never be quite the same. While the pristine facade of the city did not change, the way people viewed the little town was altered by the slowly growing realization that a murderer might lurk among their number. One of *them* may have perpetrated this incredibly violent crime. An uneasy mix of imagination and paranoia had a way of suddenly turning neighbor against neighbor. And there was fear that one of them might just kill again.

* * * *

Sleepy little Marshall was shaken psychologically and physically by the explosion in the Tasty Cafe. Windows rattled across the pastoral town, blocks away from the blast. The detonation of the bomb that killed Nola Puyear caused cars to screech to a halt on Michigan Avenue, as shards of glass rained across the street. Most people would claim they thought it was a gun going off or perhaps thunder—oddly out of place on the hot sunny day. Robert Beller, who owned the photographic studio just down from the diner, recalled, "At first I thought two cars had hit. But when I ran down the street I saw smoke puffing out of the front of the cafe, and Mr. Puyear came out into the street crying for help."[3]

Some people dodged fate that morning. Reverend Nye enjoyed breakfast at the Tasty Cafe several times a week. He had planned on stopping there that morning, but for some reason, he changed his mind and walked over to Oaklawn Hospital instead. As he reached the hospital, he heard the man-made rumble of dynamite thunder. Birds in the stately trees near the hospital broke into immediate flight at the retort. While he didn't know the source, he knew something was wrong.[4]

People poured out onto the streets. Some suspected a gas explosion, most were unsure what had happened, and all were curious. At the Tasty Cafe, as bluish smoke drifted out through the openings where the front windows had been, Richard Lockwood, a patron of the restaurant, staggered outside to get away from the blast, his ears ringing from the explosion. Richard had been reading the newspaper and had not seen the arrival of the postman. He had seen Mrs. Puyear take the package to the back of the cafe. All he remembered of the bomb was that "it was neatly wrapped." Suddenly there was a roar, and Lockwood was knocked around but otherwise uninjured. He recounted, "I ducked down, covered my head, because I could hear things falling, and ran out the door."[5]

One dazed man wandering in and out of the gutted restaurant was Paul Puyear. He had been at the grill when the bomb had gone off and had been injured himself by the force of the blast. He rushed out in a daze, slightly bruised and cut. His lack of injuries was remarkable—to some people, *too* remarkable.

At some point, Paul Puyear made his way back to his restaurant and took a seat near the front door. To many, he appeared to be in a state of shock and hysteria. Many took note that while Paul was outside, no one saw his wife, Nola. The entire town reeled for a moment, but soon everyone was heading toward the source of the smoke. No one was sure what to do. They only knew they had to do something.

A call went to the Marshall Fire Department at 9:05 a.m. Marshall's small fire department was already out on a call at the Robert Ulrich residence on Marshall Avenue. A faulty extension cord had caused a mattress fire. In the middle of the firemen's efforts to get the Ulrich children out of the burning home, there was the call for an explosion on Michigan Avenue. Fires were thankfully rare, but having two incidents at once overwhelmed them. Half of the town's modest fire department was sent off to the Tasty Cafe, while the rest of the firemen remained to finish the work on the Ulrich fire.

The fire engine sirens added to the commotion outside of the ruined diner. No one knew it was a bomb at first, despite the tang of gunpowder that hung in the air. Fearing a gas leak, the fire department went in to clear the upstairs apartments, as the police evacuated the surrounding buildings. Glen Siefke, who rented the third-floor apartment, had been home at the time of the explosion and was evacuated by the police. "The blast shook me up a bit," he reported, "but that was all."[6]

Herold Reuss, the assistant police chief of Marshall, was at the corner of Park and Michigan, at Fred's Standard Station, when the call came in that there had been a blast at the Tasty Cafe. Reuss was a cop's cop and was proud of his role as one of the officials of the small police force that kept Marshall peaceful. Dressed in his "summer whites"—a white short-sleeved uniform shirt—on that hot morning, he felt that he was ready for the heat of the day. His only real concern was for the upcoming county fair and the strains it put on the tiny police force. A few minutes earlier, he had heard something coming from several blocks away, a loud report, a crack like a sudden burst of thunder in a summer shower. When he got the call, he understood what had caused the sound—there had been an explosion.

Reuss was one of the first officials to arrive at the scene of the blast, and despite his years of experience, he was shocked at the carnage and chaos. The Tasty was filled with smoke. Glass covered the sidewalk and street in front of the cafe. Paul Puyear, who Reuss knew, was in a daze, sitting on the steps that led to the upstairs apartments over the restaurant. Puyear was shaken but insisted that Reuss go inside the establishment. There was no sign of Nola at first. Given the damage, there was a moment when he must have suspected her fate.

Reuss entered the cafe and could taste the tang of gunpowder on the back of his tongue. That odor told him this was not a gas leak but something else, something more sinister, a dynamite explosion. While the fire department evacuated the upstairs apartments, Reuss climbed over the rubble of the once pristine restaurant. There, near the back of the establishment, he found the remains of Nola Puyear, eviscerated by the force of the explosion. Herold Reuss was a tough man, a rugged officer, but nothing had prepared him for the scene he found, where Nola's remains lay all around him. He backed out of the Tasty.[7]

Calhoun County, where Marshall was situated, only had a murder or two a year. The last murder in Marshall had involved a farmer who had killed his terminally ill wife before taking his own life, and that had been three years before Nola Puyear's death.[8] Those killings had been tidy compared to what had happened in the Tasty Cafe. The bombing had been savage, brutal, leaving Nola's body hardly identifiable as that of a human being.

Lewis (Louie) Shellenberger arrived in the midst of the growing chaos. His ambulance service had been called in along with the fire department. In those pre-911 days, Marshall's ambulance service was a separate, private business not tied to the city, and Louie was accustomed to responding when the fire department was summoned. Louie, like Reuss, was an icon in Marshall, a known figure, an official. The crowd parted for him to approach the Tasty.

Louie stopped for a moment with Paul Puyear to see if he was injured. Sitting on the steps, Paul did not want any assistance. Instead, he insisted that Louie go inside. Like Herold Reuss, Louie initially thought there might have been a gas leak, but the smell of gunpowder in the air told him that gas was not the culprit in this blast.

Shellenberger had witnessed a lot of bloody accidents in this age before seat belt laws and air bags, but little prepared him for what he found

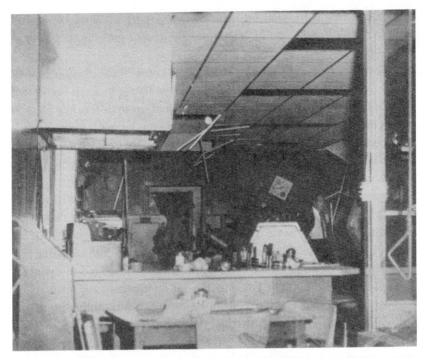

The effects of the bomb blast that killed Nola Puyear inside the Tasty Cafe. (*From the* Ad-Visor & Chronicle, *with permission.*)

inside the Tasty Cafe. Nola had been "opened like a side of beef." The counter had been flipped over, and she was leaning over it. Shellenberger left the restaurant for a moment and returned to his ambulance. He took out a plain white sheet and returned to Nola, draping the sheet over what was left of her, as if to preserve her dignity—or perhaps to spare the public shock if anyone saw her. Normally, he would have tried to take her remains out immediately, but the stench of gunpowder told him that this was a crime scene. There was no point in attempting to get Nola to the hospital. Instead, he turned his attention to Paul Puyear.[9]

He found Paul in a state of shock, muttering, "It was a bomb. . . . My God, who would want to do that to Nola?" One member of the crowd, Richard Waidelich, had been in Navy ordnance in World War II and said the odor he smelled reminded him of plastic explosives.[10] Already, speculation was beginning as to the source of the explosion. Paul's mention of the bomb trickled into the crowd, passed by word of mouth. Like in a childhood game of Telephone, the rumor grew as each person passed it on.

Gently, with respect for the older man, Louie Shellenberger helped Paul Puyear to his ambulance. Herold Reuss, trying to keep the crowd back and control the crime scene, only picked up on a few key facts in Nola's murder: that it had been a bomb delivered by mail. Reuss was already having problems controlling the scene. Some key witnesses, such as Richard Lockwood, left the crime scene, presumably to avoid public attention.

I was particularly touched at how Shellenberger dealt with Nola's body when he found her. That kind of reverence is something that made me respect the work he did. He gave Nola a moment of dignity with his simple action. It was the kind of gesture that only a friend, someone in a close-knit community, would have made. That he managed to maintain such presence of mind left a strong imprint on me as an author.

Postman Donald Damon continued on his route, oblivious to the contents of the package that he had delivered. There was a lot of commotion in town—sirens and the gathering crowd of people—but Damon was focused on keeping his daily routine. At around 10:15 a.m., local dentist Dr. Bob Heidenreich came out of his office and said, "Don, that package you delivered just killed Nola Puyear!" Damon wasn't sure how to react to the news. To him, it just didn't seem possible. Damon ignored Dr. Heidenreich's warning and continued on his route, dutifully delivering his mail.[11]

The Marshall Police Department was ill equipped for such a murder, especially one this complicated, and Herold Reuss knew it. The call went out for help—any help. The first Calhoun County deputy to arrive on the scene was Sergeant Fred Ritchie. A veteran of the Albion Police Department, Ritchie had been in the Calhoun County Sheriff's Department since 1957. Ritchie remembers, "When I got there, everybody was walking in and out of the scene. At that point, the thinking was that this was a gas leak. We had everybody wandering in and out of the restaurant, curious neighbors, gawkers, and police and fire. . . . So I got a fireman to cover the back door, and I got everyone out of there so we could preserve the crime scene as much as possible." Ritchie's actions most likely preserved the evidence that still remained in the restaurant.[12]

Other officers, such as Marshall officer John Carroll, rolled out of bed to come to the crime scene. Officer Carroll had been patrolling the streets all night and had just crawled into bed when Chief Beattie called him to come to the Tasty Cafe and to bring his camera. Carroll was the official photographer for the Marshall Police Department. He came from a family of civil servants; his father, Ed, was a captain in the Marshall Fire Department. When John arrived, he found a grisly scene of death and chaos. He took a few photographs of the victim and was told to go to the hospital along with another officer, to interview Paul Puyear. It would be long hours before Carroll ever got to sleep.[13]

* * * *

Word of the bombing spread through Marshall by telephone and radio at first, whipped like a wildfire in a stiff breeze. The police moved to block off Michigan Avenue, essentially shutting down business on the main street of the town—which only seemed to draw more attention to the crime scene. People came out to see what had happened. Fueled by the rumor mill in the town, fear began to grow. The bombing had been seemingly so random that people began to wonder if this was simply the first of many bombs to go off. After all, the Puyears were respected business people with no known enemies. If someone could attack them, anyone might be a target. As one witness on the scene said, "People that would do such a thing ought to be put to sleep. Nobody's safe when people like that are allowed to go free."[14]

Donald Damon continued his postal rounds as if nothing had happened. Until someone told him otherwise, he still had a job to do, and people counted on their mail. When he returned to the post office around 10:25 a.m., he noticed the commotion across the street at the Tasty Cafe. Before he set out again, Postmaster Reyer grabbed him and told him that indeed there had been a bombing and that it apparently involved the package he had delivered. The gravity of what had happened settled in on the postman. The postmaster told him to only discuss the matter with the police. Within the hour, Damon had been hustled down to the Marshall Police Department, where he began to relate everything he knew about the package he had provided the Puyears.[15]

Many people knew Nola Puyear, and the thought that someone from outside of Marshall would kill her seemed alien to the citizens. Little, quiet, idyllic Marshall had someone in its midst who killed a member of the small community, in a horribly violent manner. Paranoia became the norm that Friday morning—paranoia and stark fear. Suddenly, every package began to look like a potential bomb.

At Ketchum Park, some five blocks from the explosion, Bobby Lewis was celebrating his fifth birthday. The plan was for the kids to play at the park and then go into town to the restaurant where his grandmother worked and have cake and ice cream. For the mothers, the tiny park in Marshall had always been safe, nestled within view of downtown, with the fairgrounds visible just up the road. On a typical day there, the biggest fear was that a child might fall into the waters of Mill Creek above the tiny dam nearby. The mothers gathered for the party could hear the sirens and commotion coming from downtown a few blocks away but only gave it a curious glance now and then. A police cruiser swung into the park and informed the mothers that there had been an explosion at a restaurant downtown. As the car sped off, they were left with no details.

The mothers were suddenly paralyzed with fear. One turned on her car radio to try to learn what was happening, but the reports were vague at this point. While it was only five blocks away, no one was willing to run into downtown at the onset of the emerging crisis. "Was this little Bobby Lewis's grandmother's restaurant?" they wondered. For the time being, the mothers kept their kids in the park and away from the chaos of the scene.[16] They tried to hide their fear—tried and failed.

Paul Puyear had been taken to Oaklawn Hospital, where it was determined that his injuries were not life threatening. Oaklawn was the pride of the community. In 1967, the hospital had a whopping sixty-nine beds in it, thanks to a recent expansion. Various ladies' church groups had made the curtains and pillow covers for the new wing two years earlier, when it opened.[17] Quaint little Oaklawn was used to dealing with farm injuries or those from an automobile accident. Now it was dealing with bombing victims, both living and dead.

When Paul Puyear arrived, he was hysterical to the point of being almost incoherent. Dr. Archie Humphrey, who was on duty, sedated him. While Paul was being examined at the hospital, he was heard to moan, "Why did they want to hurt her? Why did they do this to her?"[18] While alone with Dr. Humphrey, he said, "My God, why did this happen to her? The package came in, she was opening it, and it exploded. There were two or three 20 cent stamps on it." Dr. Humphrey took note of the details for the Marshall police, stretching the nature of the patient-doctor privilege.[19] In small-town Marshall, where everyone knew each other, such sharing of private information was expected as the norm.

Within an hour, the local television stations began to arrive and conduct interviews for the nightly news. This only added to the confusion that had already started to spread on the street. Remote hookups and remote tapings for television and radio in 1967 were complicated affairs, with bundles of cables and extension cords draped everywhere. People from the surrounding parts of town sauntered to Michigan Avenue to see what might happen next. With school out of session, a large number of children either walked, ran, or rode their bikes downtown to see what was happening. By evening, there would be two television news crews and three radios broadcasting or filming from Marshall's main street.[20]

Marshall police chief Darrell Beattie had arrived to take immediate command of the scene and assist Herold Reuss. Beattie found himself overwhelmed with issues that rarely confronted a small-town chief. Beattie's tiny police force was dealing with rescue, investigation, and crowd control. At 10:25 a.m., he reached out for and got help from the Calhoun County sheriff, but it took an hour or so for the manpower to get in place.[21] In the meantime, key witnesses had wandered away.

Word spread slowly throughout Marshall by word of mouth. Rumors took hold faster than facts. One rumor circulating that afternoon said that the bomb had been packed in a tub of ice cream. Another rumor was that someone had thrown the bomb through the window. Details were sketchy, and radio broadcasters speculated as to who was involved and which restaurant had been the scene of the explosion. Initially, even the name of the restaurant was not announced, and with six diners on Michigan Avenue, it was a guessing game as to which one had been the target of the bomber. The Marshall police and the Calhoun County Sheriff's Department struggled to get practical information out, but the rumor mill in the small town worked much faster.

After an hour, the name of the restaurant was finally spread on the radio. Those gathered for Bobby Lewis's birthday party were relieved to learn that his grandmother's restaurant, the Hutchins Cafe, had not been the target of the explosion. Their relief was coupled with the realization that a seemingly random act of violence had been perpetrated on Marshall. The birthday party came to an abrupt end. It was much better to get the children home so that the mothers might stop worrying. It was a day when all mothers instinctively wanted to make sure their children were in sight.

* * * *

At the murder scene, the county's assistant medical examiner, Dr. Phillip Glotfelty, had been called in. The job of assistant medical examiner was part-time in Calhoun County; there simply was not enough crime to warrant a full-time position. Dr. Glotfelty was a young doctor, for whom the job paid additional income that was always welcome. Where Nola Puyear had been standing, there was little that could be used to fully identify her. Followed by Herold Reuss as he moved through the scene, Glotfelty fulfilled his grim formal duty—declaring Nola dead so that her remains could be moved.

A call also went to the Court Funeral Home two blocks away. Elliott Court and Frederick Wiessner arrived at 12:45 p.m. and, with delicate care, gathered up Nola's body. There would be an autopsy at the funeral home later, but there was little point in taking her remains to the hospital immediately.

By the afternoon of that confusing day, Chief Beattie realized the jurisdictions that were going to need to be involved. The bomb had been delivered by the post office, meaning that the federal authorities needed to be included. Most of the crimes his police force dealt with were related to driving or simple assault, limited to the narrow confines of the Marshall city limits. This was murder, a sophisticated murder. Beattie had not had a murder in town in over a year. This one was going to need laboratories, analysis, true detective work—something his small-town police force was ill equipped to handle. He had reached out to the state police for their assistance. The Calhoun County Sheriff's Department was committing resources to the investigation as well.[22] While Marshall was the county seat, even the sheriff's department realized that the scope and complexity of this crime were going to require more resources than the small southern Michigan county could muster.

The one thing Chief Beattie could control was the crime scene. He ordered the Tasty Cafe boarded up. A local contractor put up plywood to fill the space where the blasted windows and doors had been. He used a padlock to lock up the cafe and turned the keys over to Marshall's assistant chief of police, Herold Reuss. Michigan Avenue was busier than normal. People wanted to drive by and observe the scene of the crime themselves—some out of shock, some out of morbid curiosity.

Reuss and Beattie felt the weight of the community on their shoulders. Murder had come to Marshall, and the entire community expected them to find the killer as quickly as possible, before he struck again.

2
Collateral Damage

I was fortunate enough to interview Herold Reuss, the assistant police chief in Marshall at the time of the bombing. Reuss remembered incredible details of the morning, details that helped me describe the event. He stressed to me how well the investigators got along. Despite all of the jurisdictions that suddenly were thrust together, there was very little territoriality. These men were crisp professionals, finding themselves in a situation that was way beyond their expertise.

When I met with Robert Kenney's kids, they told me about their father as a man. Up until then, I only knew him as the author of hundreds of pages of reports. After an afternoon with his children, I felt I knew him. It took a special kind of detective to take on such a complicated case as the Puyear murder.

Help for the beleaguered Marshall Police Department came from the Michigan State Police post in nearby Battle Creek. In the early afternoon, Detective Sergeant Robert Kenney and his partner, Detective Leroy Steinbacher, responded to the call by Chief Beattie. Kenney arrived as the chaos started to wane, in the hot midday sun.

Kenney was from Amasa in Michigan's Upper Peninsula, a "Yooper," by contemporary slang—though the men referred to him and another officer as the "Cedar Savages," a reference to the isolated and wooded U.P. In the 1960s, the Michigan State Police resembled a military organization; troopers were often rotated around the state to communities where they had not been raised. That was how Kenney had ended up in the Lower Peninsula, in Battle Creek.

A tall six foot two, with Italian features and a stiff crew cut—"cop hair"—Kenney had no idea that he was starting on an investigation that would dominate his career for the next four years.[1] What little he did know was that there had been a bombing/murder and that he was there to coordinate the efforts from the state police. How he did that was up to him.

Det. Robert J. Kenney   **Det. Leroy S. Steinbacher**

Michigan State Police detectives Robert Kenney and Leroy Steinbacher, along with Sergeant Fred Ritchie of the Calhoun County Sheriff's Department, formed the core of the investigation team on the Puyear murder. (*From the Kenney family, with permission.*)

Detective Steinbacher—"Stein," as he was called—was a huskier-built man who wore his hair slicked back. He had a square jaw and was seven years Kenny's senior on the force. Steinbacher was from Battle Creek, so he knew the area and the people well. When he worked a case, he was a bulldog, locking his jaw on the evidence and running the perpetrator to ground. Steinbacher was not a flashy man, but he was tenacious in his actions.

Three members of the Calhoun County Sheriff's Department, as well as Herold Reuss and two officers of Marshall's tiny police department, were present when Kenney and Steinbacher arrived. A postal inspector from Kalamazoo named Minor Myers arrived along with Sergeant John Lohrstorfer and Trooper Williams of the Battle Creek state police post. This was the first bombing murder ever in Calhoun County, and no matter what their backgrounds, this crime was well beyond their individual skills. All of the investigators were in uncharted territory.[2]

Detective Kenney entered the restaurant knowing that the crime scene had already been tromped through and somewhat tainted. He was accompanied by Donald Bennett of the Michigan State Police Crime Laboratory in Lansing. The damage from the explosion made sifting through the debris searching for evidence difficult, and the job was made worse by the oily and bloody bits of tissue mixed in. Kenney and Bennett made meticulous notes of the scene, unsure if any detail might prove to be an important clue. With the heat and humidity of the August sun, the food in the Tasty Cafe would have to be checked carefully for any evidence and then discarded.

They worked in the dim light — the electricity had been shut off, and the windows boarded up. The heat made the task even more uncomfortable as they delicately climbed over the remains of the interior of the cafe and Nola herself. What they found initially were tiny bits of brown paper scattered like confetti in the debris, they assumed from the wrapper of the bomb itself. These were carefully recovered and bagged. Some of the bits were large, including one piece marked "OOKS," most likely part of the word "BOOKS." Bits of the stamps and some pieces with writing, most likely the address, were also recovered painstakingly from the floor and debris. The indelible red penciling survived the detonation, with the Puyears' home address still legible.[3]

Mixed in with the debris were much smaller bits of brown paper that had a waxy coating. Bennett's experience told him that these were possibly from the wrapping of dynamite. These were also carefully recovered and saved. Some bits of masking tape from the wrapping of the package were found. Small pieces of metal and splintered wood were collected as well, each a potential piece of shrapnel from the murder device. Two more of Nola's rings were found amid the ruins of the counter and were given to Assistant Chief Reuss to return to the family.[4]

The drop ceiling in the rear of the cafe had been tossed asunder by the concussive force of the bomb. In one of the upthrusted panels, Detective Kenney found an alligator clip with a piece of wire and some black electrical tape that looked eerily out of place. The true ceiling of the restaurant held bits of human tissue and tiny fragments of Nola's dress. Other bits of electrical tape were found scattered about, oddly out of place for the cafe. Kenney and his colleagues carefully measured the area of the explosion. An area six feet by eleven feet had been devastated by the bomb, giving them a good idea as to how much explosive was involved. Paul Puyear was only a few feet away, yet somehow he had escaped almost unharmed. Photographs of the interior were taken, to accompany their meticulous notes. The clock on the north wall was frozen at 9:13.[5]

The state police investigators found another package wrapped in brown paper in a cupboard not far from the epicenter of the explosion. This was a small, seemingly innocent cardboard box with a bottle of white capsule pills inside. The package had been addressed to Mrs. Paul Puyear at her home address, and even a cursory glance seemed to indicate that the handwriting on this package and that on the bomb seemed to be written with the same type of pencil.[6] Was it possible that this package had been sent by the murderer? If so, what was the connection?

Elliott Court, the owner of the Court Funeral Home, where Nola's remains had been taken, arrived at the crime scene at 4:30 p.m. If you met Elliott outside of his place of work, you knew his profession by his demeanor and bearing.[7] He had a firm but reassuring handshake and the kind of soothing, almost rolling voice that calmed even the harshest of nerves. As a funeral director, he was used to gruesome scenes, but this crime exceeded even his expertise and experience. Earlier in the day, Elliott had been in contact with the medical examiner, Dr. Walters, to arrange for the autopsy at his funeral parlor. Dr. Walters had recovered bits of glass, wood, and metal during his brief autopsy.

Elliott's reason for showing up at the crime scene was to gather up the rest of Nola's mortal remains, showing as much respect and giving her as much dignity as possible. It was a horrid job, working in the heat and humidity and darkness, mostly by flashlight, gathering up the tiny pieces of a human being. The air would have stung with gunpowder residue and a meaty aroma—not food, but human flesh.[8]

The officers, led by Detectives Kenney and Bennett, accompanied Elliott to the funeral home that evening to recover the shrapnel that Dr. Walters had found. The decision was made that Nola's remains should be x-rayed for other possible evidence. The task fell to Dr. Glotfelty in his role as assistant medical examiner. Elliott oversaw the transport of Nola to the hospital, where her body was checked one last time. On the films, tiny twisted pieces of aluminum were spotted near her rib cage, one driven as far back as her midback. These were extracted gently from her body by Dr. Glotfelty and turned over to the state police.[9]

The Calhoun County Sheriff's Department also contributed support for the investigation. Their help came in the form of Sergeant Fred Ritchie, who was the first deputy on the scene the day of the explosion. Detectives Kenney and Steinbacher connected with Ritchie after he had been formally assigned to the case. On that first day, they convened a quick meeting at the sheriff's department. Detective Kenney was blunt and to the point, saying, "Look, you know this area and the people a hell of a lot better than we do. So, who do you think is capable of doing something like this?"

Ritchie thought for a moment. Marshall didn't have a long list of criminals and had definitely seen nothing on the scale of the bombing that took Nola's life. After some consideration, he said, "Enoch Chism." Chism was known in the county, mostly for his wife beating and a recent arson conviction. Enoch had never committed a crime of this magnitude, but in Ritchie's mind, he was the one man "squirrelly" enough to do it.[10] Kenney and Steinbacher noted the name. At some point, they would have to find a reason to meet with this Chism.

When you read police reports of this crime, you often glean a level of clinical detail in them. They are cold, impersonal pages describing horrible situations. It takes special men to be detectives and to deal with the business of death and not let raw emotions get hold of them. The officers on this case were meticulous in their detail in documenting the gruesome events. It was tedious, painstaking work, requiring men with the right personality to pursue the details. Slowly, the physical evidence of the murder and the team that would eventually crack the case was starting to come together.

* * * *

Gathering physical evidence was only part of what had filled the first day of the investigation. Within the first hour of the explosion, the police agencies had begun to gather preliminary information regarding the Puyears and preliminary statements from witnesses who were still around.[11] Having ascertained that there was a bomb, they wanted to talk to the employees of the restaurant, to see if they had any thoughts as to who might want to kill Nola. This task was headed up by the local Marshall police.

By 11:45 a.m., several officers met with Paul Puyear at the hospital. The short, white-haired man was still shaken by the events that had taken his wife while he physically was unharmed by the explosion. They initially drilled him with questions about the package containing the bomb: the size, the weight, how it was wrapped, and the types of stamps used on it. Any thoughts or memories he might have could prove useful.

Their questions turned to Nola. Was there anyone who might want to hurt her? Paul was as stumped as they were. Nola had no enemies that he knew of. He did know that she had received a package in the mail about six or seven months earlier that contained a bottle with some pills inside. There had been no return address on that package either. As far as he knew, the pills were still inside the Tasty.[12] Paul had even complained about the pills to the postmaster in Marshall, but the package could not be traced. To the officers involved, it seemed that there was a connection between these pills and the bomb.

Paul Puyear could offer no motive for anyone to want to hurt him or Nola. This was not a simple crime, though. This was exceedingly violent. The police felt that whoever wanted Nola killed had to have powerful emotions behind these actions. Also, this was a crime that required planning, making it a premeditated act.

The police wanted to go through Nola's address book. Paul said that it was kept in his wife's purse. The officers knew that the scene was a gruesome mess. Paul asked that Nola's friend Marg Warsop and the Reverend Samuel West go and recover the purse. For the two of them, who had known Nola, the crime scene had to be unnerving to walk through. Herold Reuss escorted them into the Tasty Cafe. They found the purse, along with $485 in cash, a large amount for the time, indicating that Nola may have been using it for making change.[13]

Officers turned their attention to the employees of the cafe, starting with Josie White. Josie was an older woman who had worked at the Tasty Cafe for the last two years and was contacted quickly by the police. She worked there from 10:30 a.m. to 4:30 p.m. on Tuesday through Saturday, working a split shift on Friday and Saturday. She had been scheduled to come in that Friday but had heard about the blast on the radio and had stayed away. She didn't know of anyone who had an issue with Paul or Nola, but she admitted knowing about the mysterious pills that had been sent Nola. The bottle contained five capsules filled with some white substance.

Josie offered a glimpse into life at the Tasty Cafe with Paul and Nola. She said that she felt that Paul was irresponsible and not very interested in the restaurant or working at it. He never worked afternoons and left every Friday, right after the noon rush, to go up north to his trailer. She also informed the police that Nola had seemed distracted and bothered during recent months. At times, Nola would say, "I'm kind of worried, but I don't know why."[14]

The Marshall police tracked down Paul's brother Mark Puyear in Battle Creek. Like everyone else, he was stunned by the murder. He knew of no one who wanted to hurt Nola or Paul. He did offer up that Paul was an avid sportsman and maintained a trailer in Barryton where he often went on the weekends. He added that "neither of them was seeing anyone on the sly."[15]

Mark Puyear offered up a tantalizing clue to the police, though—one that dominated their thinking in these early hours of the investigation. Nola and Paul had just returned from the funeral of Nola's brother, Wayne Mills, in Arkansas. Wayne's estate had totaled 1.2 million dollars, of which Nola and her sister would split three hundred thousand dollars. While Mark didn't know the exact amount that Nola had come into, it was a large enough number to garner the police's interest. Was it possible that Paul would have killed his wife to get control of her inheritance? To the police, it certainly seemed possible. Husbands had killed for much less. They began to view Paul Puyear with more scrutiny.

Another Tasty Cafe employee, Janet Embury, came forward to the police after she heard about the blast. She was a perky twenty-eight-year-old waitress who the Puyears had employed for two years. When asked about the comings and goings of the Puyears, she claimed that they were good people to work for and seemed to get along with each other. Janet informed the police that Paul left every weekend to go up north to his trailer, leaving on Saturday and returning Sunday night.[16] Nola stayed in Marshall, alone, while Paul went away.

The police became suspicious of Paul's trips up north to his trailer, a suspicion that was only confirmed as they dug deeper. Why would a happily married man leave his wife every weekend to go up north? When they met with Paul's cousin Clyde Prayor, they used a classic ploy. The officers said that they knew Paul was having an affair, to see his cousin's reaction. Prayor begrudgingly admitted that his cousin had a girlfriend in Barryton, saying, "You already know that."[17] The police didn't know it until he had confirmed it for them.

The investigators were narrowing their focus on Paul Puyear, and at first glance, the attention was justified. He was apparently having an affair, and his wife had recently come into a large inheritance. Corporal Legland Whittaker and Officer John Carroll of the Marshall Police Department went back over to Oaklawn Hospital to ask Paul directly about his extracurricular weekend activities. When confronted with the accusation of having an affair; Paul Puyear admitted that he was, indeed, involved with a woman in Barryton. Her name was Deborah Lipton*, though Paul and almost everyone else referred to her as "Bettie."

Paul reluctantly confessed that he had been "dating" her for five to six years. He was quick to add that he thought Bettie could not have had any part in the bombing, reporting, "This thing up there (in Barryton) was casual. She understood the situation and that I was married. I told her that when after the weekend's over, forget it; this wouldn't get out of hand." She had been recently hospitalized and had said to Paul, "If I don't see you again, it's been fun."[18] Her comment, if taken out of context, was enough to catch the attention of the investigators. The police quickly noted that they would need to check out Deborah Lipton and anyone connected to the trailer that Paul maintained in Barryton. Paul's strained confession of an affair only seemed to heighten suspicions that he may have had something to do with his wife's murder.

As tends to happen in all small towns, some leads the police received came from the citizens themselves. Mrs. Delores De Pue contacted the officers with information on an event she had witnessed in the Tasty Cafe that might be pertinent. Delores ate at the Tasty almost every day. She recalled that on Monday, August 14, four young "negros" had been in the restaurant, and in her mind, they had been "casing" the cafe. A group of black men in Marshall stood out. One of the youths had commented to Nola that she had a nice place there and would be seeing more of them. Mrs. De Pue came forward only because the incident stood out in her mind. She was quick to add that she "knew Paul was a woman-chaser but never around town where Nola could find out."[19]

The mention of a group of black men in Marshall immediately caught the attention of the investigators. Marshall was a predominantly white community and clung tightly to its race-based fears. Even today, the adjective *lily-white* is tossed around in describing the town's racial mix. It wasn't always that way. Marshall's black community had been larger in the 1930s, when farming was still a primary economic force in Calhoun County. When World War II broke out, there were good-paying factory jobs in Jackson and Albion, and the handful of black families in Marshall dwindled as they moved in pursuit of better-paying jobs.

Detroit, only a few hours down Interstate 94, had already had a race riot earlier in the summer, when police had raided an illegal after hours bar. The riot had lasted five days and had sent a chill through every community in Michigan.[20] The Marshall Chamber of Commerce had even held a meeting to discuss what would happen if there were race riots in their city. The city manager had said that they had "spotters checking when negroes leave Albion or Battle Creek and know if they planned to come to Marshall." Unfounded paranoid fears of a race riot in little Marshall were apparently quite real in the minds of the citizens. The city's plan for dealing with a potential riot was on par with burying its head in the proverbial sand: "We have decided the best thing to do, if we are hit, is for every merchant to go home and let the police handle it." Paul Puyear had voiced the feelings of many of the business owners in the small city: "What I have down there is my life's work. I believe every man on Main Street should be deputized, and permitted to protect his property." The Marshall city manager balked at that idea and worried about what would happen with armed men on the streets during a race riot; the picture was not a pretty one.[21]

The air of racial tension touched every Michigan community in some way, and in Marshall, the rioting in Detroit only added to the nervousness. On his last trip home to Arkansas, Paul Puyear told his cousin Gene Henderson of the fear that the riots in Detroit might spill over to Marshall, claiming, "I have a shotgun in the back of my restaurant and have no intention of letting them destroy my business. I damned sure will use it on them."[22] But the police—especially the state police from Battle Creek, which had a black community—realized that this was nothing more than paranoia.

Other witnesses came forward offering any thoughts or insights that they thought might help the police that first day. Helen Hazen, a nurse who lived outside of town and worked at the Mi-Lady's Beauty Shop, two doors down from the Tasty Cafe, came forward to say that she had been in the shop in June when Nola had brought in the mysterious pills that had been mailed to her. Like most small towns, the barber shops and beauty parlors were hubs where "social networking" took place. It was there that information and pure gossip were spread.

Nola had told Helen that she thought the pills were some sort of practical joke. Nancy asked Nola if she had tried to determine what the pills were, but she hadn't. Nola went and got the pills, and Nancy broke one open, putting some of the white substance on her tongue. It burned, and she said it tasted like alum. Nola had taken the pills to the drugstore to see if they could tell her more about them. There had been several witnesses to the discussion that day, including Nancy Church and Jean Reed. Nancy had told Nola she should have just thrown them away.[23] The Marshall police tracked down Nancy Church at the Mi-Lady's Beauty Shop, which she owned, and she confirmed Helen Hazen's story.

The importance of the pills seemed to increase as more people discussed them. Nola had made a point of showing them to others, and if they could be tied to the bombing, they might yield some additional evidence.

* * * *

Nola was not the kind of person who collected enemies. Running a cafe in Marshall required a person to have a warm and friendly disposition, and she was well suited for the role of owner. Yes, you got the occasional stranger stopping for a meal, but most business came from regulars, which meant you had to serve good food with a smile almost every day. Nola was warm and gregarious, always laughing and friendly.

A young married couple, Tom and Karen Swalwell, lived in a tiny apartment over Mitchell's Hardware next to the Tasty. They were regular customers at the Tasty—Tom favoring Nola's famous hamburger steak dinner. Nola made sure that Tom never went home hungry, providing extra helpings of side dishes. Nola baked her own pies to sell, and if she had any leftovers, she would take them to the young couple after closing. Karen later remembered, "Nola would give you the shirt off her back. She was tough too—she didn't take any crap."[24]

Stories of Nola's kindness and generosity were commonplace in Marshall. So what could someone so friendly and down to earth do to warrant a murder on this scale? The people on the street of Marshall could not comprehend who would be angry enough to kill Nola—let alone to do so in such a violent manner. Many wanted to believe it involved strangers, that this was some random act. As each hour passed, individuals began to reflect on that thought and question if it was plausible. Was it possible that the killer was one of their own community? After all, how would anyone even know Nola unless they were in Marshall? The investigators found themselves struggling with some of the same issues themselves. There were aspects of this crime that simply didn't add up

* * * *

Detective Kenney had managed to piece together the last morning of Nola's life in hopes that it might offer a clue as to her fate. She and Paul had left the house at 5:00 a.m. as usual. On their way out, they were spotted by their neighbors, Mr. and Mrs. George, who rented their house from the Puyears. Mrs. Puyear brought over a package of matches she had obtained on a recent trip to Arkansas. The Puyears had been from Arkansas, settling in Marshall in 1929. Their most recent trip was not a vacation for them. Nola's brother had passed away, and they had gone down for the funeral. They had closed the restaurant for the time they were gone, as they had on previous trips. "We are from Arkansas too," Mrs. George would later recount. "I had breakfast at the restaurant at about 6:30 a.m. Friday before I went to work and Mrs. Puyear seemed so happy and jolly."[25] If there was any hint that Nola was fearful for her life, she didn't show it. It was the last time that Mrs. George ever saw her friend and neighbor.

Nothing at all implied that Nola Puyear suspected she was being stalked by a murderer. From all accounts, the Puyears went to the Tasty that morning and opened it as usual. There was no hint of anything being wrong, no threat against them.

* * * *

The first day of the investigation had been long, complicated, and unfulfilling for those involved. Elliott Court oversaw Nola's return to the funeral parlor that evening. Her funeral would still have to be arranged, despite the condition of her remains, and a public showing was inconceivable.[26]

The officers had some directions to pursue, most of which centered on the husband of the victim—Paul Puyear. So far, they had determined that he was routinely sleeping with another woman on his weekends. His murdered wife had just come into a sizable inheritance. The violent nature of the crime also helped steer them to Paul. Nola had not been randomly shot or stabbed; she had been blown up. This was an exceedingly violent act, which implied to them that whoever had killed her had mustered a great deal of passion in murdering her.

In the evaluation of Paul Puyear as a suspect, the biggest factor that worked in his favor was that he was present when the bomb went off. Someone who had mailed a bomb to a person wouldn't want to be near the package when it went off. Paul had only been ten to twelve feet away, and he had escaped serious injury apparently by pure luck.

By 10:15 p.m., the weary police were finally done at the crime scene for the night. They went to bed knowing that they had a lot of potential leads. More important to them, it appeared that Paul Puyear's life deserved a great deal more scrutiny. None realized just where that course of investigation would take them.

The Marshall Post Office was right across the street from the Tasty Cafe. It is a stately, sandstone brick structure, almost too large for the small town. White columns mark the entrance, along with a pristine little lawn. The boarded up building across Michigan Avenue was more than a reminder to the employees of the post office; it was a warning sign.

Air-conditioning was decades away for the building. In the hot August summer, the concrete building was a hotbox. Inside, large fans moved around the sticky humid air—an attempt to create the illusion of comfort for the employees. In the large back room, under the low buzz of the heavy fans, the mail was sorted for each route. The cool concrete walls, covered in white enamel paint, would sweat in the humidity but offered some degree of comfort.

The employees of the Marshall Post Office were justifiably afraid. The bomb had come through their pillared office. Some of them had handled it. At any point, the bomb that killed Nola Puyear could have gone off and killed them.

Postal workers tend to handle mail roughly, trusting the sender to pack their parcels for the bumpy processing. That changed in August of 1967. Every package that came through was handled gingerly, slowly, methodically. Every parcel was eyed as if it were a potential bomb. Details of packages that were usually ignored were scrutinized as workers touched each box and parcel. Processing slowed down, but no one complained.[27] A bomber was loose in their community, and while others might have the luxury of being nervous, the postal workers in Marshall felt true terror.

Don Damon, the deliveryman who had dropped off the bomb, bore the brunt of the public face of the post office after the bombing. "Every time I dropped off a package, people would say things like, 'Don, don't leave until I open this up.'"[28] It was the kind of dry humor that told just how Marshall was dealing with the stress.

The day after the bombing, the *Marshall Evening Chronicle* ran its only editorial on the crime during the three years of the investigation and trial. It captured the feelings of the town and the sudden pain and loss that everyone felt.

A Shocking Tragedy

The mysterious explosion at the Tasty Sandwich Shop, 209 East Michigan Avenue, has shocked countless Marshallites.

A bombing of this type isn't unusual in Detroit, Chicago, Philadelphia, New York City, or any other large city in America, but last Friday's local bombing was something that most residents said simply, "couldn't happen here."

City police, firemen, state police attachés, and the FBI are to be congratulated for their prompt start of investigation at the tragedy scene.

The big question of this tragedy, "who sent the bomb?"

We are sure that officials will do their utmost to find a quick solution to the deadly crime.

Mr. and Mrs. Paul Puyear were highly respected citizens of the community.

As usual in a case of this sort, "Dame Rumor," starts operating swiftly.

You can count on local authorities investigating each and every tip they received.

Without a doubt Friday's bombing will be the "biggest" news story of the year and it definitely threw the entire city into a state of confusion.

We hope there is a quick solution to the tragedy which never should have happened in this relatively quiet county-seat-city.[29]

3
Small Towns and Their Dirty Little Secrets

When you read the police reports related to this crime, you can actually trace the thinking of the officers, especially when you look at the interviews chronologically. Their logic becomes clear and concise. At first glimpse, Paul Puyear looked like a viable subject. His wife had recently inherited money, and he had some extramarital affairs—not one, but many.

The affairs were the kind of thing that simply didn't fit in with Marshall's pristine and proper image. Yet oddly enough, many people were aware of Paul's philandering. It was the stuff of gossip. As the investigators followed each lead, searching for a jealous lover or a blackmailer in the wings with a motive, what they discovered was just how difficult this investigation was going to be. The web of sex and debauchery took them down many rabbit holes.

The investigators of Nola's murder became the natural team to pull in as myriad affairs surfaced, since they were already working the bombing investigation. The final team working the case came from a variety of jurisdictions. Detectives Robert Kenney and his partner, Leroy Steinbacher, represented the Michigan State Police, who nominally were in charge of the investigation. Detective Donald Bennett of the state police crime lab provided the crucial links in the evidence. The Marshall police were represented by Assistant Chief Herold Reuss. Fred Ritchie coordinated the resources of the Calhoun County Sheriff's Department.

Minor Myers, the postal inspector from Kalamazoo, was on the team, as well as Matthew J. Reinhard. The U.S. Postal Service operated as a separate government entity, with its own police force in the form of its postal investigators. Kalamazoo was ill equipped for the complexities of a postal bombing—most cities were, because such bombings were so rare. Myers was fairly laid back the first day of the investigation, preferring to let the local authorities do the initial legwork on the crime. That was about to change, though, with the arrival of Myron P. Wood.

Wood, the postal inspector from Detroit, rolled into Marshall full of energy and vigor. He was a chatty well-kempt man who looked more like a polished salesman than an investigator. Whereas Myers had been laid back, Wood understood that this bombing had violated several federal laws, and he wanted action. Wood had been involved on one other postal bombing case and qualified as one of a handful of men with some experience in the area.

The postal inspectors brought one thing to the investigation—resources. Where the state police and other jurisdictions had some limitations on what they spent investigating, the postal inspectors had much more leeway. When they led the charge to investigate Paul Puyear, they simply hopped on planes and headed to Arkansas to probe deeper into his past.

This was a very violent crime, one that pointed to a crime of passion. The other police were willing to consider Paul Puyear as a potential suspect, but it was the postal service that wanted him placed under more scrutiny. It was a decision that was to guide the first few weeks of the investigation.

While the crime shook the small town of Marshall deeply, more disturbing were the rash of pranks and false alarms that followed. The fact that the newspapers carried these incidents only added to the fears of the local community that a bomber was out there and might strike again. Each seemingly harmless practical joke heightened the tension of the citizens.

The investigators responded quickly to the scene when Herbert Irvin reported what he thought might be a bomb at Quality Restaurant Suppliers. It had arrived in the mail, and to Irvin, it was out of place—wrapped in brown paper, with no return address. Because it had come in the mail, Inspector Wood went along with the state police to check the suspicious package. At the time, the Michigan State Police did not have a bomb squad trained in explosives or disarming bombs. When such rare threats came in, the troopers had to simply deal with it as best they could.

The officers methodically and carefully cut open the package with razor blades and steely nerves. They found that the wrapped box contained an alarm clock, papers, and wires. At first glimpse, it was, indeed, a bomb. As they sifted delicately through the contents, they found that it was apparently nothing more than a carefully crafted prank.[1] But who would send such a package—and why? Was this the murderer of Nola

Puyear, trying to send police some sort of message—perhaps throw off their investigation?

Two days after the bombing, the Hillcrest Restaurant on U.S. Route 27 overreacted to a package they had been storing. Some travelers from Indiana asked them to hold a package for them in their refrigerator. Nervous over the bombing of the Tasty Cafe, the restaurant owners called in the sheriff's department, claiming that they had a "fishy" parcel in their possession. The package was indeed fishy; in fact, it was a large wrapped fish, most likely caught in a nearby lake for later consumption.[2]

The Calhoun County Sheriff's Department was forced to treat every practical joke or overreaction as if they were real threats.

To the citizens reading the newspapers in Calhoun County, these incidents were reminders of the gruesome murder of Nola Puyear and were far from humorous. The investigators were not sure if the murderer was taunting them or if some sick local citizens were playing jokes.

Two days after the murder, the Calhoun County Fair opened in Marshall only six blocks from the remains of the Tasty Cafe. The restaurant became a sideshow attraction on its own for anyone coming to the fair. Long lines of cars eased by slowly, looking at the stark plywood covering the windows, wondering and speculating as to who was responsible. The Tasty was on the way for many fairgoers, and everyone wanted to see where the murder had taken place. The cafe was an ugly scar on quaint little Marshall, a wound that stung the detectives working the Nola Puyear case. The fair was a blessing and a curse. It captured the public's attention but, at the same time, had turned the Tasty Cafe into a drive-by tourist exhibit. Even as the police continued their work, the sounds of laughter and screams from the rides echoed through the streets of town.

* * * *

The decision to concentrate on Paul Puyear as the possible murderer was driven primarily by the postal inspectors. On the surface, it was hard to ignore him as a possible suspect. Paul was cheating on Nola and would potentially profit from her death. At the same time, there were no other alternatives to be offered. The investigation began to move away from Marshall, following the leads. The first thing the investigators did was secure rights to search the Puyear home and the trailer in Barryton.

The Tasty Cafe as it appeared after the bombing. (*From Richard W. Carver via his son Raymond, with permission.*)

The postal inspectors contacted officials in Harrisburg, Arkansas, where the Puyears were from, and did what they could to obtain information on Paul and Nola's family. The long list of people to be interviewed was divided up by the various agencies involved. Paul Puyear's life was going under a microscope, and it would reveal a great deal about a sordid side of idyllic Marshall.

In my research for this book, I learned that Fred Ritchie of the Calhoun County Sheriff's Department was among the voices of dissention about concentrating on Paul Puyear. He explained, "The postal inspectors were the ones that were determined that Paul was the one who did it. I knew that wasn't the case. Paul knew that the packages sent to the house were sent to the restaurant. If you were going to kill someone, you sure wouldn't send it in the mail, knowing it would come to where you were. You sure wouldn't stay around after the package came." Yes, Paul had survived the explosion, but that was mostly a twist of fate. Still, the postal inspectors headed south to Arkansas to interview friends and family of the Puyears. In small-town America, postal delivery people were often privy to a great deal of what was happening in their community.

Paul Puyear was born in the rolling hills and lush green fields of Cal-vert, Kentucky. His parents moved to a farm near Charleston, Missouri, when he was one year old. He had two sisters, both of whom had died in his youth. His sister Eula drowned in 1918, and his other sister, Vada Price, had committed suicide a few years before Nola's demise. He had three brothers—Herman, Mark, and Ray—who were still alive and kept in close contact.[3]

When Paul was fourteen, his family moved to Harrisburg, Arkansas. Harrisburg was located in the Mississippi River valley and had a popula-tion of around nineteen hundred. An agricultural community that pros-pered from soy, cotton, and rice farming, it was the kind of town that made Marshall look like a big city.[4] Flat farmlands surrounded by thin lines of trees marking property boundaries characterized this floodplain.

Paul met Nola Mills in Harrisburg. Paul and Nola lived next door to each other, and he dated her for five years before they married, on November 3, 1929. Paul had been away from Harrisburg for a year and a half, and their relationship had been a long-distance one during that period. Nola was the oldest of the Mills family. She had three siblings, Wayne, Ruby (Roberts), and Willie (Bunkus).

Paul lived in Harrisburg until 1928, when he set out looking for work. By his own description, his family was poor. He went to East St. Louis, Illinois, seeking a job, while Ray and Mark Puyear moved to Bat-tle Creek. Paul suffered from asthma, and the Michigan climate proved to be helpful for his condition. He moved to Marshall in 1928 and even-tually got a job at Eaton's, where he worked for seventeen years, making valves for Ford Motor Company. It was factory work, involving con-stant repetition—hot humid work during the summers, hot boring work in the winters. In 1929, Eaton's moved operations from Battle Creek to Marshall, which is where Paul and Nola settled in. Their son, John Paul, was born in 1942. Paul and Nola wanted to have other children and tried, but with no success.

Paul quit Eaton's in 1945. He explained, "I had had it as far as factory work was concerned. I was fed up. I wanted to do something differ-ent. I quit Eaton's with no idea of what I would do."[5] Nola had already been working for eight years at the Dug-Out Restaurant. Nola seemed to be born to be in the restaurant business. She was socially outgoing and developed a good rapport with Marshall's citizens. David Avery*, a friend of the Puyears, owned the Tasty Sandwich Shop, and he offered to sell the business to Nola and Paul. They purchased the tiny diner for $8,750. The business was doing well, but they opted to move it to a better location, on Michigan Avenue, in 1953. Nola was the "headman" of the business; of that there was no question. She did all of the buying and maintained the books. According to Paul, "Nola had the brains."[6]

Paul fit into the Marshall community. He joined the Masonic Order, but his weekend trips to Barryton every week limited his ability to participate much in community affairs and events. According to Paul, Nola encouraged him to go to the trailer every weekend; she was content running the restaurant. Where the Tasty was the center of Nola's entire life, Paul's seemed to orbit around the little trailer he kept up north.

The Puyears returned annually to Harrisburg to visit family. Nola was particularly close to her brother Wayne Mills. Paul was known to pal around with Bunkus whenever they were in Arkansas. From all indications from the Mills family, Paul was a caring husband, and there were no known issues between him and Nola.[7] It seemed there was very little in Arkansas that could explain the violent and brutal murder of Nola. This forced investigators to turn their attentions elsewhere. The police decided to turn up their focus on the relationship that Paul had with his wife.

It was clear Paul loved Nola, though it was rare for them to demonstrate it publicly. Many of the individuals the police interviewed said that Paul and Nola never held hands or kissed in public. There were indications, though, that Paul loved his wife a great deal. While she was working at the Dug-Out, a man named Alabam who worked at Eaton's was making passes at her. Paul knew him from the factory and came to the defense of his wife. He went to the Dug-Out and told him, "You are my friend. You will still be my friend. But if this happens again, you know what I will do." For a few moments, learning of this incident offered investigators hope—of a potential suspect. Then Paul told them that Alabam had died in 1960, ruling him out as a possible murder suspect.[8]

In the last few years, Paul and Nola's sex life had dropped off. Paul had ample drive, but Nola simply did not show an interest in sex. "Like a lot of people our age, it didn't happen very often," Paul reported. He attributed their lack of intercourse to the long, hard hours working at the Tasty. In his mind, his wife was simply too tired for sex.[9] Paul, however, had a very healthy sex drive, one that would emerge as the police attempted to see if he was Nola's murderer.

Paul was ten years older than Nola and was looking forward to relaxing in retirement, but he had to admit that he was alone in that thinking. Five years before the bombing, he had asked Nola about shutting down the restaurant on the weekends and joining him up north as a way of easing into retirement. His wife would have nothing to do with it, saying, "I'd rather not. I am happy right here in this restaurant and this is my life." Paul said, "I am getting to the age, if I don't enjoy the fruits I worked for I'm afraid I never will." She told him to take off every weekend and go assuring him, "there will never be a word said from me. I want you to do the things you want to do."[10] In the coming days of the investigation, the investigators would begin to wonder just how much Nola knew of the events in which her husband was involved each weekend.

Paul saw their relationship more candidly. As he said to his friend Keith Flowers*, "If she wants to work all of the time, let her and I'll do the playing."[11] Based on what the police were learning in Barryton, this was not a boast but a way of life for Paul.

As investigators probed into Paul's sex life, they had already discovered that the trips to the trailer in Barryton for "fishing and hunting" were really for Paul to stray from his wife. Many people in Marshall knew about his multitude of indiscretions; these were known but talked about in veiled whispers by the community. The trips up to Barryton were not well-kept secrets in Marshall—they were simply talked about with discretion. As in all small towns, there was an image and reputation that the community protected.

If you weren't looking for Barryton, you'd most likely never find it. Barryton defined the phrase "a wide spot on the road." It sat in the middle of nowhere, on the mitten of the Michigan map, little more than a postal station, a library, a gas station, and a tiny grocery store. It was only a short distance from Chippewa Lake, the headwater for the Chippewa River. Like so many communities "up north," it survived on hunting and fishing—usually from people coming up from southern Michigan. The ties between Barryton and Marshall were apparently quite strong, as the investigation would reveal.

The investigators speaking with Paul began with his admission that he had been "dating" Deborah "Bettie" Lipton in Barryton. The fine veneer of Paul's image as a discreet businessman began to crack almost immediately as the police dug deeper. Yes, there were other women. Yes, he was doing more than dating them—his relationships involved intercourse. The more the investigators poked and prodded at the goings-on in Barryton, the more they realized just how broad Paul's affairs were.

Over the course of a dozen interviews with the investigators, Paul slowly began to confess his infidelities to the police, one sordid affair at a time. At first, he claimed that the first time he wandered from Nola's arms was with a woman in Sikeston, Missouri, in 1958. His mother was at the hospital, and he was at a hotel nearby to check in on her. He met the woman at the hotel and had a short affair with her while he was in town.[12] Paul could not remember her name.

An interview with Tessie Pridgeon, a clerk in the Barryton Post Office, offered up another name that Paul would confess to when presented the information by police, Eve Jones*. Tessie said that most folks in Barryton knew about Paul and the "goings-on" at his trailer. Like Marshall, Barryton was a small community that kept its secrets near and dear. Tessie reported that it was well known that he "ran around" with Eve Jones and Bettie Lipton. Paul's preference in woman chasing was to go after divorcées or widows.[13]

When police confronted Paul with Eve's name, he initially claimed that he had a casual relationship with her. But when pressed by investigators, he admitted that he had slept with her. His friend Keith Flowers had introduced them. Paul went out with her for five to six months, on the weekends when he would go up to the small trailer he had moved up to Barryton. To most people, a trailer was simply a wheeled weekend cottage of sorts, but for Paul, his had quickly become a place for him to have his affairs. Eve worked in nearby Big Rapids, and when investigators found her, she only spoke fondly of Paul. Eve had terminated their relationship when she met another man, one that was available to her more than just on weekends. For investigators, it was another dead end.

Paul confessed a 1957 affair with Jane Marie Morton*. He had gone out with her for a year and a half and had broken up with her. When he had later met her daughter on the road, and she had said, "Mother would like for you to come back and see her sometime." He drove up to her house, and Jane curtly called out to him, "You don't need to get out.

Back up and go about your business. You are not wanted here anymore." To the police, it sounded like she was a jilted lover—a potential suspect. Investigators tracked her down and discovered that the chubby fifty-six-year-old had remarried and apparently did not have any ill will toward Paul but also didn't want anything to do with him.

Paul began to rattle off the names of women he had dated to the police. There was a woman named Velma Harter* who Paul went out with a few times.[14] Paul remembered another short affair around the same time period, with a woman he only remembered by her first name, Etta. She lived seven or eight miles east of Barryton, but he had heard that she recently had remarried.[15] Another woman Puyear admitted that he had an affair with was Gertrude Westhaven*. He was quick to point out that this had only been on two occasions three to four years ago, while he had been seeing Bettie—an admission that he had been cheating on Bettie as well.[16] Barryton seemed to have no shortage of older lonely women looking for comfort, and Paul was more than willing to fulfill their needs.

In 1961, Paul decided his old trailer in Barryton was too small for his activities. He purchased a larger, two-bedroom trailer, one that would allow him to invite other Marshallites up north. He kept the trailer parked on Chippewa Lake. Still somewhat small and cramped, it was barely comfortable. The other trailers on the lake were more like hunting lodges or summer cabins. The Puyear trailer was more like a hidden sex den, tucked away in the shade of the trees along the edge of the lake.

Paul confessed that he had met his longtime girlfriend, Deborah "Bettie" Lipton, around 1959–60. Bettie was short—five foot one inch in height—weighing 141 pounds. She wore glasses and had a bubbly personality. She was divorced and had three children, two who died at birth and one in the Air Force, like Paul's own son, John. Her son, Robert*, sometimes hitched a ride with Paul from Battle Creek up to Barryton. Puyear visited Bettie often, even when she was in the hospital. When Wayne Mills, Nola's brother, had died, Paul had his friend Jack O'Grady* relay a message to her that he wouldn't be up to Barryton for the weekend. His dating of Bettie was far from a secret, nor was he very discreet about the relationship.

The investigators wanted to see if Paul was indebted to her or if she was in any way blackmailing him. They coyly slid in questions in their talks with him about how much money changed hands between them. He admitted that he had given her money on certain trips, fifty dollars for Christmas, ten dollars for Mother's Day and for her birthday. To the investigators, this, too, seemed to be a dead end—money was clearly not the motive.

In more than one interview session, Paul wanted to clarify that he did not think Bettie was at all involved with Nola's death.[17] The team investigating the crime was not entirely convinced on Paul's word alone. After all, he had concealed his affair with her. But on further probing, he had disclosed numerous affairs in Barryton. Inspectors traveling up to Barryton found Bettie Lipton to be more than willing to discuss her relationship with Paul.

Deborah Lipton was born on July 27, 1929, in Flint, Michigan, and was thirty-eight years old in 1967. Her nickname, "Bettie," was one a relative had given her at an early age, and she had gone by it ever since. Bettie had been divorced for twelve years and had been going out with Paul since 1960, when Eve Jones had introduced them. When asked if she loved Paul, she gave a very noncommittal response, saying she thought as much of him as she could any man. Her response was far from passionate. Perhaps years of being the other woman had taken from her all of the passion. Bettie was openly forthcoming with investigators about the numerous affairs in Barryton between Paul, his friends from Marshall, and the local community.[18] Her admissions, combined with his, defined their relationship to one word: sex.

Paul never talked marriage or the future with her, and she did not harbor any illusions about the future of her relationship with Paul. It was clear to her interviewers that she was still bitter over her first marriage. When they asked her about Paul's thoughts toward her, probing for a possible motive, she replied that Paul would say he loved her, but usually in a casual manner. There was no commitment between these two older people. All they had was the weekends and the torrid affairs in the trailer. In many respects, it was simply sad.

Paul told Bettie that Nola was "married to the restaurant." When she pressed him about Nola, he said that their relationship was "like that of a brother and sister," that they had not been as man and wife since around the time his son, John, was born. Paul insisted that he had tried to get Nola to retire but that she would not do it.[19] He admitted to Bettie that he would not fight with Nola; instead, he would just walk away.[20] To some of the investigators, these were not the words of a man who was planning to blow up his wife. However, the postal inspectors did not let up their digging into Paul's life.

When asked about her commenting to Paul, "If I don't see you again, it's been fun," she said that the line was a standing joke between them, which one or the other would usually use whenever they parted ways, and that there was nothing else to it. The last time she spoke with Paul, he had said, "If I can't come up Friday, I'll call you." She had replied, "I'll see you Friday."

Inspector Myron Wood of the postal service pressed the true question home, asking Bettie whether she or Paul had anything to do with the murder of Nola. Her response was no—flatly, categorically no. She said that Paul couldn't have had anything to do with it, because he was far too kind and gentle.[21] The inspectors interviewed Bettie's son and former husband to see if either of them had any motive to strike out at Paul, but what they found was another disappointing dead end.

The spotlight of the investigation was still on Paul Puyear and his extramarital affairs. To the investigators, it seemed to be the best place to explore. In their minds, whoever killed Nola had to have a strong emotional reason for such a brutal death. If Paul had not murdered Nola, that posed a serious complication to the police. It meant that the real killer may have struck randomly—that he may not have had a connection to his victim. It meant that the answers to the crime might yet lie in the tiny community of Marshall.

In photographs, Paul Puyear looks like a genteel bespectacled grandfather, not a Lothario with a harem of lovers. But the more the officers poked and prodded into his private life, the more he revealed. Each interview brought more people into the web of the investigation. It became apparent that Paul Puyear's extramarital activities involved not just him but other members of Marshall's private community.

While several teams of investigators fanned out in rural Barryton to track down each of Paul's affairs, the police in Marshall decided to dig deeper into Paul's love life locally. Were there any women in Marshall who Paul had fooled around with? Could he have only fooled around in Barryton? They pressed the small older man with a flurry of questions, and Paul hesitated, admitting that there were indeed some local affairs.

He had slept with the wife of one of his best friends, David Avery, from whom he bought the Tasty Cafe. Nearly twenty years before, he had met a Marshall woman named Emily Judith Martin* and carried out an affair with her. Paul seemed to hesitate in talking about her, more than most of his other conquests.

Emily—who, at various times, had had the last names Martin*, Jackson*, and Carmichael*, dependent on her volatile marital status—was a younger woman. A skinny woman, she was often described as a "hillbilly." Paul admitted that she had always been putting the squeeze on him for money. She commented once that her son had a lot of the same features as Paul and had been born just after they broke up—implying that he had fathered the boy. In a Marshall bar, one witness heard her say that Paul Puyear was paying for her apartment and that Paul was her son's father. Another patron noted that she was quite drunk at the time and implied that either Bob Avery* or Paul Puyear was the father of her son, and she was upset because both Bob's and Paul's sons had so much more than hers. Emily was considered a loose woman and was laden with problems of her own. She was out on bail on a prostitution charge and was evicted, making it harder for the police to track her down.

From talking with several friends of Paul, they got a similar story. Bob Avery, who knew Paul from when they worked together at Eaton's, claimed he didn't know about the affair, but he later confessed that Paul had taken Emily to Barryton several times.[22] Further probing produced witnesses who claimed that Bob had also had an affair with Emily and that she accused him of fathering her son as well. Other inquiries to people who knew Paul in Marshall produced others who claimed they had heard a rumor that Paul was the father of her son and had paid her a considerable amount of money.[23] Josie White, who worked at the Tasty Cafe, had heard the same rumor from her sister, Thelma Patterson, who ran Thelma's Cafe in town.[24] Marshall's rumor mill had plenty to say about the clandestine affairs of its citizens.

Paul vigorously denied Emily's accusation of fatherhood. Yes, Emily had pressed him for money, and he had, at times, given her small amounts, but he had never paid her off. Emily had her own police record for disorderly conduct, had left Ceresco where she had lived, and had married again and moved on.[25] The last time Paul had seen her was two years ago, when she had stopped by the Tasty.[26] She was the only one

of Paul's mistresses who blatantly came to the Tasty Cafe or ever had
contact with Nola.

It took the police three weeks to track Emily down in nearby Battle Creek, where she was living with her new husband, a black man—
violating yet another social taboo of the time. She was thirty-seven years
old, meaning that when Paul had dated her, she may have been a minor,
which may explain why he had been reluctant to discuss her with investigators. She was a shapely 130 pounds, with brown hair and blue eyes,
and her criminal record showed she had a rough life. When investigators
interviewed her, she denied ever knowing Paul Puyear and was unco-
operative with the officers beyond providing a sample of her handwriting. From what the investigators could tell, Emily didn't have the skills,
motivation, or expertise to create a bomb.[27] She was a sad young woman
searching for some hope of happiness in life, a search that seemed to be
far from complete.

The discovery of Emily's relationship with Paul attracted the attention of the investigators. She was local to the area and had a police record. She had been trying to wring money out of Paul in the past. If
she was innocent, what about her son? Was it possible that he believed
Paul to be his father and was striking out at him? He was brought in for
an interview with Sergeant Ritchie. The young man said that he knew
Paul Puyear and had known him since he was a young boy. Ritchie carefully danced around the issue of Paul's fatherhood, and the boy, Robert,
claimed that his birth father lived in Florida. From what Sergeant Ritchie
could tell, the young man did not know about his mother's insinuation
that Paul Puyear might be his father. Ritchie obtained a sample of Robert's handwriting and ruled him out as a possible suspect.[28]

Paul also admitted that a regular customer at the Tasty Cafe, Violet "Sene" Buckner, had flirted with him. But he said that nothing had
come from it. Sene and her husband, Bruce, hung out a great deal at
the restaurant, and for a long time, Paul claimed, he had not returned
her overtures. Two times, she had come over to him, pushed away the
newspaper he was reading, sat on his lap, and kissed him. She had said,
"That was pretty good, I'll have another one," and kissed him again. On
his birthday, she made a point to give him a big kiss. When Nola had her
cataract operation, Sene came by for drinks and kissed him good-bye.
Paul remembered her saying, "Stop by anytime."

On one occasion, Sene came to the Tasty on a Friday afternoon carry-ing a bedroll, claiming that she was going to go up north to the trailer with him. Before he could react, she and Nola cracked up—both of them being in on the joke. Sene dressed provocatively, for 1967, often wearing shorts or slacks that made her stand out on the highly conservative Marshall streets. Sene was an incendiary character and outright daring by small-town Marshall standards. Her flirtatious attitude and bubbly personality clashed with a town struggling to cling to the norms of the 1950s.

Paul wanted to make sure that the investigators understood that he had never fooled around with Sene. Given the number of extramarital affairs he was involved with, it had to have struck them as odd that, for some reason, he and Sene had never hooked up. Paul exposed Sene's own affairs to the police, adding that she was known to have a boyfriend outside of Marshall named Dave Hart*.[29]

In another interview with police, when pressed about other trysts locally, Paul confessed that he had also slept with LuLu Simmons* in Marshall. She was a single woman at the time when he had a relation-ship with her. Their affair had lasted eight to nine months during World War II, and Paul had not seen her since.[30] She apparently had remarried and left town.

Paul contacted Inspectors Wood and Myers to clarify a point. He was worried that the police thought the affair with Bettie was serious, and he assured them it wasn't. To emphasize his point, he said that on one night, both he and Oscar Sharp* took turns sleeping with her. That night, Sharp had relations with her three times, and Paul slept with her once.[31] It was an odd way for him to try and prove the nature of his relationship with Bettie—by implicating her with others in Marshall.

What Paul didn't realize is that he had suddenly made the investiga-tors aware that others were visiting the trailer in Barryton and that other affairs were taking place up there. Rather than clarifying anything, Paul had expanded the number of people who the police needed to talk to. Worse, they were going to find out that the goings-on in Barryton by Marshall's men were much more perverse. The image of pure and inno-cent Marshall was slowly showing its cracks and weakness.

The police revisited several interviewees and added to their list of persons of interest. Bettie Lipton informed them that Hollie White, Josie White's husband, had been to the trailer several times and, when there, dated a local woman, Gertrude Westhaven. They would go over to the Idle Hour Bar in Weidman for fish suppers on Friday night; it was one of the few places to dine out in the area.[32] Gertrude already had had an affair with Paul at the time. Hollie was from Harrisburg, Arkansas, the same town as Paul and Nola. He knew most of the members of the Mills family and had known the Puyears for twenty-five years. Hollie was employed as a janitor at Sherer-Gillett Company in town.

At first blush, Hollie White vigorously denied he knew any women in the Barryton area or had a girlfriend on his trips to the trailer. When Inspector Myers told him that he had information to the contrary, Hollie reluctantly changed his answer. Yes, he had taken up with a woman named Gertrude three or four times about six or seven years ago. She was a small, chunky woman with glasses. He assumed she was keeping house for a farmer.[33]

Paul indicated that one of the women he had dated, Velma Harter*, had dated Ed Royale* a few times when he visited the trailer he kept next to Paul's.[34] Suddenly, the investigators began to wonder just how many of Marshall's good male citizens had some sort of connection with Barryton via Paul's tiny trailer. One of the men who Paul mentioned to the police as a visitor to his trailer was seventy-year-old Felix "Fritz" Hoffman*. Hoffman knew Paul for forty-five years and was well known in Marshall. He went up north with Paul about three years before the bombing. Like many people in town, he knew Paul kept company with Bettie Lipton. Fritz had stopped visiting up there, because his wife had put a stop to it.[35] Like many of the men who went with Paul up north, he initially and defiantly denied any wrongdoing up at the trailer.

Fritz denied any knowledge of the carnal activities in Paul's trailer until Sergeant Fred Richie told him that the investigators knew what had happened there.[36] This information was courtesy of the information Bettie had provided investigators. Faced with this and the gravity of the murder investigation, he changed his story. Fritz had been "dating" Eve Jones on his trips up to Barryton.[37] Apparently, Mrs. Hoffman's decision to put an end to his trips up north was a good instinctive hunch on her part—either that or someone in Marshall had tipped her off.

Some of the tips that came in on the case bordered on the bizarre. One local wag, Harry King*, reached out to the postal inspectors with some information. He was insistent that he could only speak with the postal inspectors and arranged a rendezvous at the Mar Creek Bar in Ceresco, nestled between Battle Creek and Marshall. When Inspector Wood arrived, he found a man wearing a slouched hat sitting in his car, wearing dark sunglasses to obscure his identity. The cloak-and-dagger meeting seemed to add credibility to the story he was going to tell. King introduced himself and tried to establish himself as "in the know." He had known Paul Puyear for forty years and was sure that Paul never "stepped out." He had known Nola just as long and was sure that she was faithful as well. Then again, he pointed out, "still water runs deep," and he wouldn't be too surprised if she had a man on the side.

King had been married to a woman who had left him for another man, Oscar Sharp. King insisted that Sharp was the man who had killed Nola. There were a few reasons for this. King had hooked up with his ex-wife, and when he had run behind on his alimony, Sharp had raised a ruckus over it. According to King, Sharp had driven his wife crazy, quite literally. She had been institutionalized for some time now. According to King, he had once seen Sharp take two eight-gauge shotgun shells and convert them into a potent bomb. King hypothesized that Sharp had gotten his mentally imbalanced wife to address the package for him.

The story was fanciful but had to be investigated. Wood was surprised to learn that King himself had been institutionalized recently as well. Samples of handwriting were obtained from both King and his former wife, and neither matched that of the bomb.[38] At first glimpse, this appeared to be another dead end.

Oscar Sharp, however, was a man who Paul Puyear said frequented his trailer, which meant that he needed to be interviewed by investigators. The forty-nine-year-old man had known Nola and Paul Puyear from when they all lived in Arkansas. Sharp's initial response to the allegations of sexual activity by visitors to Barryton was in line with his peers—he denied everything until confronted with the testimonies of others. Bettie had already informed the police that Oscar had dated Abbie Raymond* of Barryton.[39] Like those on the long list of Paul's friends interviewed before him, he admitted to having an affair up north.

Another friend of Paul whose name surfaced was a rugged truck driver named Jack O'Grady. The interview with O'Grady started out with police delving into the details of a small loan he had taken from Paul. Money was always a powerful motive for murder, but in this case, they knew the amount was paltry. This was a classic police ploy aimed at putting him at ease—asking him a safe, easy question to answer. Jack opened up readily, admitting that he knew Paul was involved with Bettie Lipton. He had enjoyed going up to the trailer in Barryton so much that he had purchased his own trailer, parked just a short distance from Paul's. Initially, he denied any affairs or illicit behavior on his part.[40] For the investigators, this was a familiar pattern for the Marshall men.

Paul, however, had already offered a more intimate clarification of their relationship, and the investigators were armed with that knowledge. About a year ago, Paul went to the trailer with Jack O'Grady, who had brought along his wife, Donna. Once there, Jack encouraged Paul to have intercourse with Donna while he watched. Paul did so on two or three occasions. Jack had done the same with Oscar Sharp, who had also had sex with Donna.[41] Paul said that after he witnessed Jack beating his wife on one trip, he didn't want her brought to the trailer.[42] This had led to the reason for Jack to purchase his own trailer in "friendly" Barryton.

In a follow-up interview with police, Paul said that Jack was known to be "real moody." On one occasion, he had completely ignored Bettie at the trailer, upsetting her to the point where she left for the night. When Paul had confronted Jack about it, he flew into a tantrum, yelling, "Goddamn it Paul, you are on the wrong side of the fence." He threw objects about the tiny trailer. As the investigators spoke with him, Paul said that Jack had become so angry at him that he would not sleep with *him* that night. To the investigators this seemed odd. After all, it was a two-bedroom trailer. Unless . . .

Playing a hunch, they asked outright if Paul was involved with Jack homosexually. He admitted that they had had such relations. He added that Jack had even suggested that Paul dump Bettie and move in with Jack and Donna. Paul didn't believe that Jack was in love with him, but he knew Jack had strong feelings for him. Jack had slept with Bettie and with Eve Jones. When Paul would be making love to one of the women, Jack would fondle him. These "parties" were something that Jack enjoyed a great deal.[43] On at least one occasion, Jack had convinced Oscar Sharp to make love to his wife while he participated in the wings.[44] On one night, Oscar and Paul had taken turns with Donna while Jack watched.[45] The sex in the tight confined space of the trailer was far beyond a simple affair and fed the police investigation into Nola's murder.

Was it possible that Jack was so in love with Paul that he had killed Nola out of jealousy or to have Paul to himself? The police didn't feel that was likely, but it was hard to rule him out. The postal inspectors went to Mrs. O'Grady's place of business, the Shaeffer Bakery Company, and checked her signature in her personnel record. It was not a match for the handwriting on the pills or the bomb package. In many respects, Nola was not a real threat to his relationship with Paul—whereas Bettie was. Nola seemed to look the other way at her husband's indiscretions or was oblivious to them. Jack was known to be violent and emotional, though, and as a bisexual, he would remain a potential suspect for some time.

* * * *

Detectives Steinbacher and Kenney spoke with airman second class John Puyear, Paul and Nola's only son. Their questions were light compared to those that had been directed at his father's infidelities. Did he know of anyone who might want to harm his mother and father? No. John was forthcoming that he had heard rumors about his father's extramarital affair but had never been able to confirm it. The police checked to see if John Puyear had been trained in explosives in the Air Force, but he had not—his specialty was in recreation and athletics.[46] Just to verify his account, they pulled his service records. John also informed them that he had only gone to Barryton a few times with his father, and then only for hunting and fishing.

The only thing that seemed to provide any motive for John to have done the crime was tied to a job that he had held before going into the Air Force. John Puyear had worked for the Twentieth Century Guaranty Life Insurance Company of Battle Creek and wrote a policy on Nola for twenty-one thousand dollars in the summer of 1965. Paul was the primary beneficiary, and John was the contingent.[47] While the amount of money was significant in 1967, it simply didn't seem to be enough to justify murder.

The search for a motive had preoccupied the first few weeks of the investigation. As perverse as the sexual escapades in Barryton were, none of them gave the police what they were looking for—someone with a motive to kill Nola Puyear. To the officers involved with the case, the affairs in Barryton had been a costly and somewhat embarrassing distraction for the investigators. All they had managed to uncover in their investigation was the involvement of a small cadre of men from Marshall and willing women of Barryton in isolated orgies on the weekends. They had learned that Marshall and Barryton had a lot of dirty little secrets, but they had not learned much more. After a short time investigating in this area, several of the officers involved continued to focus on the physical evidence.

The search of the Puyear home on 857 East Michigan Avenue by Sergeant Richie and Detective Steinbacher took five hours and produced little information. Paul Puyear slept in a separate bedroom from his wife. They found some wiring in the basement and garage that potentially could have been used in the making of a bomb. In the basement, they discovered two cans filled with gunpowder, but they found shotgun primers and loading equipment nearby, indications that someone was loading their own shells. Still, the material was gathered and sent off to the state police crime lab.[48] The most tantalizing item found, in the eyes of the postal inspectors, was the book *How to Murder Your Wife*, by Henry Williams. The book was a light comedy novel that Fred Ritchie found in the home. In any other context, it would have meant nothing. But to the postal inspectors on the case, it only solidified their suspicions about Paul Puyear.[49]

The search of the trailer in Barryton had yielded some potential evidence. Postal inspector Matt Reinhard and Officer Erland Wittanen found eight aluminum blasting caps used to set off dynamite, a partial roll of masking tape, and ten magazines of different types.[50] These were sent off to the crime lab, and Paul Puyear was questioned in regard to them. Paul said he had no real experience with dynamite other than trying to blow up a piece of concrete next to his trailer. He had purchased the blasting materials to take out several stumps he had near the trailer.[51] The story seemed plausible, and there were no other potential bomb-making materials at the trailer. Still, the investigators were not entirely convinced by the explanation.

An additional search of the Tasty Cafe was undertaken discreetly, out of the eyes of the newspaper reporters. With the exception of the food that had been removed and discarded, nothing had changed since the restaurant had been sealed by the Marshall police. For the investigators, the search revealed a small book in a cupboard that had been overlooked earlier. The book, labeled "Atomic Shocking Book," was actually hollowed out and rigged with some sort of battery-driven device. When opened, it delivered an electrical shock to the person holding it.[52] Paul Puyear had no idea where the book had come from. He assumed someone had given it to Nola as a practical joke—either that or she had gotten it in the mail. The police studied it with a detailed eye. Could such a device have been used to trigger the explosion that had killed Nola? For Assistant Chief Herold Reuss, the book triggered not a bomb but a memory, one that would prove important later in the investigation. He kept quiet for the time being, as the jury-rigged book was sent off to the state police crime lab.

Thanks to television shows and highly public trials, we are lulled into familiarity today with the high-tech aspects of police work. As I labored through the case files for the Nola Puyear murder, I was struck at how much of the police work was good old-fashioned legwork. Interviews, hunches, and suspicions were all carefully pulled together with a framework of logic. Digging into the details of this crime, one gains a healthy respect for the work the officers did and for how urgent it was for them to find the killer.

Nola Puyear's funeral was on August 21, 1967. An approximate eight carloads of relatives came up from Arkansas to attend her services. A family friend, the Reverend Charles Lewis of Harrisburg, Arkansas, traveled to Marshall and assisted Pastor Myril Ross of the Calvary Baptist Church in delivering the ceremony. Nola's funeral was one of the largest in recent memory, its size contributed to by the coverage in the newspapers. She was laid to rest at Oakridge Cemetery. Pastor Ross said that she was known as "a woman whom everybody loved."[53] The grim reality was that at least one person in the community did not love Nola and had taken extreme measures to kill her.

The investigators were present as well, stalking the shadows and fringes of the service. Marshall police went to the funeral home and discreetly wrote down the license plate numbers of everyone who attended. Checks were made at the local airport, Brooks Field, to see who, if anyone, had flown in. Likewise, checks were made of all the local hotel registries, for potential suspects. The investigators spoke with Paul and John Puyear and received from them the condolence book from the

Court Funeral Home and the sympathy cards. They wanted to know who had been to the funeral home and where they had stayed, on the hunch that the killer might be among them. The traced license plates provided the investigators with names of people they might want to interview.[54]

The Calhoun County Fair came to an end a week after opening, a milestone marking the end of summer and the start of fall. The carnival rides were loaded on trailers for their next gig, and dozens of winners of ribbons went home and proudly displayed them. The *Marshall Evening Chronicle* had covered the events at the fair in lieu of coverage about the murder investigation. Merrie Kapp was judged the grand champion and junior grand champion in livestock for 4-H. Bernard Jones of Battle Creek had swept ten of the fifty-two categories of the floral competition. The photos of harness racing and prize bulls and horses seemed almost surreal compared to the horror that had been unleashed on Michigan Avenue two weeks earlier. The fairground outside of town was abandoned for the season, prepped for the coming chills of fall and winter. Marshall was slowly trying to move on, though the paranoia that gripped the community lay just under the surface.

As the fair crowds disappeared from Marshall, there was still no sign from the police that they were closer to finding Nola Puyear's killer. What was clear was that Marshall's own people were starting to turn on each other. Suspicion and paranoia festered as the citizens started to wonder who in their number could have done such an act. Suddenly, a community that had trusted each other only a few days before saw potential murderers everywhere.

Blanch Velliquette lived across the street from the Puyears and came forward to offer her opinion to investigators as to an area to consider. Blanch told them that a family by the name of Delaney moved into the neighborhood twelve to fifteen years ago and that Paul and Marg Warsop had circulated a petition among the neighbors to keep them out. The petition was not well received by their neighbors. The Delaney's son, John Delaney Jr., had caused trouble on one occasion about some shrubs growing over the Puyear's property line. According to Blanch, he had said that "some day he would get even." Since then, he had married and moved away.[55] To the investigators, this was intriguing but seemed to be another lead that went nowhere.

The police tried to turn the focus away from Marshall to the nearby communities, looking at the usual suspects—known criminals. That part of Calhoun County did not have a long list of felons or people who were worth checking into. There was an airman who was AWOL from Selfridge Air Force Base and happened to be a demolitions expert. He was found and ruled out after he provided a solid alibi. Several other former criminals were contacted and at least interviewed. None seemed to have any ties to the Tasty Cafe or the Puyears.

One of these former criminals, brought in on August 28, was Enoch Chism. A sullen, brooding man, he had been called in because of his involvement in an arson just a few years before, when he had burned down his brother's house in Marshall. Chism had the distinction of being one of the few convicted felons on parole near Marshall, making him one of the usual suspects. Chism's name had come up the day of the murder, when Fred Ritchie had told Detectives Kenney and Steinbacher that he was one of the people who might be capable of committing such a crime.

Chism was known to be a troublemaker. The county sheriff's department had been out to his home on C Drive North several times for domestic disputes. Enoch had a temper and was known to be calm one minute and moody the next. His only tie to the Tasty Cafe was that his mother-in-law, Josie White, worked there.

Chism outwardly appeared relaxed and cooperative. He was five foot eleven, weighed 200 pounds, and had brown hair and steely blue, piercing eyes. The tip of his right index finger was missing, the result of an accident with a power saw fourteen years earlier. He had a small scar near his right eye where a piece of steel had been removed. Enoch spoke in a low soft tone, with no hint of emotion. He said that he had never been to Barryton in his life but knew that his father in-law Hollie had gone up there with Paul on several occasions. According to Chism, everyone liked Paul and Nola very well as far as he knew. He said he never saw Paul with any other women, but there was a rumor that Paul had dated a slim dark-haired girl named Simmons. His mother-in-law, Josie, never mentioned any trouble between Nola and her patrons or tenants.

The police asked for a handwriting sample, which changed his demeanor. He appeared nervous to the officers when he wrote, sweating—wiping his strong hands in his lap when he finished. Chism wrote very deliberately while giving his handwriting, as if possibly to disguise it.

His efforts were so nerve-racked that he broke the pencil lead. He must have sensed the police noticing how slow and ponderous his writing was. Enoch simply told them that he had only graduated the third grade and that writing was not something he was good at.[56] His writing sample was turned over to the postal inspector's handwriting expert, who immediately ruled it out as the match they were seeking. This interview, like so many they had been through, appeared to be a dead end.

In their search for any potential lead, the officers made inquiries at the Battle Creek and Marshall libraries, to see if they had any books on bomb making and, if so, who had checked them out. Both libraries said that they didn't carry such books, and Battle Creek's Willard Library said that they had had only one inquiry on the subject ever, by a seventeen-year-old that had asked about the subject four years earlier. Every avenue they explored led investigators nowhere.

On the same day as Nola's funeral, the investigation team was pulled together with the Calhoun County prosecutor, John Jereck, to review the status of the case. Assistant Chief Beattie, Detectives Robert Kenney and Leroy Steinbacher, and Inspector Minor Myers were all present. The meeting, which took place in Chief Beattie's office at the Marshall Police Station, was held to bring Jereck up to speed on their efforts so far and to perhaps get a new perspective. Detective Kenny was confident that the state police crime lab would be able to reconstruct most of the packaging of the bomb. Kenny's instincts told him that the physical evidence was going to be the key to solving the crime and obtaining a conviction.

Later that day, Myron Wood and Matt Reinhard stopped by the state police lab in East Lansing to meet with Detective Don Bennett. They had been to the Barryton area, wrapping up interviews, and hoped to review the photos of the evidence from the first parcel at 2:00 p.m. that day, but the photos were still drying. Bennett pulled together the other physical evidence while they waited for the photos.

Bennett had identified a Fisk battery from the shards recovered at the Tasty Cafe. It was the opinion of the state police lab that the torn and twisted fragments of the battery were the culprit in detonating the bomb. In Michigan, the Fisk brand was sold only at the K-Mart stores.

The wrapper for the bomb had been pieced together best as the lab could do. The parcel had been addressed with crayon or a dry marking pencil. The name was written in longhand, whereas the address and the word "BOOKS" had been printed. The paper was ordinary brown paper identical to that used in paper bags. The lab technicians had recovered additional fragments that didn't fit the bomb package, one piece of which had the marking "Viking" on it. Bennett had determined that the additional paper pieces had come from a nearby wastebasket that had been blown apart in the explosion. Additionally, brown paper with orange residue recovered was determined to be from the dynamite.

The masking tape used to wrap the package was one inch wide. On one piece were the wavy lines of the postmark roller. The letters "MAR" and "HAL" had been found. Wondering if Nola's family might have been involved, the postal inspectors did a quick check of Arkansas post offices that could have sent it, which implicated only Waldenburg, Arkansas, and then only if you inverted the M and ignored some of the other recovered pieces.

The postmark was applied with a roller type assembly, which limited where it could have been done. There were twelve Marshalls in the United States at the time. They were able to determine that the package had been canceled by the rollers, meaning that it had to have come from Marshall, Michigan.[57] Nola's murderer had been in town the day that the bomb was mailed—that much they now knew. While it seemed to be a complicated way to prove the obvious, it was going to be necessary to validate the origins of the package for certain if the evidence went to trial.

The address on the package had been ripped to confetti. But the lab technicians had pieced together a considerable amount of it. They had "aul P_year," "7 E. Michigan," and "Marshall, Mich."

Several screws, five small fragments of aluminum, and one larger strip of metal about seven by one-half inches were recovered and assumed to be part of the mechanism that triggered the bomb—either that or intended as shrapnel. Some wires and a tiny spring were found, too. An alligator clip had been found driven into a ceiling tile. This, too, was assumed to be part of the bomb, along with several pieces of electrical tape. White electrical cord and rolls of black electrical tape recovered from the Puyear residence were being evaluated. Paper tape, red tape, rubber electrical tape, a black-colored felt marking pencil, the Puyears' telephone bills and bank statements, pieces of plastic, and other, unidentified debris were all being checked as potential evidence.

The other significant piece of recovered evidence had nothing to do
with the bomb; it was the package of pills that had been sent to Nola. The
state police handwriting analysts validated Detective Kenny's suspicions;
they were sure that the address on the bomb matched the handwriting
on the pills package. This was key to the investigators. The bomb had
simply been an escalation of attempts to kill Nola Puyear. Her killer had
struck before and failed.

The pills themselves were in a plastic medicine bottle with a plastic
top. It was determined that the pills were in a type of bottle that was usually used to hold Coricidin. The label on the pills read:

24 tablets
Edwards Brand
Tran-Vex tablets
For relief of nervous tension, restlessness, irritability, non-habit
    forming.
Edwards Drug & Chemical Company
Detroit, Mich—Distributors

The address on the pills package eerily matched that of the bomb. But
the package had been postmarked in Detroit. If the murderer was from
Marshall, he or she had traveled to Detroit to send this package to Nola.

When the photos of the pills package were dry, the police and inspectors reviewed them to see if there were any other details that they may
have overlooked. Nothing seemed to stand out.[58] The physical evidence
gave them quite a bit to work with—namely, handwriting. Linking the
pills to the bomb showed that the attempt to kill Nola was not a onetime
affair. More important, it gave them two samples of handwriting to work
from. Suddenly, the pills were as important as any piece of shrapnel from
the bomb—they were linked to the same murderer.

They decided that they would gather handwriting samples in all of
their interviews of witnesses. Myron Wood said that the postal service
employed a top-notch handwriting expert, who he would ask to be assigned to assist the case, though the state police had their own expert.
Among the first handwriting samples recovered were those of John and
Paul Puyear, who were quickly ruled out as having addressed either
package.

The handwriting sample taken from the pills mailed to Nola months before her bombing murder. *(From the Chism Defense Files.)*

When they discussed the pills with Paul Puyear, he could offer little about them or their origins. Nola had received a parcel about the size of an ordinary package of cigarettes that contained capsules that were all dried up. He couldn't find any postmark and took the wrappings to the postmaster, Mr. Reyer. Paul remembered distinctly sitting in Reyer's office discussing the package with him, but the Marshall postmaster did not remember the discussion. According to Paul, the post office said they couldn't trace who had sent the pills.[59]

Mrs. Nancy Church, who co-owned the Mi-Lady's Beauty Shop a few doors down from the Tasty, proved to have additional information beyond her initial interview. Nola had brought the pills down to the beauty shop to show them to the women there. In the packaging was a note that read, "Nola, take these for your nerves." Later that day, Nola took the pills to Carrington's Pharmacy at the insistence of the women in the shop.[60] Helen Hazen, who worked in the beauty shop, recorded the date in her diary as May 4.

The police went back to Josie White to verify from her what she might know about the pills. Josie remembered that she had been washing dishes when Nola showed her the pills. Nola said, "Look here, what I got from Detroit."[61]

Sene Buckner remembered that when Nola opened the parcel and looked at the pills, she said, "I wonder if —— could have sent them." Trying as hard as she could, Sene could not remember the name of the woman Nola mentioned. Sene was quick to point out that she was referring to the *first* package of pills that Nola had received.

This was important to the investigation team. There definitely was more than one package that had been sent to Nola. Sene was pressed by Inspector Wood if she could describe the package she had seen. According to her memory, it was three to four inches in length, two inches wide, and one inch in depth. Sene remembered that the first package of pills contained solid pills, not capsules.[62] She told Nola not to take the pills. It was another two to three weeks later when the second package of pills arrived, the one that the police had in their possession.[63] Apparently, Nola had discarded the first package of pills but had kept the second one, showing that one around to the ladies in the beauty shop and to customers. It was now clear to the investigators that the bomb was the *third* attempt to kill Nola Puyear.

Opal Conrad came forward to the police to offer what she knew about the pills. According to her memory, several months ago, Nola showed her a small package that she got in the mail. They checked the wrapper, and Opal was sure that it was postmarked from Detroit. Nola told her that she was supposed to take the pills for her nerves, per a note. Jean Reed tested them, and they burned her tongue. Nola showed Opal the package and asked, "Doesn't that look like Paul's handwriting?"[64] The state police crime lab had already looked at numerous samples of Paul Puyear's handwriting and had ruled him out as the addresser of the packages.

The state police lab had confirmed that the pills recovered from the restaurant were lye. Three doctors were consulted, and they concluded that if someone took one of the pills, it would have caused death. It was an easy-to-purchase form of lye, and it was impossible to determine the exact brand. The commercial product most likely to have been used was Drano.[65]

A few days later, Detective Bennett called Detectives Steinbacher and Kenny and told them that the laboratory had found a human hair under the masking tape used on the bomb package. It was about two inches long and was not pubic or negroid hair. The hair might be used to link a suspect to the bomb package, if a suspect could be found.[66] The biggest problem was that the police still did not have a suspect. With each passing hour, the murder case of Nola Puyear seemed to be growing colder.

The police reports do not capture the mood when the realization came to the investigation team that they were dealing with an orchestrated plot to kill Nola. The bombing had simply been the latest attempt on her life, and this one had worked. I have tried to picture the discussion between the officers when they perceived that this was not just a bombing but the act of a dedicated killer who obviously had a deadly grudge with the victim. Who could it be? There seemed to be no one who had anything bad to say about Nola Puyear, let alone anyone furious enough to make multiple attempts to kill her.

The police knew that someone was executing a prolonged campaign to kill Nola—the lye pills were proof of that. In their questioning of her friends and regulars at the restaurant, they began to learn that Nola had apparently been receiving threats for some time. She had never filed any reports with the police about them, probably considering them nothing more than pranks. Still, any one of these threats could have come from the person who killed her.

Between July 28 and August 1, Mrs. Denise Reish stopped by the Tasty to visit with Nola and show off her new baby. She was a bright, energetic twenty-three-year-old and quite proud of her newborn. While she was in the Tasty Cafe, the phone rang. Denise couldn't hear the other party, but the call stuck in her memory. Nola had said, "If you don't quit threatening me, I am going to call the police. I don't think it is funny. I mean it, I will call the police."

Denise remembered that the call came in between two and four in the afternoon. After she hung up, Nola didn't seem concerned.[67] When she came by Denise's booth after the call, Denise asked Nola if it was some crank, if some kids or someone was threatening her, or if someone was bothering her. Each was a separate question, and Nola said no to each one.[68]

Sene Buckner's husband, Bruce, remembered that one of the Puyears' tenants had been behind on paying his rent and had locked horns with Nola—always a stickler for money. His name was Bill Courtwright. An interview with him did not yield anything more than a handwriting sample. Sending a bomb to Nola would not have solved his financial problems at all.[69]

Mrs. Velma Southward came forward to the police about a chronic complainer who she had witnessed in the Tasty Cafe. The man had complained about a piece of glass in his Swiss steak. Josie White was in the restaurant at the time and showed Velma the steak after he left. There was nothing more than a sliver of bone in his food.[70] Checks were made of other local restaurants to see if they had any patrons who were known to complain of food on a regular basis.

In one of his interviews with investigators, Paul said that Marg Warsop, Nola's close friend, had told him that Nola was afraid of a man who had been in the restaurant. This piqued the investigators' interest. Perhaps Nola had a good reason to fear this man. The investigators followed up with Marg Warsop again.

Marg was an older woman, southern in her upbringing, with red hair and buck teeth.[71] She and Nola had been close friends for years. Marg remembered the incident with the Swiss steak. The man was described as being around thirty years old, five foot nine, wearing glasses, slender, and sunken chested. Marg said he drove a beat-up Chevy with Michigan plates. Josie White gave a slightly different description of the same man, as two inches taller, weighing 160 pounds, and about forty-five to forty-eight years old.[72]

About five weeks before the bombing, Marg was in the Tasty with Nola when she witnessed this man making Nola uneasy. Sene Buckner was with Marg and recalled that the man seemed to "undress all the girls and women with his eyes" as they came into the restaurant. Nola had said that the man had been coming to the restaurant for ten days or so.[73]

The thought that some patron who had gotten a bad meal had been driven to murder was a stretch at best, but the investigators were willing to explore any avenue at this stage of their hunt. The police pulled

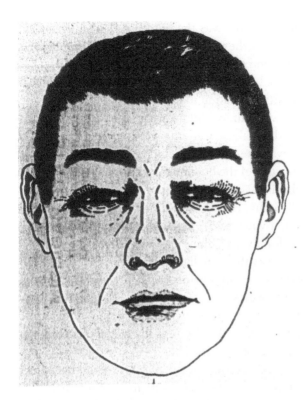

The police composite of the customer who was labeled a chronic complainer at the Tasty Cafe. (*From the Michigan State Police Files— Nola Puyear Murder Investigation.*)

together a sketch of the man based on the descriptions that Marg and Josie had provided. It wasn't much, but it gave them something to work from. Because the man could not be directly tied to the case, the police did not release the sketch to the newspapers. Unfortunately, the sketch could have been just about any person walking down Michigan Avenue.

The police visited the six restaurants in town to see if their drawing or description matched any diners at the other restaurants. Josie's description matched that of a man who had been a semiregular at Thelma's Cafe. The man had stopped visiting Thelma's a few months prior to the bombing, though, and there were no leads as to who he was, other than that he was very picky about his meals.

Ultimately, the investigators found this avenue a virtual dead end. The threats to Nola may or may not have been tied to the crime. The one that intrigued them the most was the one that Denise Reish had witnessed. Was it possible that the person who sent the poison pills and the bomb had been calling and threatening Nola Puyear?

While the police explored every possible lead, someone was terrorizing the Marshall community in relation to the bombing. A wave of eerie phone calls began in Marshall almost immediately after Nola's murder. The police began to wonder if these were the work of children playing pranks or if the bomber was attempting to derail the investigation.

In the afternoon of the day of the bombing, Mrs. Phyllis Myers at the Hutchins Cafe on Michigan Avenue received a telephone call from an unknown male. She called out "Hello" three times with no answer, and just before she hung up, a voice said, "Remember Nola. You're next!" The voice then laughed loudly and hung up.[74] What made this suspicious to the investigators was the fact that Nola's name had only been released to the press less than an hour before the call. Was this call from the killer, taunting the authorities?

Paul Puyear indicated that he was receiving threatening phone calls at his home starting the day after the death of his wife. Sometimes he could hear breathing on the phone, then the person would hang up; sometimes the person would slam down the receiver; sometimes they asked if he had received the bomb. The calls were making him nervous, and the police arranged to place a tracking device on his phone to allow him to trace who was calling him. In those days, such devices were slow and cumbersome—impossible to use on such short calls.

Marshall resident Lottie Ellis received a call on August 30 from a male saying, "Have you received the bomb?" The call shook her deeply. Sergeant Richie of the sheriff's department checked and determined that her phone number was one digit different than that of Paul Puyear's home. If nothing else, this incident confirmed that Paul was indeed receiving crank calls.

Nola's close friends were not spared the prank calls. Several days after Nola's funeral, Sene Buckner received a threatening phone call at 1:30 p.m. It was a male, and his voice sounded distant, perhaps even long distance. The mysterious caller said, "Stay away from Paul Puyear and out of his business," then hung up.[75] The voice didn't have an accent and was not too fast or too slow. While the tone didn't sound threatening, the intent clearly was.

On September 6, Marg Warsop got a call that was disturbing as well. A man said, "This is Mr. Steinbacher. We would like to talk to you some more. Will you be home tomorrow between 2:00 and 2:30 p.m.?" Marg replied that she would be. It was only after the call that she became suspicious. The voice tipped her off. It didn't seem like that of Detective Steinbacher, so she called him, and he assured her that no one from the investigation team had called her. Another call came late that night between 11:00 and 11:30 p.m. The male caller said "Hello" and then "Good night."[76]

Was it possible that the murderer was attempting to intimidate Nola's close friends to keep them from cooperating with the investigators? People being interviewed by the police seemed to be targets of the calls. The use of Steinbacher's name in the case of Marg Warsop's crank call indicated that someone was following the case closely. Sene Buckner was also speaking with the police—though that was not known to the public. Were the police getting closer to the killer?

In reviewing these calls in the police record, I had to consider that they may not have been made by the killer but could have been a practical joke gone awry. That left me with a bitter taste in my mouth. What kind of a person does prank phone calls related to such a hideous crime? Obviously, it would take a sick mind. As I read the reports tied to these events, one thought kept coming to my mind: was this the killer at work? Was the murderer inflicting even more terror on the citizens or, better yet from the murderer's perspective, disrupting the investigation?

The investigation reached a low point in early September. Having exhausted Paul Puyear's extramarital activities as a potential catalyst for someone killing Nola, the investigators turned their attention to Nola herself. Was it possible that Nola was a lesbian and that her death was the result of a jilted female lover?

In retrospect, it is easy to see how they arrived at this line of thinking. Paul and Nola's sexual relationship was nil. Perhaps this was not just because of Paul's running around. Perhaps Nola was simply not interested in men. The question of her sexual preference was put to a number of Nola's friends, most of which were stunned by the suggestion. It was another dead end, one that no one was proud to have pursued.

On September 6, 1967, at the request of the investigators, Paul and John Puyear agreed to undergo a polygraph examination to rule them out as murder suspects. With all of Paul's extramarital activities, the exam was seen as necessary—if only to clear him once and for all as a suspect. Both took the test and were found not to be deceitful or withholding pertinent information.[77]

Well over a month and a half had passed, and the investigators sat with little to show for it other than the physical evidence gathered, the handwriting sample, and a glimpse into the seamy, dark side of life in pastoral Marshall. So far, everyone who had provided a handwriting sample had been ruled out by the state police crime lab. The decision was made to focus on the handwriting as the best way to capture the bomber.

Little did the investigators realize they had already interviewed their elusive killer.

4

The Secret Witness

Fear was palatable in Marshall in the weeks after Nola's murder. The murder was *the* subject of conversation, along with terrified speculation as to who the killer might be. The police, however, were stymied. This killer seemed cunning, and as they pressed on to search for a motive that would lead them to a murderer, they slowly came to grips with the fact that motive might not be a factor.

At the end of August, Detective Kenney went to the Kalamazoo State Hospital to interview the director of the facility, Dr. Clarence Schier. The hospital in Kalamazoo was the nearest state-owned mental health facility to the crime scene and was much more cooperative than the privately owned Battle Creek Sanitarium. While the sanitarium—"the San," as it was known—was a large facility, it always treated its clientele with utmost privacy.

Detective Kenney went to Kalamazoo for two reasons. One was to learn what kind of personality might be behind the bombing/murder. The other was to see if there were any outpatients from the state hospital in the Marshall area that he should be considering as potential suspects.

There were no criminal profilers in 1967. That field did not emerge until the 1980s and later. But there were psychiatric professionals and their opinions. The fact that Detective Kenney went to Kalamazoo was an indication of where the investigation was—dangerously stalled. In Kenney's own words, "Dr. Schier was given the known facts of the case in general for his ideas on the type of personality we should be looking for if no further evidence can be found to tie in the family or motive."[1]

Dr. Schier, for his part, was able to provide some tantalizing glimpses into the mind of the bomber. In Schier's opinion, it was most likely that the individual was a male and a paranoid. If it could be established that the killer had a motive, he would be most likely a psychopath as well. From the doctor's perspective, motive was not considered important.

The motive of a paranoid could go back to some insignificant factor or event within the last ten years.

For Kenney, this had to be sobering. The investigative work so far had concentrated on finding an individual with a motive. Dr. Schier was saying that such efforts might be a waste of time. If, in fact, they were facing a true paranoid, the motive might be nearly impossible to determine. If that was the case, the search for the murderer would have to be approached in an entirely different way.

What compelled the thinking that the murderer was suffering from paranoia was the fact that there were two kinds of attempts to kill Nola Puyear—the poison pills and the bomb. Dr. Schier advised that "a paranoid's characteristic behavior pattern would be in general cause him to keep away from his victim."[2] Such a person chose to try to kill a victim in ways that avoided direct confrontation.

The profile of the killer became even more chilling as the interview continued. The paranoid would not stand out in public. He could hold a good job and be well thought of by his employer and show no deviation in his lifestyle to the casual observer. He would be neat in his personal habits, even in his manner of dress. For all intents and purposes, the murderer might easily blend into the fabric of Marshall society and never be thought of as being paranoid or abnormal at all. Dr. Schier pointed out that the fact that another restaurant received a recent threat as well might indicate that the killer had a dislike for such establishments in general.

The killer most likely would have certain topics that would set him off, driving him to be outspoken. He could potentially be thrown into a violent rage over seemingly insignificant events or subjects. The murderer also would have above-normal intelligence. The killer was not likely to commit suicide himself.

Dr. Schier had culled the files of the state hospital and had found two men diagnosed with paranoia that were discharged to the Marshall area. He was quick to point out that he felt neither was a likely suspect. One was classified as having delusions of grandeur in which he believed he was Jesus Christ. The other individual was so imbalanced that he was given to bouts of uncontrolled rage.[3] These men with extreme cases of paranoia also had other psychological issues that, in Dr. Schier's mind, precluded them from being suspects.

In both of these cases, Detective Kenney obtained handwriting samples from their files. There was no point in taking chances. Handwriting, it seemed, was going to play a much larger role in apprehending the killer.

* * * *

The physical evidence in this case was plentiful by today's standards and technologies, but in 1967, the usefulness of the recoveries from the crime scene was limited. Fragments of the bomb and the handwriting samples were all that the investigative team had to go on. It seemed to be a daunting task.

The handwriting was deemed to be the best course of action to pursue. Matching the handwriting on the bomb packaging to someone in Marshall would tie him or her directly to the bombing. The U.S. Postal Service offered its services to assist in the arduous task. This help came in the form of James Dibowski, the director of the Post Office Laboratories.[4] Dibowski hailed from Cincinnati, Ohio, and was considered one of the best resources the postal investigators had at their disposal. He had examined a quarter of a million documents in his twenty-year career, and this case was going to press that number even higher.[5]

The Michigan State Police already had their own handwriting expert tasked to the case, Captain Wallace Van Stratt. He was the man who had linked the handwriting on the remains of the bomb to that on the poison pills sent to Nola. He and Dibowski were not territorial but seemed to work together to divide and conquer the ever-growing list of handwriting examples. Both men seemed to acknowledge that they needed to agree on any "hits" they got in their search. If they didn't agree, it would come out in trial and cause problems for the prosecution down the road.

As one state police detective on the case said of the murderer, "It could have been anyone who came through here. The killer doesn't have to be anyone who lives in Marshall. He simply could have eaten at the cafe and, somehow, built up some feelings of hatred towards Mrs. Puyear. But all those signatures and samples, there must be over 50,000 handwriting samples to go over."[6] Dibowski did not seem daunted by the task facing him. As he told one interviewer, "I didn't think the job would be simple. Now let's get started."[7]

They started with the samples provided by everyone interviewed by the police and in the Puyear family. Every interviewee in the case was asked to provide handwriting samples. By September, all of the interviewees had been cleared, including many of the women who Paul Puyear had slept with and the men from Marshall who had traveled up to his trailer for their sexual escapades. Even the children of the women and men involved with such affairs were sampled by the police. Other sample sources that Paul Puyear turned over to the police were the sympathy cards from his wife's funeral and the condolences book from the Court Funeral Home. None of these proved useful.

Dibowski and Van Stratt were going to cast a large net in their efforts to find the murderer. Dibowski was given access to voter registration cards, driver's license applications, and even dog licenses to attempt to find a match to the distinctive handwriting on the package. Van Stratt worked out of his office in East Lansing, while Dibowski set up on a desk in the basement of the Marshall Post Office, right across the street from the remains of the Tasty Cafe. In the basement, Dibowski would work for hours, poring over each sample signature, looking for distinctive ways that letters were made. Each crossing of a *t*, dotting of an *i*, or sweeping tail of a *y* or *g* was placed under intense scrutiny. Each day, as he finished, he would come upstairs and look across Michigan Avenue to the blasted remains of the Tasty Cafe.[8] Every morning, he went back into the basement with his magnifying glass, working through reams of paperwork, looking for a clue. Despite the efforts of these experts, they were no closer to solving the case in early September than in the first week of their work.

Something had to be done to generate new information or leads in the case. On September 7, Prosecutor John Jereck and the U.S. Postal Service announced in the Marshall and Battle Creek newspapers that they were offering a reward of two thousand dollars for information leading to the arrest and conviction of the person responsible for Nola Puyear's murder.[9] In 1967, two thousand dollars was a considerable amount of money, and the hope was that it would shake loose new tips in the case.

The result of the announced reward was an influx of tips—none of which were particularly useful. One man was turned in by his neighbors because of his knowledge of electrical components. The surprised man was an amateur radio builder and operator and was willing to provide a handwriting example. Some Marshallites turned in regular patrons of the Tasty Cafe, thinking they may have some secret motive for killing Nola. Five of these were tracked down by the investigators and questioned. Their handwriting samples were submitted to Dibowski for his grueling scrutiny, none showing any of the characteristics of the bomber's writing.

The effect of the reward on the small community was only to heighten attention to the case and the suspicions that the citizens held of each other. Marshall was turning on itself. Neighbors who had suspicions about neighbors quickly submitted names to the investigators once money was offered. One man whose name was submitted was an individual who was routinely turned in for crimes in Marshall. "He is well known in the city as the town drunk. In interviewing this subject found that he also is also a 'mental,' possibly from his drinking."[10] Other men were turned in because it was known that they used dynamite. While this seems rare now, farmers often used explosives to remove stumps and so on in the 1960s. One of these men refused to provide a sample of his handwriting, but his employer, a taxi company, turned in his application for a taxi permit.[11] This gave Dibowski a good sample, which he used to rule out the man.

The mention of the pills in the newspapers expanded the scope of potential suspects. One Battle Creek resident turned in his neighbor who had mental problems and claimed that people were trying to poison him. Detective Steinbacher spent a long evening in the man's home talking to him but ruled him out without a handwriting sample. The man had lost both of his arms in the Korean War and was not capable of addressing a package or building a bomb.[12] Despite this obvious disability, his neighbor had turned him in.

The owner of the Galloway Bakery in Battle Creek turned in the name of a man who frequented his coffee shop from time to time and would sit and draw pictures on napkins, talking about pills and bombs and so on. The man complained often that the owner was trying to poison him. "If this man is not the bomber," the bakery owner claimed, "he should be put away anyway as he is definitely a dangerous character." The police tracked down the man, a veteran, and while they found him quirky, they did not feel he was tied to the Marshall bombing.[13]

By September 14, working in the basement of the Marshall Post Office, Dibowski was still pushing ahead. He reported, "I've examined 5,000 samples from the license records and we've already looked through the signatures of all county parolees, several thousand at two local plants, mental patients, all voters in the last elections, and members of a construction crew working nearby."[14] While some of the signatures looked close, further samples proved them to be false positives.

Myron P. Wood, the postal inspector assigned to the case, added his own perspective: "I've worked on bomb cases for 19 years and frankly I wouldn't want to put one of those things together. I'd be afraid it would blow up in my face." Wood pointed out the problem they were facing: "We're not making much headway. We can find any number of suspects but no motive. But one thing we won't do is quit. We are going to crack this thing."[15] Privately, both Wood and Dibowski had to know that searching for the signatures without a tip was akin to looking for a needle in a haystack.

* * * *

Today, it is not uncommon to hear about cold cases—violent crimes that remain unsolved. There are entire TV series dedicated to cold cases. It wasn't always that way, though. Calhoun County only had two unsolved murders at the time of Nola's death. One was a man killed in the 1930s. The other was from 1963 and only eight miles down the road from Marshall—the brutal murder of Daisy Zick. It was impossible to talk about Nola's death without someone trying to link it to the slaying of Daisy Zick. Her brutal stabbing was still being pursued and was still the talk of Battle Creek. The last thing the police wanted was for this new crime to remain unsolved and open. They were determined to find Nola's killer.

In January of 1967, the *Detroit News* began a new program in conjunction with law enforcement. The program, titled "Secret Witness," was designed by the *News*'s editor, Martin S. Hayden, and city editor, Boyd Simmons. Recently, a death in New York City had been witnessed by twenty people, but no one had summoned the police or gone to the female victim's aid. As Boyd put it, "Too many killings are unsolved, too many violent crimes committed in homes, at work, or on the streets. The crimes are unsolved because there is no link between the killer and the victim. But in almost every one of these cases, somebody knows who the criminal is. What we have to do is find a way of allowing people with information to pass it along without fear of reprisal."[16]

The Secret Witness program did just that. Information on unsolved crimes was published in the *Detroit News*. Individuals with information related to the crimes were able to submit their tips anonymously. Rather than provide his or her name, a tipster was encouraged to write a secret six-digit code on the letter containing the written tip, then to tear off the corner of the letter and write the same six-digit code on the corner and keep it. If an individual was then convicted of the crime based on the tip, the tipster would be able to claim a monetary reward by presenting the torn-off corner and code that matched the rest of the letter.

The *Detroit News* claimed that the Secret Witness program was designed to help solve crimes. To the public, that was a satisfactory explanation. In reality, the hundred thousand dollars that the newspaper had set aside to fund the program was aimed primarily at selling newspapers. The *News* staff would get the inside track on any tips they received that helped resolve crimes. Scooping their competition would sell newspapers.

The Secret Witness program worked in Detroit. Since it had begun in January of 1967, there had been thirteen cases for which the *News* had run stories under the program's banner. Of these thirteen, five had received tips that had led to arrests.[17] Detroit, however, was a long way down Interstate 94 from little Marshall, and the only link between this case and Detroit seemed to be the clue that the poison pills sent to Nola Puyear had come from there. Other than that, this was a small-town crime, and the *Detroit News* was a big-city newspaper. Only the sensational nature of the crime—a bombing—kept it running in the Detroit newspapers.

Myron Wood was from Detroit, however, and familiar with the Secret Witness program. Based on that knowledge, he did something that caused some ire with the rest of the investigation team. On his own, on September 18, he went to Detroit to meet with Boyd Simmons to elicit his help. Would it be possible for the *Detroit News* to include the death of Nola Puyear in its Secret Witness program? The slender Simmons was a cigar smoker who used to cover the crime beat in Detroit and was intrigued by the details of the mysterious bombing/murder.

Despite their appointment, Simmons had been summoned away on a hot story. John Nehman of the *News* met with Wood to discuss the case. Nehman was noncommittal in the meeting; after all, Detroit was a long way from Marshall. The only thing that seemed to get his attention was the fact that it was such a strange case, a bombing that happened on the main street of town. The peculiarity of the crime stuck with Nehman, and he said that he would speak to Simmons.

The next day, a *Detroit News* reporter and photographer showed up in Marshall and met with Wood. The *Detroit News* was prepared to put up an additional three thousand dollars in reward. To help augment the campaign, the *News* wanted a sample of the bomber's handwriting and any clues the investigators may have already gathered. Wood agreed.

The members of the usually close-knit team of investigators were taken aback by Wood's arbitrary action to engage the *Detroit News*. Making matters worse, on September 19, Wood issued his own press release that the *Detroit News* would be publishing information on the crime as part of the Secret Witness program. This press release was like a bombshell for the investigators and for young prosecutor John Jereck.

Before Jereck could react, the two local newspapers, the *Battle Creek Enquirer and News* and the *Marshall Evening Chronicle,* reacted for him. Both were extremely upset that they were being scooped by the *Detroit News*. Why had they been cut out of the details of a local case in favor of a newspaper not even from the area? Calhoun County was small, and suddenly the *Detroit News* was getting the inside story of this local murder. While they would be able to republish the story from the *Detroit News,* both local papers were inflamed by the arbitrary action and let Jereck know it.

The press release that Myron Wood put out consisted of several specific details that the investigators had kept from the public up to this point. First was the pills sent to Nola Puyear months ago were laced with lye. Second, the handwriting on the pill package and that on the bomb were identified as having been written by the same person. Wood allowed the *News* reporters to photograph the handwriting on the reconstructed bomb package and gave them a photograph of the pills and the bottle for publication.

For the first time in the investigation, the well-oiled team of investigators experienced internal turmoil on how to handle the investiga-

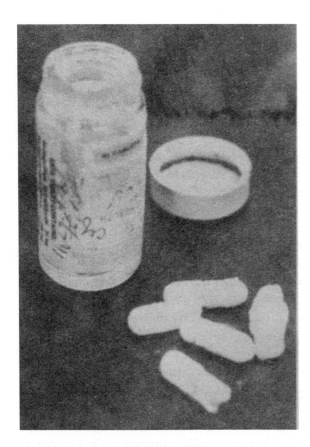

The poison pills mailed to Nola. The handwriting on the package these were sent in matched that on the bomb. *(From the* Ad-Visor & Chronicle, *with permission.)*

tion. It wasn't that what Wood had done was wrong. It was that he had not coordinated his actions at all with the prosecutor or the rest of the investigation team. There were jurisdictions enough attached to the Puyear case, and this point of conflict was sufficient for Detective Kenney to type up a summary report of it, pointing out that Wood had not informed the rest of the team or Jereck of his actions.[18]

There was no way to put the genie back in the bottle, and there was no way to deny that the investigation was becoming stagnant. Culling for signatures at random, despite Dibowski's doggedness, was not obtaining results. Perhaps upping the reward to a total of five thousand dollars and providing a means for someone to respond anonymously might prove to be a useful approach. It is conceivable that John Jereck could have stopped the *Detroit News* from running its subsequent articles on the case but didn't. Like the other men on this case, Jereck wanted to see justice done and done quickly.

On September 20 and 21, the *Detroit News* ran two articles on the Puyear murder—complete with writing samples. Both of the local papers in Calhoun County ran the articles and photographs as well. The net was slowly closing on Nola's killer.

At around the same time, Paul Puyear had been contacted by a local resident, Thomas Guy, about the Tasty Cafe. Guy wanted to lease the restaurant and reopen it. Puyear agreed to the lease terms. He had no desire to return to running the Tasty Cafe, not after all that had happened there. For him, it was a chapter of his life that he was putting behind him. Thomas Guy went about the work to refurbish and rebuild the Tasty Cafe. No matter how much paint he put on the place, though, he could not cover the memories of the bombing in the minds of the citizens of Marshall.

The community had to be tantalized by the new details that were emerging in the case. Rumors had sprung from beauty parlors and barber shops in town regarding the poison pills sent to Nola, and now they were plastered on the front page of the *Marshall Evening Chronicle*. The size of the reward caught attention as well. The handwriting sample provided was the talk of the town.

The publication of the handwriting sample and the larger reward appeared to have one effect that was totally unintended. On October 3, Marg Warsop, Nola's friend, received a crank call just before midnight. A man with a deep voice said, "Why Rogers, Arkansas?" then abruptly hung up.[19] Rogers, Arkansas, was near where Paul and Nola Puyear hailed from. Marg was a close friend of Nola's, and she was shaken by the call. Rogers had only been mentioned in one of the newspaper articles about the murder or the investigation, and then only as a passing reference. This call, to Nola's friend, seemed to be someone attempting to intimidate someone tied to the investigation, albeit in a strange manner.

These mysterious, almost haunting phone calls to the people who were talking to the police were not taken lightly. Yes, other prank calls were made, more often than not by a handful of sick individuals, usually kids. The calls that were more related to the police investigation, however, were seemingly aimed at people close to the case. Was this the killer attempting to intimidate possible witnesses? Or was the murderer taunting police?

The community as a whole was more than willing to help. Mrs. Ruth Bruce of Battle Creek phoned Myron Wood in his motel room and offered her technical services. She was a graduate of the University of Michigan and had worked for nine years as a handwriting analyst. She asked a question almost embarrassing for Wood—had any of the investigators had handwriting analysis done on the samples published in the newspapers? The answer was no. While Wood was uncomfortable discussing the case over the phone, he agreed to meet with Mrs. Bruce.

Using the copies of the material printed in the *Battle Creek Enquirer and News,* Mrs. Bruce had prepared the following summary of her analysis of the handwriting on the pill package in regard to the personality of the person who wrote the address label.

FORMATION	INTERPRETATION
35 degree slant	The writer is intensely emotional and expressive, an extrovert, impulsive and moody.
Ascending and descending baselines	Either writing under the influence of alcohol or drugs—or—writer is manic depressive and excitable.
Irregularity of spacing and sizes of letters	Either under the influence of drug or alcohol or electrical activity in the brain is severely damaged.
Angular strokes	Aggressive
"Club-like" I dots	Brutal
Hooks at the beginning of letters.	Greedy
Hooks at ends.	Tenacious
Low capital letters	Lack of self assurance usually caused by failure to succeed or youth and inexperience.
"P" in Puyear is small	Symbolic of low self esteem of family last name.
Mind-tent-like structures, v-structures—large writing—retracing.	A quick thinking, curious and critical person who becomes frustrated because he cannot concentrate and therefore loses the value of his thinking ability.

| Precise punctuation | Excellent memory, fussy, detail minded. |
| Death symbols show in "x"s | The writer thinking in terms of death usually forms x's the way this writer did in his printed M's and number 8. |

Bruce summarized, "Because the writer began writing in suppressed formation and then broadened to unrestrained, irregular writing, it can be assumed that he was writing under the influence of alcohol or drugs. Basically, a keen, alert mind, but has erratic sense of proportion and so his sharp mentality is used in a negative way. This writer is highly emotional and un-secretive, expansive and broad minded when either feeling in high spirits or intoxicated. The mostly uphill ascension of the writing indicates a feeling of exhilaration when writing caused by emotional mood, instability or artificial stimulant."[20]

The results that Mrs. Bruce had developed meshed well with the profile that Dr. Schier had provided. The impulsive nature of the writer, combined with the paranoid description from the doctor, gave the investigators a grim portrait of the person they were looking for.

* * * *

The effect of the handwriting sample being run in the paper spurred attorney Ronald DeGraw into action. Since the day of the explosion, he had suspected that Enoch Chism might have had something to do with it. He ordered his staff to pull out everything he had that might have Enoch's handwriting on it, for a comparison to what was printed in the paper.

One of his secretaries, Shirley Lawcock, had already made the connection on her own. The signature published in the paper the night before looked familiar to her. She had purchased a fishing boat for her husband recently, and the handwriting photograph in the *Marshall Evening Chronicle* looked like that of the man who had signed over the title to the boat, Enoch Chism. She and her husband looked over the photograph of the bomb wrapper. He still had the title in his wallet. Taking it out, they could tell, even with untrained eyes, that the handwriting was a match.

Mrs. Lawcock mentioned the title to DeGraw, who asked her to go and get it. When he saw that sample, DeGraw knew he had a perfect match for the handwriting. He called across the street to the post office and spoke with Myron Wood. When DeGraw told Wood that he had proof that the bomber was Enoch Chism, Wood was hesitant, saying, "We already ruled him out." But Wood knew that if he disregarded De-Graw, it might discourage other people from coming forward, given that DeGraw was a respected attorney in Marshall. Just to humor DeGraw, he came over and picked up the boat title to put in front of Dibowski's keen eye.[21]

In the basement of the post office, Inspector Dibowski was set up on a massive nine-foot-long table, looking over every voter and car registration in Calhoun County. Wood slipped the title in front of him. Dibowski looked at the handwriting on Shirley Lawcock's boat registration, then turned to the two men and said, "That's the one!" Wood informed DeGraw of the rewards offered and said that his tip qualified. At his prodding, DeGraw followed the procedures of the Secret Witness program outlined in the *Detroit News*.[22]

Two days after the *Detroit News* and the local papers ran the Secret Witness program's articles on the case, a plain envelope arrived at the *News* addressed to the program. Boyd Simmons opened it and saw that the corner had been ripped off. The letter plainly stated, "The name of Nola Puyear's killer is Enoch Chism. I saw the handwriting in the picture and recognized it from an official document I saw Enoch write." The paper was signed by a six-digit sequence. Boyd Simmons locked up the letter and contacted the investigators with the tip, though they already knew the name from DeGraw's visit. For the first time, they had a tangible suspect in Nola's death—Enoch Dalton Chism.

5

A Wolf among Sheep

The death of Nola Puyear was so brutal, so violent, that anyone analyzing it would want to balance it with the conviction of a person who is equally as evil and cunning. Somehow that would make it right, allow it to make sense. In many ways, Enoch Chism provided that balance. Clever, devious, brutal, savage, and smart—all in one deadly package—he seemed to be a killer who offset the violence he unleashed. It didn't make Nola's death easier to deal with, but his depth of evil makes it somehow balance in the analyst's mind.

Enoch Dalton Chism was not an unknown character in Marshall. At Sergeant Fred Ritchie's urging early in the investigation, he had been brought in for an interview and had provided a writing sample—one that Dibowski had already discounted. Chism was in the back of all of the investigators' minds as a potential suspect, but there had been nothing that had tied him to Nola Puyear other than his mother-in-law, Josie White, working at the Tasty. To the seasoned police officers, anyone who killed someone so violently needed to have a good motive. There had to be a reason that anyone would choose to kill someone in this manner. Chism, on the surface at least, didn't seem to have one.

What complicated matters for the investigators was that there were two Enoch Chisms: the one who the police knew and the Chism who only his family experienced. From the investigator's perspective, the Calhoun County Sheriff's Department and the Marshall Police Department felt that they knew Chism far too well. He was a known domestic abuser—a wife beater, by the nomenclature of the day. There had been a number of times that sheriff's deputies had been out to his house on C Drive North, responding to urgent calls claiming that Enoch was attacking his wife and threatening his family. The Marshall Police Department knew him from the 1965 arson of his brother's house in town. The general consensus was that Enoch was "squirrelly."[1] To many people who knew him, Chism was not believed to be mentally stable, but there was little that tied him to Nola Puyear in late September of 1967, other than the fact that his mother-in-law, Josie White, worked at the Tasty Cafe.

To acknowledge his reputation is not to say that Enoch always stood out in public as an agitator or an aggressive person. In fact, quite the opposite was true. He was an active member of his church and often did volunteer construction projects or other activities. Enoch coached a boy's baseball team, and to the young men he coached, he was support-ive, even friendly. A soft-spoken man, Chism was not known to lose his temper. To some people, Enoch was simply another member of the com-munity with a wife, good job, and children. Clearly, there were multiple aspects of this man.[2]

Before the police and the prosecutor could charge him with the crime, they had to do some additional digging. There had to be something else that linked him to the murder. If nothing else, they were going to need to get additional handwriting samples that could confirm him as the per-son who addressed the bomb and the pills. The tip that they had received from the Secret Witness program energized the police, giving them a concentration, a focus of their consummate skills.

* * * *

What the investigators on the case learned about Enoch Chism's life was pieced together mostly from their peers who had been called out to his house for numerous domestic issues. The grapevine in Marshall talked about the issues with whispers. People didn't talk about "wife beatings" or "spousal abuse." Instead, gossip circles referred to "family squabbles" or "wife and husband problems." It would be decades before Michigan enacted any domestic abuse laws. Before that happened, the victims of such abuse simply did whatever they could to survive in their environ-ments.

The police—with the exception of those who met Enoch—struggled with him a little as a suspect. It was a big leap to go from abusing your family to murder. There were signs that he was escalating in his crimi-nal activities. Chism had been convicted of arson only a few years ear-lier. Perhaps he was expanding his violence. As Herold Reuss said, "We knew he was a wife beater. The sheriff's department was out there all of the time. Generally speaking, people who beat their wives don't carry through with violence with other people. They prefer to rule through intimidation at home. Outside of the home, they are pretty mild. That just wasn't the case with Chism."[3]

Piecing together what they knew of Chism was easy for the investigators. In 1951, Enoch's wife, Bernice, had threatened to file for divorce. Enraged, Enoch had shattered the windshield of her car while she was behind the wheel, cutting her in the process. The sheriff's department was called because the Chisms lived just at the edge of the Marshall city limits, in Marshall Township. Enoch was arrested and charged with assault and battery.[4]

The tight-knit Marshall community thought that the Chisms were simply a typical family, and many were unaware of the turmoil that was unfolding behind closed doors. That wasn't to imply that everyone was in the dark. Enoch was known to confront his wife in restaurants or at work, sometimes cursing loudly at her, sometimes slapping her. Enoch was jealous over his wife, and this often fueled him to acts of violence against her. Bernice worked a late shift at Bell Telephone, almost opposite of her husband's shifts. Enoch was obsessed with her comings and goings, suspecting that she might have someone on the side, despite her assurances of the opposite. Enoch's obsession with Bernice led to constant violent confrontations.

* * * *

Starting in 1963, Enoch slowly succumbed to his personal demons and began a cascade of events that, the investigators found, propelled him to kill Nola Puyear. Enoch's brush with the law in that year was no minor offense but, rather, a crime committed by him remotely. Several of Enoch's brothers had moved to Michigan and Ohio, and he maintained close relations with them. His brother Carl owned a house in the Marshall city limits, at 114 North Fountain Street. Enoch acted as his brother's landlord, performing maintenance on the house and collecting the rent.

The tenant left the house empty, and a few days later, on November 27, 1963, a neighbor reported seeing smoke rising from the structure.

The Marshall Fire Department was on the scene quickly and entered the smoke-filled structure. Chief Bruce O'Leary reported that the firefighters found a black oily substance spilled about the house and found several towels that had been soaked in the same material and used to start the fire. From the smell in the air alone, the chief could tell that it was some sort of oil.

The quick action of the fire department saved the home. They had responded within five minutes and were able to put the fire out. Whoever had set the blaze had done so with some sort of fuel oil. Crawling on the floor of the burning building, Captain Ed Carroll located a Unico oil can through the smoke and haze. He had the presence of mind to get it out, preserving it as evidence.[5] The towels soaked with the substance had been placed on the furnace and in the kitchen and living room. Whoever had started the fire had done so with some sort of fuse or contraption that had failed to ignite the fuel oil entirely. The damage had been contained to the living room, kitchen, and bedroom—all of which had been doused with the oil. What had saved the residence was the fact that fuel oil had a high ignition point, which the heat of the fire simply did not have time to reach.

Chief O'Leary knew arson when he saw it and was careful to preserve the oil can and samples of the fuel oil. He reported that the fire was "incendiary in origins" and contacted the police. He tried to track down the landlord of the property, Enoch Chism, and discovered that he was in Battle Creek, some twenty minutes away, at work at the Kellogg Company.[6] Enoch feigned amazement at the news of the fire.

The home's former tenant, Lynwood Hunt, was quickly located, and he informed the investigators that he had left the house empty and clean and had never seen any fuel oil cans there when he had been living there. The Calhoun County deputies and a state police detective visited Enoch at his home to ask him what he knew about the fire. When they arrived, his garage door was open, and they noticed several Unico oil cans identical to the one recovered at the crime scene.[7] The sight of those fuel oil cans made Enoch Chism their immediate suspect.

Enoch attempted to get out of appearing at his trial altogether. He filed a note from Dr. L Harold Caviness, who said that Enoch was being treated for a nervous and emotional condition. Dr. Caviness said that the stress of attending his trial might prove too much for his patient. The judge, however, was not going to allow Chism to dodge attending his own trial. Having a defendant not appear in court would have been basis for appeal. Chism was told that regardless of the stress it might cause him, he needed to attend.[8]

For his part, Enoch claimed innocence. He told the investigators that his brother had advertised the vacancy in the house in nearby Albion, Michigan. From what Enoch said, the ad had read that the home was open to renting to either colored or white tenants. In a quirky turn, he added that he had been kidded at work a great deal about the advertisement. Racial tensions in Michigan were building slowly, and lily-white Marshall had very few black residents. Ironically, one of them rented the house adjacent to his brother's property on North Fountain Street. For the investigators, Chism's response to their questions about the arson seemed odd and only drew more attention to him.[9] Detective Joseph Terze came right out and pressed Enoch with a blunt query, "Did you have anything to do with the fire?" Enoch asked, "What would happen if I did do it?"[10] These were hardly the words of an innocent man.

Researching this book forced me to learn a little bit about the law. Gillespie's *Michigan Criminal Law* (page 1,395) explains, "Arson, however, from the very nature of the offense, is not a crime that is committed in the presence of witnesses." It was eerie how this aspect of the crime mirrored the murder of Nola Puyear by mail bomb.

The Unico oil can recovered at the scene of the fire was fingerprinted, and Enoch was asked to contribute his fingerprints. There were three prints on the can: one from a Marshall fireman and two from Enoch Chism. Enoch was arrested and charged with the crime of arson. He was represented by James Tompert, who did what he could to defend the headstrong Chism.

Enoch claimed he had an ironclad alibi—he was at work at the time the fire started. He alleged that on the morning of November 27, 1963, he left for work at Battle Creek on old U.S. Route 12. He stopped and used a pay phone to call his brother Carl at 6:30 a.m., then went to Kellogg, where he clocked in at 6:50 a.m.

Dragging in the Kellogg Company meant that their records were subpoenaed and that employees there were interviewed as well. Enoch claimed that he had a solid alibi by being en route to work at 6:22 a.m., when the alarm was sounded with the Marshall Fire Department. He further claimed that the trip between Marshall and Kellogg was a thirty-minute trip and that this fact, combined with his call to his brother (the same brother who owned the home), made it impossible for him to have set the fire.[11] In Enoch's mind, it was an ironclad defense. There was no way that he could be convicted.

Chism waived his right to a jury trial and arrogantly felt that the trial was a mere formality—that his word and his alibi were enough. The prosecution felt differently. They timed the trip between Chism's home and Kellogg at that time of day and found it to take just over twenty minutes. Even with a short phone call, it was ample time to make the trip. In addition, the way the fire had been started seemed to have been done with a contraption of sorts, a device to delay it from starting right away. Chism's alibi seemed to melt away as the prosecution looked into the case. His fingerprints were on the oil can used to start the fire, and the former tenant solidified through testimony that he had left the home empty. Chism refused to take the stand in his own defense. On October 26, 1965, he was found guilty of arson.

Enoch Chism should have been sent to jail. He should have faced severe punishment. But Judge Ronald Ryan spared him, explaining, "I feel that it was a most unfortunate situation that you got involved in and I also feel that you had some matters in your family life and elsewhere that really brought about a mental condition or mental problems that have seriously affected your way of life to a certain extent, on the other hand, you have had a steady job at the Kellogg Company over quite a long period of years, and you have a good work record. You had, of course, matters affecting domestic relations and there is a divorce case pending, of course, at the present time. . . . Certainly after reviewing all of the factors involved with this case, and I spent a great deal of time with the probation officer, and I have also talked with your counsel and he has talked with me in your behalf, it is the sentence of the Court that you be placed on probation for a period of two years."[12] Chism was also forced to pay a fine of fifty dollars, one hundred dollars in court costs, and an additional five dollars to the state police training fund.

Enoch got little more than a pitiful slap on the wrist for his arson conviction. Years later, Marshall police chief Herold Reuss reflected with me how this arson trial was a foreshadowing of what was to come: "What bothered us all was that we had gotten a solid conviction on this guy and the judge had set him loose. We were frustrated because we knew if he had been in jail, she [Nola] never would have died." As Reuss confided to me, "It was a miscarriage of justice."

Even the lenient Judge Ryan sensed that there was something not quite right with the defendant. He stipulated, "But there is one condition to the probation that the Court feels is important and that is that you attempt to obtain some psychiatric treatment wherever you think that it can be obtained. I think you had some experience before at the Sanitarium. So it is a condition of the probation that you make another attempt to see if there is some help and assistance that you can receive from a psychiatrist to straighten out some of the problems that are seriously affecting you in connection with your routine of living. So that will be part of the terms of probation." The judge continued, "I think that if you cooperate with the probation officer and do your part, that a lot of these matters that are affecting you will be straightened out. You can continue to hold your job and I hope that you can so rearrange your life that you can proceed forward without having so many of these problems that affected you so much. So I am sure that you will cooperate."[13]

In the research of this book, I spoke with two officers who looked back at the arson very differently in light of the murder charges leveled at Chism. Hindsight, as it seems, is an enlightening thing. Was the fire really arson or a botched attempt at murder? Marshall had only a handful of black families living in town, and one of them lived adjacent to 114 North Fountain Street. Enoch demonstrated his extreme prejudice toward blacks as part of his defense. Was it possible that he had set the fire in hopes that it would spread to the family in the adjacent home? Looking back, more than one official attached to the case is convinced that Chism's real intention was to burn out the neighbors. This possibility offers a glimpse into the twisted deviousness of Chism's thinking. As one official put it to me, "Enoch never came straight at you, he always came from behind or the shadows."

* * * *

To say that Enoch abused his wife is almost to downplay his actions toward her. In the 1960s, a wife abuser was called a "wife beater," and this description fits Chism perfectly. The Calhoun County Sheriff's Department had been out to the Chisms' home on several occasions to break up Enoch's attacks on his wife and daughter. This was an age when domestic violence was seen as a family problem. The police rarely stepped in and arrested the aggressor. They more often tried to calm the situation down, sometimes sending one of the parties away for the night to defuse the situation. As Sergeant Fred Ritchie put it years later, "We went out to the Chisms' house all of the time. You know, it was family argument stuff—typical—a husband arguing with his wife. We'd show up and calm everything down and leave."[14]

On one occasion when the deputies showed up, Chism had been chasing his wife in his car and run her car off the road. He had then attempted to use his car to hit Bernice. On another night, Enoch had gone after her with a knife; the deputies disarmed him and made sure that he calmed down, then let him go. Bernice filed for divorce on May 1, 1965. Divorces in the 1960s in Michigan were not fast things, though. There were built-in cooling-off periods, and in this case, the cries for divorce were not coming from both parties. Enoch did not want to let Bernice go. His behavior began a slow cascade, and his violence began to leak out into the Marshall community.

The police were called once more to the Chism household on May 21, 1965. Once more, Enoch had escalated. When the officers received the call to the home, it was because Enoch had a shotgun in a cloth bag and was threatening to kill his wife and the officers. When they arrived, Enoch did not have the gun. The deputies suggested that Enoch spend the night somewhere else. He claimed to need to get a few things and went to the bedroom. One of the deputies was a little suspicious and went back to the bedroom to find Enoch loading the shotgun. Enoch claimed he was putting it away so that the kids couldn't get hurt with it. The deputy carefully took the weapon away from him. Enoch left for the night, and his wife, most likely out of fear, did not offer to press charges.[15]

On August 24, the sheriff's department once more arrived at the Chism house. Enoch had exploded in a rage, shouting and cursing at his wife and daughter. He had thrown things around the house, breaking dishes. He chased Bernice and his daughter, Sharon, off the property. This time, Bernice had him picked up and put in jail on a forty-eight-hour hold, a cooling-off period. During that time, two Marshall doctors provided him with some basic psychiatric evaluations. One felt Enoch was a risk, while the other thought he was just fine. In Bernice's words, "he had snowed them."[16] After his temporary separation, Enoch was released and allowed to return home.

* * * *

The investigators had access to additional information on Enoch as a result of his arson conviction—namely, in the form of his parole reports. Chism was required to regularly check in with Neil Finley, his parole officer. While parole officers today are seen as burdened by massive caseloads and unable to monitor convicted criminals, such was not the case in the 1960s in Marshall. Finley not only maintained regular meetings with Enoch but did some of his own investigation work on this man.

In May of 1966, the Chisms separated. This time, Bernice moved in with her parents, Josie and Hollie White, who lived next to the Chisms at the time. For a few weeks, Enoch lived with his sister Ruby Bagwell in Battle Creek, then, on May 6, he obtained permission from his parole officer to move in with his brother Whitman Chism in Toledo.[17]

A month later, Enoch returned to Calhoun County and almost immediately became involved with a ridiculous moneymaking scheme. A man by the name of Jones in Jackson, Michigan, claimed to know another individual named O'Connell who possessed a machine or device that could take in one-dollar bills and convert them to twenty-dollar bills. On the surface, this seems like such a scam that even a child would question it as a parlor trick. Enoch claimed, though, that he was convinced of its legitimacy and invested five thousand dollars of his own money in the counterfeiting device. Enoch claimed that the elusive Mr. O'Connell had skipped out on both him and Jones, taking fifteen thousand dollars from them.[18]

Jones, however, told a different story, claiming that Enoch was involved and had even orchestrated the theft. The finger-pointing between the men went nowhere, as neither was willing to press charges. Even more incredible, Enoch recounted the entire affair with his parole officer, who labeled it a "scheme."[19] Enoch seemed to lack the common sense to avoid telling an officer of the court that he was planning on undertaking a criminal activity—in this case, counterfeiting.

There was a part of Enoch Chism's personality that harbored the belief that a windfall of money might somehow make matters in his life better. Interviewing Chism's parole officer, Sergeant Ritchie reported that "the victim of arson attempt [that Enoch was convicted of] was Chism's brother, Carl Chism, and after the insurance paid off the property was deeded to Enoch free and clear with no charge to Enoch. It was subsequently sold by Enoch, indicating a possible conspiracy in this arson. It is Findley's opinion that Chism would not be above any venture for money, legal or illegle [sic]."[20]

On July 30, 1966, Enoch Chism was fired from his job at Kellogg. His dismissal came from violating the company policy—Enoch was caught drinking on the job.[21] In August, he took a job working for the Clark Oil station on Capital Avenue in Battle Creek. He leased the station for one month but quit the job there by September, claiming that Clark Oil had not lived up to its agreements with him. Much of his time at the service station was spent mailing out credit card applications—tedious work at best. With Enoch, the blame never rested with him but always fell to someone else.

Frustrated with the opportunities around Marshall, Enoch moved in with his brother Orville in Detroit in October 1966. He got a job working construction at R. E. Dailey and Company in Southfield, Michigan, performing steelwork. After only a few weeks in Detroit, he moved back to Marshall.

Enoch was able to get a job working at Clark Equipment Company upon his return, on October 17. It was not a job that he was happy with, especially since it had him working an opposite shift from Bernice. From his interview with Chism's parole officer, Sergeant Ritchie reported, "Chism is violently jealous of his wife and accused her of all sort of infidelities but Findley was unable to obtain any evidence of unfaithfulness."[22]

By December of 1966, Enoch and Bernice were back together again. Perhaps it was the fact that he was able to stabilize his work life. Perhaps he was attempting to make some changes. Regardless, Enoch was back in her life, and there were no calls to the sheriff regarding domestic disputes.

* * * *

The investigators of the bombing that killed Nola Puyear still had a lot of work to do to tie Enoch Chism to the scene of the crime. By the first week of October 1967, the investigators were beginning to piece together a more complete picture of the man who had become their only suspect in the murder. What they found was a man who was slowly escalating in his violence, one who was losing control of his life and, quite possibly, his anger.

Enoch's brushes with the law seemed almost trivial compared to the bombing murder. While the police visited his home often to protect Bernice and his children, his actual arrests were small, including one in 1951 for assault and battery. The arson arrest and conviction in 1965 stood out as the most prominent crime—a long way from a bombing. He was arrested twice in 1965—in May and August—during the time of Bernice's filing for divorce. Since then, there had been nothing. Even the calls to the sheriff's department had dropped off. For law enforcement in Calhoun County, it seemed as if things at the Chism home had maybe settled.

Then came the tip from the Secret Witness program. In looking at Enoch Chism as a suspect, investigators thought he seemed to possess a volatile temper that might lead someone to violence, and from his work in maintenance, they gathered that he might have the technical skills. But Jereck and the investigators didn't have enough to pull Chism in immediately. They needed to confirm his handwriting sample, especially since Dibowski had already cleared him once before.

Also, there was still a missing motive. Why would Chism want to kill Nola Puyear? The question hung in the air with the police and the prosecutor, nagging at them. For such a violent crime, they had a need to have a compelling reason to commit such a murder. What they knew of Enoch Chism offered no reason at this stage of the investigation.

For the investigators, there had to be more to the story about this man. Some of those facts would surface as they dug deeper; others would remain secret to them for years to come. One thing was for sure: they had a great deal of work ahead of them before they could arrest and convict Enoch for Nola's murder.

6

A "Vile and Unpredictable Temper"

There was a distinct difference between what the investigators knew about Enoch Chism and the real man. They were limited by the information that they had access to at the time. Now, over four decades later, details can be brought to light that reveal the hell on earth that Enoch Chism unleashed on his family and eventually on his community.

Enoch Chism was from Lepanto, Arkansas, less than thirty miles from the hometown of the Puyears. Oddly enough, they never seemed to have known each other, but it was a coincidence that captured the attention of the investigators. Born to Columbus and Joyce "Ludie" Chism on May 18, 1924, Enoch came from a family of farmers. The family had been in America since the 1750s, starting in South Carolina, moving to Mississippi, then concentrating in Arkansas. Enoch was the eleventh of fifteen children born to his parents.

His father, Columbus, was a farmer, working for the Weona Farming Company. Enoch's formal schooling was limited—depending on who he was talking to, Enoch said he completed either the third or sixth grade. Whereas his father worked a company farm, Enoch worked a farm for himself, eking out a living through World War II.[1] By his own admission, Enoch was not very close to either of his parents. He described his parents' marriage as "average" until later in life, when his father began to drink. Enoch reported about his father, "He would get quite violent. When he was sober, you couldn't ask for a nicer guy."[2]

At the age of twenty-one, Enoch married Bernice Louise White, on March 24, 1945, in Marked Tree, Arkansas. They were married by a local minister.[3] Almost from the start of their marriage, Enoch and Bernice seemed to have issues. He explained, "We didn't get along as well as my mother and dad. She's quite domineering . . . quite independent. When we try to talk thoughts out I have quite a temper too. I can go quite a long time but when I explode I do things I shouldn't."[4]

Enoch had moved to the Marshall area in 1946, building his own little ranch home on C Drive North. Enoch eventually secured a job at the Kellogg Company in Battle Creek. Kellogg was one of the largest employers in Calhoun County. Getting a job there or with Post Cereals was considered to be fortunate, thanks to their wages and benefits. Chism was a maintenance man, performing repairs on the cereal production lines. His work life, at least for a few years, seemed perfectly normal, though many people who knew him commented that he was "queer" or "not right in the head." Chism kept to himself, and from what his coworkers knew of him, that was just fine.[5]

His wife, Bernice, was the polar opposite of him in many ways. Bernice was the foundation of stability in their family. They had two children. The older, Sharon, was born in 1946, and his son, Michael Chism, was born in 1953. Outwardly, they appeared to be a normal family. They attended church regularly, and Bernice and Enoch attended typical community events, such as high school plays and so on.[6] Bernice's parents, Hollie and Josie White, moved in next to them when they first relocated to Michigan. Sharon eventually married a local man, Bruce Norton. Her husband was in the service, and she continued to live at home.

Enoch's early encounters with the law were limited to his confrontations with the police when he attacked Bernice. His arrest in 1951 for assault and battery was one in a string of events erupting in their house. His conviction of arson in 1965 forced him to seek psychiatric counseling. To the outside world of Marshall, Enoch claimed that he had nothing to do with the fire, that he had been framed by forces unknown. The evidence of his fingerprint on the fuel oil can used as an accelerant was glossed over. Privately, he admitted to his wife that he had indeed set the fire.

To those treating him, Enoch presented an entirely different story. He claimed that the entire community had turned against him, that the police, lawyers, and everyday citizens were "harassing" him. He reported, "I felt kinda embarrassed. I didn't want to face the public. I even dreaded to walk out of the house to see my neighbors. . . . It got to where I couldn't get along with anybody. I got irritable. I didn't trust anybody. Seems like everybody knew and were talking."[7] All of this was the product of Enoch's mind.

Paranoia began to set in. Enoch told his doctors that the police had tapped his telephone line and that detectives had been planted at Kellogg to spy on him. Chism began a withdrawal from society, turning inward on his family. He reported, "I became quiet. I didn't care too much about bothering people I wanted to be by myself."[8]

Matters at home were far from stable. Enoch was obsessed with the thought that his wife was having affairs behind his back. His suspicions resulted in eruptions of rage. At first, Bernice's family actually sided with Enoch—he was so convincing in his imaginary stories that their daughter was running around. By 1965, they began to see the truth about their son-in-law. Bernice, with the children in tow, would seek shelter with them after his violent explosions. He would come over and plead for them to return, begin to cry, and eventually cajole Bernice to return, with promises that he would treat her better.[9]

Once Enoch saw that he could no longer count on his in-laws to support his allegations, he turned on them. He threatened both of the seniors, swearing to kill them. The Whites finally moved away, unable to live next door with the constant threats.[10]

In early May of 1965, during one of their fights, Chism jumped through a door and window at one point when his wife had locked him out, cutting his arm so badly that he nearly slipped into shock and had to be taken to the hospital for fifty-two stitches.[11] Matters had reached the boiling point for Bernice, who contacted Ronald DeGraw to file for divorce.

Bernice's petition for divorce painted a dark, grim picture of life on C Drive North. In her lawyer's words, Enoch Chism was the most sadistic man he had ever known.[12] On one occasion, Bernice believed that Enoch tried to poison her. She had returned from work, and Enoch had made coffee for her. She poured a cup, tasted it, and said it burned her mouth like it contained some chemical substance. She poured the coffee out and found a white substance mixed in with the coffee grounds.[13]

Her divorce outlined the range of violence that he was capable of. Her divorce filing claimed that he had "abused the petitioner [Bernice] and the parties' minor children both physically and orally." Enoch beat Bernice about the face and head with his fists and, on several occasions, threatened to kill her. One night, he attacked her with a knife. He threw a heavy monkey wrench at his daughter, Sharon, apparently aiming at her head.[14]

At home, Enoch swore loudly at his family one minute, then threw himself on the floor and cried like a child the next. On one occasion, he attempted to injure himself by throwing himself down a flight of stairs. Several other times, he would remove his belt, pulling it tight around his neck to hang himself. In his explosive outbursts, he broke furniture and dishes, throwing them around their home.[15] The Chism family lived in a constant hurricane of conflicting emotions, raw terror, and ever-present fear.

Not all of Enoch's rage was contained to his home. He would go to Bell Telephone, where Bernice worked, and accost her there, slapping her in front of the other employees. He would stalk her at lunch in restaurants and curse at her, causing a scene and embarrassing both of them. One night, he ran her car off the road. When Bernice got out of the car, he tried to run her down with his own vehicle. When he couldn't get to her, he tore the radio antenna off her car.[16]

The filing for divorce was a wake-up call of sorts for Chism. Up until that point, Bernice's threats to leave him had been academic. This time, she was serious enough to file paperwork, and the effect on Enoch was immediate.

Dejected, swinging between rage and fits of crying, Enoch checked himself in at the Battle Creek Sanitarium for treatment. There was no sign of violent outbursts. His treating doctor, Doctor L. Harold Caviness, noted, "He has a terrible temper, beats wife, impulsively grabbing her by the hair and slapping her around. Before outsiders he presents a sweet and innocent person."[17]

Enoch's ability to control his personality in public was incredible. He had been able to localize his rage, only unleashing it on his wife and children. "He has been able to maintain a perfectly normal behavior pattern at work and away from the house," Dr. Caviness noted. Only when the doors were closed did the true Enoch Chism emerge. Even in the hospital, he took part in group therapy and recreational activities. Dr. Caviness reported, "Patient is pleasant, quiet, makes no complaints is, 'almost too perfect a patient.'"[18] Whatever personal demons he struggled with, Enoch managed to pretend to be perfectly normal.

The psychological tests Enoch undertook were not something he could bluff his way through. While he felt he had outfoxed the staff, the tests were another matter. During his interviews, Enoch admitted that he was now "always angry." Sentence completion tests underscored his feelings of weakness, hopelessness, and failure. One doctor reported, "He has no hope of achieving any satisfaction or joy in this world and awaits for the end." Enoch was described as a hypersensitive, lonely, and unhappy man perceiving himself as living in a very unfair and cruel world. The same doctor wrote, "He has managed thus far by blunting his emotional life, denying much and otherwise detaching himself." Enoch was said to be a paranoid, with a chronic lack of patience and inability to control his temper. To Enoch Chism, the world was a threatening, unpredictable, and unsafe place.[19] The image his doctors arrived at was of a man who was on a collision course. With what, no one could say.

Chism's IQ was normal, but emotionally and in his ability to cope socially, he was listed as "dull." Rorschach tests did not brighten the picture for the professionals. Enoch showed "considerable evidence here of explosiveness and instability." Machover tests demonstrated that he was at a primitive level of emotional development. One doctor noted, "This is a three year old emotional creature who feels overworked and encased in a very tired 60 year old body."[20]

Today, Enoch Chism would likely have been arrested at the first instance of domestic violence. There might have been batteries of tests done on him, and he might have received doses of medications that would have smothered his inner beast. The law might have ensured he never got close to his family or posed a risk to them. This was the 1960s, though. Such protections simply didn't exist then. Thus, a dangerous killer, a ticking time bomb of a man, was allowed to be stalking the streets of Marshall.

* * * *

On May 19, 1965, Enoch was visited in the sanitarium by his daughter, Sharon. She had had some sort of confrontation with her mother and, according to Enoch, had been bruised in the process. Enoch was no longer able to maintain his front for the doctors. He began to break down, bursting into tears, worrying about what was happening at home. What no one documented was how much of this threat to Sharon was in his own mind.

Two days later, he met with Dr. Caviness and decided to check out of the hospital and return home. His doctor recommended a structured return, to minimize the chance of any conflicts. He thought that Enoch did not display any psychosis, "but rather a passive aggressive schizoid personality pattern with a low frustration tolerance, a lot of conflict about dominating, provocative, frustrating females and some brittle controls indicating the probability of occasional explosive temper outburst."[21] The prognosis noted in the doctor's discharge painted a grim outlook: "Guarded, unless it is possible to bring about environmental changes or inaugurate parallel casework for the wife."[22] The doctor told Enoch in blunt language that he should stay away from his wife.

That night, Enoch threatened his family with a shotgun and was arrested again. There is no way to know just where the incident might have gone if not for the intervention of the sheriff's department.

His time away from the sanitarium only lasted until May 29. Enoch admitted that he had gone home too soon, that he had "got upset with his wife"—a euphemism for another beating event. He had tried to go to work but was too nervous and returned to readmit himself.

By June 8, Enoch had approached his doctor about attempting to convince Bernice that she should not divorce him. Dr. Caviness noted, "He has become obsessive compulsive kind of fellow which is rather very difficult to change his mind or accept any reality, rather he would prefer someone else to change instead of him."[23]

Bernice finally met with doctors, who found her petite, attractive, and very controlled. She told them that she was going to pursue a divorce—that she was done with all of the beatings. The cruelty had become too much for her. There seemed little middle ground in the relationship.

Enoch's response was unpredicted. The next night, he broke out of the Battle Creek Sanitarium, going AWOL to return home. Enoch was caught when he broke back in that night. His doctor later reported, "I told Mr. Chism that he had built up a reputation of being a very clever lock picker by the way he got on and off of our ward."[24]

In late June of 1965, Doctor Caviness secured a copy of the arrest report from May 21, the night of the shotgun incident, and read it before speaking to his patient in a follow-up meeting, not telling Enoch that he knew the deputies' version of events. Enoch attempted to minimize what had happened in the episode, ascribing it to his wife's exaggeration. The police report told another story, with Bernice badly bruised on the neck and wrist from his assault prior to the sheriff's arrival. Enoch tried to dismiss or downplay the confrontation that led to his arrest, claiming that it wasn't his fault—it was all Bernice.[25]

Doctor Caviness attempted to help him cope with the reality that Bernice was most likely going to pursue the divorce. He wanted to help stabilize Enoch, strengthen him for the stress that the divorce was likely to bring. The doctor observed, "He cannot quite give up the hope that a reconciliation could yet be affected and claims that as late as a day or two after her interview in my office, she asserted to him that if he could change with the help of psychiatric treatment, she would be willing to drop the divorce action. I told him if I wondered if this were not wishful thinking on his part but I could not actually call him a liar. I therefore asserted he must not count on it."[26]

After that advice, Enoch began to miss his appointed follow-ups. Disregarding the advice of professionals, he immediately went to his home to confront Bernice over the alleged abuse to Sharon. The matter boiled over, forcing the sheriff's department to show up and arrest Enoch once more, holding him for forty-eight hours. The next day, Bernice was awarded a preliminary injunction against her husband as part of her divorce filings. This injunction described Enoch in the most unflattering terms: "The defendant possesses a vile and unpredictable temper." The injunction required Enoch to "keep away from molesting, interfering, with the personal freedoms, threatening their person and property, swearing, calling them names, and from entering the dwelling."[27] Enoch only spoke to his psychiatrist two more times, missing more scheduled appointments than those he made.

* * * *

By May of 1966, Enoch and Bernice had reconciled and once again had another blowup. This time, Bernice moved in with her parents. For a few weeks, Enoch floated between the residences of his sister Ruby Bagwell in Battle Creek and his brother Whitman Chism in Toledo.[28] What was missing was his friends. Simply put, there were none. Enoch had to rely on his blood relations. There was no one else who would take him in— no coworkers, no pals, not even members of his church.

His attempts to get involved with the moneymaking scheme to convert dollar bills into twenty-dollar bills underscored Enoch's deep-seated thoughts that money might solve his problems.[29] As Sergeant Fred Ritchie told me, "One of Enoch's biggest issues was that his wife was high maintenance. She had a good job, made good money. He just felt that that the work he got was below him."[30]

Enoch was fired from his job at the Kellogg Company on July 30, 1966. His dismissal came from violating the company policy by drinking alcohol on the job.[31] He told conflicting stories about the reason for his termination. Enoch claimed he had been given the beer by a coworker and had been set up for the dismissal. Two years later, his family would tell police that Enoch had struck his supervisor after being caught and that this was the reason for the termination.[32] The last vestige of stability in his life was suddenly gone, lost due to his own inability to control himself.

Much of this information about Enoch Chism and his character was hidden from public view at the time of the investigation into the bombing death of Nola Puyear. In many respects, the police investigating the bombing did not fully understand the man they were about to deal with.

7

To Catch a "Tiger"

The investigative team did not immediately arrest Enoch Chism. They had
to make sure that their case was solid before they moved in. This was not
the typical criminal after all. This was a brutal murderer who had, so far,
evaded them. Arresting Enoch Chism was going to be a carefully planned
and executed operation.

On October 6, 1967, most people in Marshall were looking forward to the
home football game against neighboring Harper Creek. Marshall's chief
rivals in high school football were Albion and Harper Creek—mostly
due to the proximity of the schools. Redskins football always brought
out the entire community, and fans always looked forward to the duel
with the Harper Creek Beavers. The game, which required heavy coats
and blankets due to the chill in the air, would be a good diversion from
their own insecurities about who Nola Puyear's killer was.

On October 6, the investigators minds were far from football; they
were beginning to feel more confident that their prime suspect was indeed the murderer of Nola Puyear. John Jereck met with the investigators and laid out a strategy to solidify their case. They needed writing samples from Chism, samples produced when Enoch did not have
investigators watching him. He worked at Clark Equipment, and one
team was sent there to obtain his job application. The request was done
discreetly so as to avoid tipping Enoch off. Another team went to the
courthouse to obtain his driver's license paperwork and any other official court documents that he had written or signed. From his application
at Clark Equipment, they knew he had worked construction in Detroit
for a month at R. E. Dailey and Company—so records from that business
were also gathered. Jereck wanted to make sure that he had a significant
number of samples for Dibowski and Van Stratt to analyze.

Both of the teams hit pay dirt, coming back with untainted samples of

Chism's scrawled and jagged handwriting. In the case of the documents obtained by the sheriff's department, Jereck took the precaution of making sure that the sheriff's deputies at the Driver's License Bureau, Betty Kedo and Ellen Palmer, could be counted on to swear that Chism had indeed written the documents in question. In a chilling discovery, Enoch had filled out his latest application for a driver's license on the day that the bomb had been mailed to Nola. It was entirely possible that the signatures and the addressing on the bomb had happened within hours or even minutes of each other. His two booking sheets for previous crimes were also secured.[1]

Several of the investigators were sent out to check the hardware stores in the county to see if any had sold Chism any dynamite. The store records and degree of accuracy varied widely, but Enoch Chism's name did not appear on any of their rolls. Nearly fifteen hardware and supply stories were checked in the process, though the trooper performing the search did not reveal who he was looking for. The investigators knew this was a difficult course to follow. In the 1960s, almost every farmer had access to dynamite for removing stones or stumps, and there was no requirement to check identification when purchasing it. Every hardware store of any size carried and sold it upon request.

Detectives Steinbacher and Kenney spoke with the supervisor of Marshall Township, Charles Quick, who attended the same church as the Chisms and said that Enoch had been in church the weeks following the bombing. When he saw him on September 24, "Chism appeared withdrawn, as though something was bothering him." Quick also stated that Chism's neighbor had once told him that Enoch had used dynamite on his septic tank recently, with destructive effects.[2]

A discreet meeting with the Chisms' neighbor James Herman confirmed that story. Chism didn't get along with Herman—they had squabbled before over the fence that separated their properties—and he was more than willing to assist police. Earlier in the spring, Enoch had been digging in the yard with a posthole digger, after which Herman heard several explosions. In talking with Chism, he learned that Enoch had been trying to unclog his septic tank using dynamite. Rather than remove the obstruction, Enoch had admitted that he had blown the tank up. The police were able to confirm the story further by talking with the local business that had replaced the blasted septic system.[3]

This became important in the minds of the investigators. While they could not find documentation that Enoch had purchased dynamite, he was known to have had it and used it in the spring.

The handwriting samples gathered were passed on to James Dibowski, who was meticulously working on a massive table in the basement of the Marshall Post Office. When given the first new samples on September 27, he noted that there were similarities in the samples and that he wanted to study them more before rendering a decision. He pointed out that the similarities appeared in the writing on both the bomb package and the package of poison pills.[4]

* * * *

Ronald DeGraw agreed to be interviewed by authorities—not as the "secret witness," but as Bernice Chism's divorce attorney. He told them that Chism was the most sadistic man he had ever known. He beat his wife and had even tried to poison her by mixing something into her coffee. For the investigators, this was new information, and it piqued their interest, given that poison had been mailed to Nola weeks before the bombing. During their divorce proceedings, Chism threatened to kill not only Bernice but DeGraw as well if she continued with the divorce. Bernice had folded only six weeks before the divorce would have been final, not out of love, but out of mortal fear for her life. There was seemingly no escape from Enoch and his obsession with her.[5]

DeGraw didn't tell the investigators at the time that Enoch had nearly attacked him once, right on Michigan Avenue. During her 1965 attempt to divorce Enoch, she had come to DeGraw's office for a meeting. Enoch showed up in the lobby, and Shirley Lawcock had called back to him to tell him that he was pacing around the office, refusing to sit down. Enoch was wringing his hands and muttering to himself. Shirley was nervous.

DeGraw decided it was best to walk Bernice to her car, which was parked a few blocks away, by Cronin's Department Store. Enoch followed. Walking backward, he pleaded with Bernice to take him back. He told her to ignore her attorney—that lawyers made their living off the grief of others. When they reached Peck's Drugstore, across the street from Bernice's car, DeGraw said, "Enoch, you've had your say. Now we're leaving." Taking Bernice by the arm, he started across Michigan Avenue.

The sound of running footsteps were coupled with Bernice turning and looking over DeGraw's shoulder, then saying, "Oh, God, here he comes." At the last moment, DeGraw spun around quickly, braced for an assault. "You get the first shot, Enoch. Make it a good one!" he warned. Chism backed off immediately once the men were facing each other. Bernice got in her car and left. The last time DeGraw saw Enoch that day two years earlier, the latter was sitting on the curb, crying.[6]

Despite a peace bond, a form of restraining order, Enoch broke into Bernice's home and threatened her. Both of Bernice's parents, Hollie and Josie White, were in fear of Enoch as well, thanks to his threats to kill them. On one occasion, he had tried to burn Bernice with a hot iron. He had threatened to kill the entire family once—pulling a pistol out of a bag he had brought with him, to intimidate them. On one particularly horrific night, August 21, 1965, Enoch had broken a broom in half to use as a weapon, broken furniture and dishes, and thrown a wrench at his daughter, Sharon.[7]

Once when Bernice went out and had her hair done, he became so enraged that he wrestled her to the sink and rubbed sugar and coffee into her hair. He was so unstable that he broke down a locked bathroom door one night while she was taking a bath—simply to get at her. Only police intervention had stopped Enoch from inflicting more harm that night.[8]

Detective Kenney, Inspector Myron P. Wood, and M. W. Hammond sat in on the interview with DeGraw. For the first time, they got a more in-depth understanding of what Enoch Chism was capable of. Even for seasoned investigators, it had to be sobering to hear about the rage the man possessed.

Inspector Wood was concerned for the man who had tipped them off to Chism—especially since it would be several days before they would be ready to apprehend Enoch. Marshall was a small town, and with each passing day, there was a risk that the grapevine might discover that Chism was a suspect. If Enoch suspected that DeGraw had turned him in, he might extract revenge.

Wood gave DeGraw a book on car bombs. The best advice it gave was to use two pieces of Scotch tape on the hood of your car. If the tape was broken, then someone had opened the hood of the vehicle and possibly planted a bomb. That day, Ronald DeGraw began putting tape on the hood of his car and checking it before he turned the ignition.[9]

* * * *

I was struck by the meticulous and deliberate approach of the investigators that was evident in the police reports related to this case. They were sure they had the right man, even if they didn't understand why he had committed the crime. But they didn't rush in to apprehend Enoch. Instead, they circled him like wolves stalking their prey. They gathered the evidence bit by bit and prepared carefully. After all, this killer was capable of using explosives to do his dirty work.

John Jereck met with U.S. district attorney Harold Beaton on October 9 to discuss just who was going to prosecute Chism. There were multiple jurisdictions involved with this case, since sending a bomb through the mail was a federal offense. The men came to the conclusion that Jereck should go after Chism first for the murder of Nola Puyear. If he failed to get a conviction on the murder at the state level, the federal authorities would go after him for the postal bombing.[10]

For several mornings, troopers discreetly tailed Chism's 1964 Ford sedan to get a feel for his driving and work routine. They knew the roads and exits he took to get to and from work daily. When dealing with a bomber, they wanted to make sure that when he was taken into custody, it was done smoothly, quickly, and efficiently.[11]

By October 10, the investigators laid out what they had on Chism in the office of the Marshall police chief, which served as a makeshift conference room. Enoch was a character who certainly possessed a penchant for violence. He had access to dynamite, too. Most important, both Dibowski and Van Stratt had reviewed the body of handwriting samples. There was no doubt in their minds: Enoch Chism had written the address on the bomb package and the package containing the poison pills.

That afternoon, John Jereck authorized a warrant for Chism's arrest for murder in the first degree. Detective Steinbacher walked it over to Judge Alfred Stuart, who signed off on it. The plan was to take down Chism in his car as he came home from work.[12]

* * * *

The morning of October 11 was cold, with a hint of white frost on the browning grass of a Michigan autumn. The plan to apprehend Enoch

Chism was highly orchestrated and organized. A surveillance car would tail him for a short distance heading west along Interstate 94 from his job at Clark Equipment, then pass the tailing on to an interceptor car containing some of the arresting officers on the case. Using multiple cars for the tailing would reduce the chance of Chism detecting that he was being tailed. The last thing they wanted was for Enoch to realize he was being followed and react.

From their surveillance, they knew he usually exited the highway at U.S. Route 127. At the stop before this, on Twenty-Six Mile Road, the car filled with the arresting officers would be waiting on the entrance ramp. They would slide in behind Chism and pull him over at the top of the ramp when he exited at Route 127. The original tailing car and the interceptor car would wedge in behind and in front of Chism's car. They knew Enoch had previously owned a shotgun and was a potential bomber, so the goal was to get him out of his car quickly, to reduce his chance at possibly setting off a bomb or drawing a weapon.

The troopers in the interceptor car, number 4611, included Sergeant John Lohrstorfer and Trooper Hutchins. Detectives Kenney and Steinbacher and Sergeant Richie, who had been on the case since the start, were in the surveillance car that was tailing Chism from work. For Kenney, Steinbacher, and Ritchie, Chism's arrest was a chance to bring some degree of closure to the case they had been working since August. For Ritchie, there had to be more than a hint of satisfaction. The day after the bombing, when asked, he had said that Enoch Chism was the first person he had thought of as the murderer. For Marshall as a whole, Chism's arrest was bound to calm nerves and allow the little town to return to some semblance of normalcy.

Chism did not seem aware of the tailing state police car behind him, and at first, everything seemed to be going as planned. But just after 7:10 a.m., Enoch suddenly exited in his Ford at Twenty-Six Mile Road. It was a divergence in his pattern and was enough to make Detective Kenney nervous that someone may have tipped him off. That might mean that Enoch was prepared for them, a situation none of them cared to face. Worse yet, Sergeant Lohrstorfer and the men in his car were on the exit ramp, and Chism was now *behind* them. Kenney made the call: they had to take him down on Twenty-Six Mile Road.[13] Sergeant Lohrstorfer threw his patrol car into reverse and gunned the engine, roaring backward up the exit ramp to the top, where Chism had turned south and crossed over Interstate 94. As Chism came off the overpass, the state troopers swooped in, blocking his car and forcing him off the road.[14]

Unflinching, Sergeant Lohrstorfer approached the car and extracted Enoch from the vehicle. Detective Steinbacher was waiting with a pair of handcuffs. They tossed him onto the trunk of his car and quickly patted him down. Steinbacher gave Chism his Miranda rights.

All of the investigators were convinced that Enoch must have been tipped off as to his apprehension and had changed his pattern accordingly. They were equally convinced that he could have wired his car to explode. Detective Kenney drew the nerve-racking task of inspecting Chism's Ford for any suspicious wiring or bombs. He checked under the car, under the hood, and in every possible space, to ensure that Chism did not leave a last-minute surprise for them all. The other investigators stepped clear, but after a few minutes, they determined that there were no bombs.[15] When I interviewed Trooper Lohrstorfer, he spoke glowingly of Detective Kenney: "It took a lot of guts for him to get into that car knowing we had a bomber in our hands, but that was just the kind of guy. Bob wasn't about to ask anybody to do that task. We didn't have bomb squads in those days—so that took a lot for him to poke around in that car."

Chism's demeanor was sullen and defiant with the officers, which struck them as strange. Most people are suddenly confused or at least feign innocence at the moment of arrest. Not Chism, he seemed almost combative. When asked why he had exited at Twenty-Six Mile Road, he said that he was going to stop off at an orchard to pick up apples—despite the fact that no orchards were open at that hour of the morning.

After Chism was put in the police car, on the way to the jail, he began to ask questions about the charges being leveled against him. The officers told him that the car was not the place to talk about them, but Enoch, ever wanting to wrestle control of a situation, insisted, "I want to talk about it, you have got it all wrong."[16] Enoch said he fully understood his rights, but he continued to talk. His comments were disturbed, to say the least, including "Why don't you kill me" and "Take me out and shoot me."[17] Much to the officers' surprise, Enoch talked the entire way back to the courthouse. He told them that he hardly knew the woman killed, Nola. He claimed that he had only been in her restaurant about six times in his life.[18]

The 1967 arrest photo
of Enoch Chism.
(*From the Michigan
State Police Files—
Nola Puyear Murder
Investigation.*)

A man who abused his wife, he openly feigned concern for her, saying, "[I] hate to put my wife through this again." In his simple words,
he was saying that *he* did not cause his wife any anguish, that it was
the legal system that was inflicting this on Bernice. His own culpability
was tossed out with the truth. Enoch babbled on with the officers as if
to sway them, taunting, "I bet you a million dollars you will pin this on
me as you did on the arson case."[19] Despite the fingerprint evidence that
proved he had set that fire and the fact that he had been found guilty of
the crime, Enoch still refused to accept any responsibility for it. According to him, the conviction for the arson was not his fault; he blamed his
lawyer, saying, "I have no use for lawyers such as Tompard."[20] Chism
was caught in a mental tornado of denial, blame laying, and refusal to
deal with reality—as if he could talk his way to freedom with the of-

ficers who had spent almost three months pursuing him. To Detective Kenney—who had made the visit to the Kalamazoo State Hospital and had gotten back the profile that the man they were looking for was a paranoid, someone who felt everyone was out to get him—Enoch Chism most certainly fit his diagnosis.

The citizens of Marshall, who had been living under the specter of a murderer in their midst, were greeted that October morning with a surprise announcement on the WALM 1260 AM radio news broadcast: "The Prosecutors' Office announced this morning that they have picked up a suspect in the bombing of the Tasty Restaurant which took the life of Mrs. Nola Puyear. The name of the man will be released later today. Keep tuned to WALM 1260 on your dial."[21] They would have to listen until the 11:00 a.m. news to get the name that the community had been waiting to hear, "Enoch Chism."

That night, the *Marshall Evening Chronicle*'s headline read, "Enoch Chism Held in Puyear Bomb Slaying."[22] For the first time in three months, the tiny community could let out a collective sigh of relief. Some of the locals were stunned, saying that Chism was "a quiet kind and courteous . . . a man that wouldn't harm anybody." Those who attended his church knew him to be a quiet man, seemingly composed.

For many in Marshall, the announcement was not a complete surprise. Enoch's abuse of his wife was no secret—it was fertilizer for the town's grapevine. His abuse of her in public gave many Marshallites a glimpse of what Bernice was facing at home. While they had talked about it in hushed whispers, no one had taken any action in defense of Bernice. Chism's arson conviction suddenly had context, it was part of a pattern of behavior that apparently had led to the death of Nola Puyear. Some who had witnessed Enoch's darker side said he had a dual personality—that he had "a tiger in him"—and that he was "mentally imbalanced."[23] Somehow, the announcement of Chism's arrest just made sense.

Paul Puyear was contacted before Chism's name was released. Yes, he knew Enoch Chism, mostly through Chism's father-in-law, Hollie White. No, he knew of no reason why Chism would have wanted to kill Nola. About a year earlier, when he had been remodeling the restaurant, he remembered hearing that Enoch wanted to buy it. He told the investigators he didn't remember who he had heard it from.[24]

No bail was set for Enoch. His crime was deemed too severe to grant him any degree of freedom. This was especially true in light of his arson conviction. For the first time, the community was acknowledging the threat he represented.

For the prosecutor and the investigators, there was still a great deal of work to do. The evidence they had was mostly circumstantial, and there was still a lack of a motive. While a substantial part of their work was done, there was still a long way to go to ensure that Enoch Chism faced justice.

8

The Quest for a Motive

Enoch Chism was evil, a dark, brooding kind of evil. He was the kind of smart evil that is particularly dangerous. He was simply brutal, especially to his family. Yet under all of that viciousness was a mind capable of building a sophisticated bomb. Just having him in jail gave people some relief, but ultimately, getting him tried and convicted was what was necessary for the people of Marshall to sleep peacefully at night. One question remained: why had he done it? It was a question that would plague the investigators for months to come.

Enoch Chism was interviewed initially by Prosecutor Jereck, Inspector Wood, and Detectives Kenney and Steinbacher. He refused to provide another writing sample and was adamant that these charges against him would "kill his family." All throughout the discussion, he denied having anything to do with the murder.

John Jereck had never tried a murder case, let alone any case this complex. But this did not daunt him. Enoch Chism was cunning, so Jereck had to have his best game face on at all times. He presented Enoch a number of handwriting samples—from his boat registration to his job applications at R. E. Dailey and Company. He asked what seemed to be an innocent question to the prisoner—"Was this your handwriting?" Enoch said it was. Chances are he didn't realize that those samples could link him to the handwriting on the packages containing the poison pills and the bomb.

Jereck did not allow himself to be sucked into the debate about Enoch's guilt. Instead, he stayed the course. Would Enoch give them permission to search his home and vehicles? Enoch agreed and signed off on a waiver for the search, which Jereck already had prepared. Enoch insisted that he had nothing to hide from the police, that he was innocent.

The police peppered Enoch with questions about his relationship with the Puyears, which he claimed was almost nonexistent. His mother-in-law worked at the Tasty Cafe, but that was the depth of his relationship. They tried to pin him down on his whereabouts on August 16 and 17 and got a jumble of responses from him. Throughout the morning of October 11, he staunchly denied having anything to do with the bombing murder of Nola Puyear.[1]

* * * *

While most of the officers were concentrated on Enoch, Sergeant Fred Ritchie and Detective Steinbacher went to Michigan Bell to inform Bernice Chism of her husband's arrest and to secure her permission to search their property—in case Enoch refused. Ritchie knew Bernice from visiting her home during Enoch's explosions of domestic violence. No one was sure just how she was going to respond to Enoch's imprisonment. Bernice was stunned initially by the news but quickly regained composure. She drove her Pontiac back to their home on C Drive North while the police followed her.

Bernice, for her part, had been waiting for them, at least emotionally. She told them that after she had seen the newspaper article with the handwriting examples, she knew Enoch had been responsible for Nola's murder. The suspicion was not new. As early as the day of the explosion, she suspected that her husband had been involved. She had even gone so far as to bring the murder up in his presence, but he had displayed no emotion about it one way or another when the topic came up. When she read about the pills filled with lye, Bernice, unsure of what to do and still fearful of her husband, threw out the Drano in the house. The stress of this knowledge ate at her. Both of the Chisms had attended Nola's funeral, but Bernice said that Enoch had displayed no emotion at all. She had lost considerable weight since the bombing, and at the news that Enoch was in jail, she seemed happy and relieved.[2]

She openly agreed to let the police search their property. When the officers contacted Prosecutor Jereck, he informed them that Enoch as well had given them full permission. By early afternoon, the officers converged on the Chism home. During that time, Bernice Chism offered the first true glimpse as to what might be a motive for the crime.

Enoch had lost his job at the Kellogg Company in 1966 due to his drinking problem. After that, he had become very depressed. She had dropped her divorce proceedings with him temporarily during that period in hopes that Enoch would emotionally turn around. There were short periods where he seemed stable, but they were few and far between. Enoch remained possessive of her and suspicious of her every move. His jealousy over his wife was beyond obsessive. Bernice said that when she would go into town to get groceries, he would accuse her of meeting another man. Enoch had no close friends, and she reported that "he had no hobbies and seemed to only follow her around."[3]

Bernice confessed that her life had been "a living hell ever since this thing happened." Fear ate at her—fear of the law and of her husband. On several occasions, she saw a policeman and had felt an urge to "scream" out her story but was simply too afraid.[4] Fear was the cornerstone of life in the Chism household.

Enoch's employment at Clark Equipment was a step down for him, both financially and from a career standpoint. According to Bernice, Enoch felt that his job there was "degrading" because it involved him getting dirty. Sergeant Ritchie had an expanded perspective of Enoch's issues with his wife: "She [Bernice] was part of the problem with Enoch. She was a supervisor at the phone company. Enoch was a factory worker. She dressed to kill every day, and he wore factory worker pants and shirts. He felt that the work he was doing was below his station."[5] It seemed that whatever business ventures Enoch became involved with somehow failed. The solution he had arrived at was to get into the restaurant business. In his mind, it was a business that the entire family could work at together.[6]

When I read this in the police reports, I was amazed. The owner of a small restaurant business needs to be personable, highly social. This was not the character of the surly, sometimes abrasive Enoch Chism. In his twisted mind, he had envisioned that his wife would walk away from her job of twenty-two years with Michigan Bell and work beside him, slinging hash. Then I realized the darker side of his thoughts. Having Bernice working with him was simply another way for him to control her.

Enoch had asked Bernice to talk to her mother, Josie White, to see if Nola Puyear would be willing to sell the Tasty Cafe. Ever impatient, Enoch went to Josie himself and asked her to speak to Nola about selling the business. Bernice was unsure of what response he received, but the death of Nola certainly painted a bloody picture for both her and the investigators.[7]

Bernice arranged for Ritchie and Steinbacher to meet with thirteen-year-old Michael Chism. In talking with him, they were able to glean a few details. Yes, his father had used dynamite. Enoch had set it up with a fuse and had dropped it down a pipe in the yard, demolishing the septic tank in the process.

In terms of his father's activities, Michael claimed to not know anything about the criminal charges leveled against his father. On August 16, his father was unexpectedly at home due to some issues at work. Enoch was working on something at his workbench in the basement, but Michael did not know what it was; he was too busy entertaining two of his friends. On August 17, his father had taken him to the dump to drop off a barrel of trash, then to the sheriff's office to get his driver's license.[8]

The officers felt that Michael was holding something back and noted that additional discussion with him was warranted. Shortly thereafter, the rest of the investigation team arrived—led by John Jereck. The time had come to go through the house of their prisoner in a search for evidence.

Discussions with twenty-year-old Sharon Norton, the elder of the Chism children, proved more useful to Jereck. She told him that when she had seen the handwriting published in the paper, she knew it was her father's. Sharon was married to a soldier and was more or less free from the controlling grip that her father held on the family. She admitted openly that Enoch had beat her mother and the children—often threatening their lives. Like her mother, she seemed relieved that Enoch was behind bars, hopefully for good.[9]

Sharon also revealed that Enoch had confessed to her mother that he had been responsible for the arson fire in 1965. He still professed to the police that he had been set up for that crime and that the real fault for it lay with his attorney. It gave the investigators yet another glimpse into his mind and way of thinking.

* * * *

The search of the Chism home was a step into the surreal. One would

A battery recovered from the nightstand of Enoch Chism's bedroom and identical to the one used in the bombing. *(From the Michigan State Police Files—Nola Puyear Murder Investigation.)*

think that the home would have been cluttered and disheveled, but it was the opposite. Bernice Chism was an incredibly tidy homemaker. The Chism home, while not plush, was pristine and immaculate. One must wonder if this was her way of combating the emotional, physical, and mental chaos that her husband brought down on their clan. The only place where the spotless nature of the home disappeared was in the basement and garage, where Enoch did his tinkering.

The sweep of the house found some items that normally would have been ignored but seemed significant to the case. In the nightstand next to the Chisms' bed was a Fisk battery—the same brand as the one used in the bomb. This was taken by the police in hopes that it could be matched to the battery recovered from the Tasty Cafe.[10]

John Jereck was there when investigators opened the garage. The Chisms had a garage door opener, something of a luxury item in 1967. The device was new technology at the time and drew their attention mostly out of curiosity. Jereck noticed that the wiring on the opener looked strange, tampered with in some way. A clock mechanism was wired into the opener.

The device made no sense whatsoever to the investigators. They worked the garage door several times before they were able to figure out

The rigging Enoch attached to his garage door opener to track the comings and goings of his wife. (*From the Michigan State Police Files—Nola Puyear Murder Investigation.*)

the purpose of the device. The clock mechanism was rigged to stop when the garage door was opened and then closed, logging the time. Enoch Chism, in his quest to track his wife, had rigged the garage door so that he could monitor her comings and goings. For Jereck, this proved that Enoch had enough technical skill to potentially build a bomb, while also confirming Bernice's stories of Enoch's possessive character toward her.[11]

The investigators combed every nook and cranny of the Chism home looking for potential bomb-making material. In the garage, in a coffee can near the shower, they found two marking pencils, red and black. The marking pencils were similar to thin grease pencils and seemed to match the writing on the bomb package.[12]

A number of other pieces of possible evidence were gathered for the state police crime lab to evaluate. Pieces of aluminum were found, along with various pieces of electrical wire. An alligator clip found on the floor of Chism's car was confiscated. Rolls of electrical and masking tape were confiscated as well. Masking tape had been used to wrap the bomb pack-

A roll of masking tape recovered at the Chism home and tied, through testing, to the bomb package. *(From the Michigan State Police Files—Nola Puyear Murder Investigation.)*

age and was of immediate interest. A pill bottle was found in the bathroom medicine cabinet with six transparent capsules filled with a white substance, all of which were quickly secured. Brown wrapping paper similar to that used to make paper bags was found and taken in for testing. Hair samples were taken from each of the Chism family members.[13]

Detectives Steinbacher and Kenney found a red plastic container on the floor in front of Enoch's workbench in the basement of the home. The container seemed to be sealed and had some sort of a stick poking out of it. From what they could see of the interior of the container, it seemed to hold electrical wiring components. For a few tense moments, the investigators thought that they had found a bomb of some sort. The detectives treated it delicately, working the lid off only after the house had been cleared of other personnel. They discovered it was simply a container—nothing more.[14] As they logged it into evidence, they experienced just a fraction of the terror the rest of the Chism family endured living with Enoch.

Looking in one box of tools, the investigators found the Chism family Bible. It was casually tossed in, as if it and its ideals had been discarded.[15]

Enoch's basement workshop, where he allegedly assembled the bomb. (*From the Michigan State Police Files—Nola Puyear Murder Investigation.*)

* * * *

Was Enoch's desire to purchase the Tasty Cafe really a motive for him to kill Nola Puyear? In all of their discussions with his family, it seemed to be the only thing that the investigators could agree on. It seemed to be a thin motive at best. Why would he so brutally murder someone just to purchase their business? While none of the investigators felt it was motive enough for murder, it was all that they had at that time.

The afternoon session of interviewing with Enoch zeroed in on his interest in buying and running a restaurant. For his part, Enoch admitted that he wanted to open an eatery. He claimed that he had lost twelve hundred dollars in his failed Clark gas station, which had left him too cash-strapped to pursue a restaurant purchase. He had visited a local chain, Dairy Isle, in Ann Arbor and had expressed an interest in their operation. If nothing else, Enoch seemed rather nonchalant about this line of questioning. It was no secret that he wanted to purchase a restaurant.

When Enoch was asked about his activities the day of the bombing, his story matched that given by his son. He remained steadfast throughout the interview—he denied sending the bomb or having anything to do with it.[16]

Back at his home, Enoch's carefully compartmentalized world was coming apart as his family became freed from his grip. The investigators turned their attention to the day before the bombing and the day of the attack, attempting to reconstruct Enoch's activities. Bernice said that on August 16, Enoch was working the day shift and ran across some bad stock on his machine. Because of this, he was taken off his equipment and put on the 11–7 shift. Enoch hated to work nights, because, in his mind, it provided his wife with the opportunity to slip out with other men.

Bernice called home in the afternoon of August 16 to talk to her son, and Enoch answered the phone from the basement extension. This surprised her, and she asked what he was doing home. He told her of the issue at work. At the time, she believed he was repairing something in the basement at his workbench there.[17]

The officers asked Bernice if she could provide them with samples of Enoch's handwriting. She produced a brown notebook and a number of cancelled checks. These would be useful in validating Enoch's handwriting.

Bernice's sister, Betty Rowe, came to the house, and the investigators spoke to her as well. She could offer no substantial information but did relate a family meeting that took place several weeks earlier at her mother's house. When the topic of Nola's murder had come up, they had discussed their suspicions that Enoch was responsible for the crime. The family had decided that until they had proof, it was best not to mention it again, because of the harm it would cause if they were wrong.[18] The fear that Enoch generated had served him well in keeping their suspicions suppressed.

Bernice's mother, Josie White, arrived at the house during the search for evidence. The police had interviewed both her and her husband earlier in the investigation, but now their focus was not her work at the Tasty or the goings-on in Paul Puyear's trailer—this time, their focus was her son-in-law. Josie was more than willing to provide them information now that Enoch was in jail.

Enoch's reign of terror encompassed not just his home but that of his wife's parents. From what Josie relayed to the officers, Enoch had threatened to kill both her and Hollie on more than one occasion. She described, in painstaking detail, his pattern of abuse toward her daughter and grandchildren. Enoch would strike at his wife and children, who would flee to Josie and Hollie's home for protection. Josie and Hollie were in their seventies, though, and posed no real threat to Chism or protection to the family. After a short period of time, Enoch would either come over or call, sometimes crying, and pull his wife and children back into his grip. Josie and her husband had lived next to the Chisms, but after years of this cycle of abuse, they had finally moved away.[19]

The questioning turned to Enoch's possible interactions with Nola Puyear. Josie said that Enoch felt his marriage would be better if he and Bernice were working together. A family-owned restaurant would accomplish that perfectly. He reasoned that if he were working in a restaurant, he would "not bring dirt into Bernice's house."[20] In his mind, the root of their marital problems was dirt—not his own inability to control himself. Bit by bit, the motive began to form for the investigators. Enoch became obsessed with purchasing a restaurant and talked about it often. Over time, he brought up the idea of purchasing the Tasty Cafe with Josie.

Over the years, Josie had spoken often about the restaurant, and she was convinced that Enoch knew that Paul was interested in selling the Tasty but that Nola was not. Whenever Chism talked about purchasing a restaurant, the topic shifted quickly to purchasing the Tasty Cafe. Enoch called Josie once and asked her to speak with Nola to see if she would be willing to sell the Tasty to him. Josie told him that Nola would not sell at that time, but Enoch insisted that Josie speak with her. This happened roughly three months before Nola's murder. Josie worked with Nola several days a week and knew that it was a pointless discussion. She never did raise the topic with Nola.[21] Eventually, Enoch prodded Josie to hear the response. Josie told him that Nola had said she would not sell the Tasty. It was a simple white lie that set off a chain reaction of events that none of them could have foreseen.

Enoch was not a man who tolerated women refusing him. He didn't put up with it from his wife or daughter, and there's no reason to believe he would think of Nola any differently. In reality, Nola knew nothing about his offer, but in Enoch's mind, she had said no to him. After a while (Josie did not know how long), Enoch called Nola at the restaurant. The call came in on a day when Josie was working. After the call, Nola had told Josie that it had been Enoch calling to purchase the restaurant and that she had told him that it wasn't for sale. Nola had further added, "I wouldn't sell it to him anyway."[22] That was the only time Josie White knew of that Enoch had tried to contact Nola. Both Enoch and Michael had come into the Tasty after the call to eat lunch, but nothing was said about the offer.

Chism had not let go of his thinking that purchasing a restaurant would solve the problems plaguing his home life. He had taken Bernice and Josie with him to Parma outside of Jackson, to look at a restaurant that he thought was for sale. As at the Tasty Cafe, Enoch found an owner who was unwilling to sell. The man said that he wanted to remain on, running the restaurant himself. Despite this, Enoch was excited at the possibility. He even asked Josie if she would be willing to drive to Parma to work at the establishment if he bought it.[23]

The skilled and experienced investigators turned their questions back to Nola. Was she aware of the problems between Bernice and Enoch? After all, Josie worked closely with Nola. Had the topic ever come up? According to Josie, Nola was intimately aware of the marital problems between Josie's son-in-law and daughter. It was a common subject in their casual conversations. There were few secrets to be kept in the tiny Tasty Cafe. Nola had expressed to her that Enoch was "sick and needed help."[24] With this intimate knowledge of Enoch's issues, Nola would have been predisposed to refuse him a chance to purchase the Tasty.

Josie was fairly certain that Enoch was aware of both her and Nola's work schedules, from experience and casual conversation over the years. She did not think Enoch was aware of the Marshall Post Office's practice of delivering the Puyears' home mail to the Tasty Cafe.

A short interview with Hollie White, Josie's husband, seemed to confirm her stories. In the twelve years they had lived next to the Chisms, Enoch had threatened to kill them on several occasions. Hollie reported, "Enoch has a violent temper and the slightest thing will set him off."[25]

For the investigators, this gleam of a motive struck them as odd. Chism had not even tried to purchase the Tasty Cafe after Nola's death.

In fact, Paul Puyear had sold the restaurant to another local man only a few days before Chism's arrest. Was this resistance on the part of Nola enough to cause Enoch to try to kill her—twice?

The investigators reached out to Nola's circle of friends who they had already interviewed. Now that a suspect had been named, did this trigger any memories? Did anyone remember Nola and Enoch ever talking or arguing? The phone calls to potential witnesses began, but almost all of their responses were in the negative. The investigators needed to find more of a link between Nola and Enoch in order to help their case.

One person from Nola's inner circle, Sene Buckner, did have a memory of Enoch Chism and Nola together. Sergeant Ritchie and Detective Steinbacher traveled out to Sene's home with the booking photo of Chism. Sene remembered Enoch having some sort of argument with Nola. This confrontation had never come up in Sene's previous discussions with the authorities. It wasn't until Enoch had been arrested that she even recalled the event.

Approximately two months before Nola's murder, Sene had been in the restaurant with Nola when Enoch had come to the restaurant. Coming in at the back door of the Tasty, he called Nola into the kitchen, and they spoke for five or more minutes. At the end of their terse conversation, both "turned on their heels" and started walking away from each other. Enoch turned and said something to Nola, and she made some reply that Sene couldn't hear.

As Chism left out the back of the restaurant, Nola poured herself a cup of coffee and sat down at the end of the counter, where Sene joined her. In all of the years that Nola had worked at the Tasty Cafe and that Sene had been her friend, this was the only time she had called Sene over to join her at the counter to share a cup of coffee. That was why it stuck in Sene's mind.[26]

Nola had started talking about Josie and her entire family, saying, as Sene recalled, that "if something don't straighten out it would drive her [Josie] crazy. And if not Josie, that it would drive her [Nola] nuts." Sene remembered that Nola mentioned the need to talk to Josie because of this. Nola never said what "this" was, but Sene assumed that it was the confrontation with Enoch.[27]

The investigators felt that they had confirmation of Josie White's story. Moreover, they had a witness who contradicted Enoch's claim that he never spoke with Nola. Chism could now be placed at the Tasty Cafe as more than a customer, confronting Nola Puyear in some way.

* * * *

With the announcement of an arrest, rumors began to boil up for the investigation team, especially since the community had a name to associate with the crime. One allegation that came in to John Jereck was that Sharon Norton might actually have been fathered by Paul Puyear. Maybe that was what had driven Enoch to murder.

It was a fanciful guess. The investigators pulled up Sharon's birth certificate and validated that, indeed, her father was listed as Enoch Chism—not Paul Puyear. Even if it had been true, why would that have driven Enoch to kill Nola? Perhaps he might kill Paul, but not Nola. No matter how ludicrous the products of the Marshall rumor mill were, each had to be explored.[28]

On the afternoon of October 13, the police once more sat down with Enoch for an interview. Detective Kenney made sure he was aware of his rights, and Chism claimed that he was. Kenney asked him if he wanted an attorney, but Enoch said he didn't know. He had called his wife, and Bernice had told him that she would not get him one. Kenney asked if he wanted a court-appointed attorney, and he said he didn't know. Chism was oddly chatty. Regardless of having no lawyer, he wanted to talk.[29] The officers offered him an opportunity to take a polygraph, to help him clear up his claim of innocence. Enoch said he did not want the test at that time but perhaps would want one later.

When the subject turned to his interest in buying the Tasty Cafe, Enoch said that he never talked to Paul or Nola about purchasing the restaurant. He claimed that he only stopped in at the restaurant to have a cup of coffee or to buy lunch.[30] The police did not tip their hand regarding Sene Buckner's memory of a confrontation. Enoch was providing them plenty of information, which indicated to them that he was withholding certain information or outright lying.

Chism was shown the brown notebook and cancelled checks from his home, which he agreed were his. The notebook had been his book of record when he had worked at the Clark gas station. He claimed that he lost twelve hundred dollars in the venture, leveling the blame at both the company and his wife. He confirmed for the officers that all but two pages in the book had been written by him, apparently not realizing that he was handing them additional handwriting samples.

When pressed about his wife, Enoch turned bitter and angry, particularly at how things had turned out during his self-committed time at the Battle Creek Sanitarium. Why had he escaped "the San"? Enoch's answer was that his daughter had come to visit him with black and blue marks all over her where her mother had beaten her with a shoe. He broke out to confront his wife about the beating. It wasn't his fault that he had escaped the facility; it was Bernice's. Enoch was simply being a good father.

Enoch went so far as to claim that Bernice had often framed him for his alleged beating incidents. She would call the police and then fabricate some lie about him threatening the entire family or abusing them. One time, he said, she had gone so far as to have him arrested. Enoch had been stunned by this. In Enoch's twisted version of events, Bernice always started the incidents and then would call in the police to get him into trouble. "It's all her fault," he said.[31]

When Detective Kenney pressed his questions regarding the bombing, Enoch claimed that he didn't know the first thing about bombs, only what he had seen on TV. Kenney reported Enoch's claim that "someone has it in for him and wanted to get rid of him."[32] When Kenney asked if it was Josie, Enoch replied no. Was it Bernice who was conspiring against him? Enoch said that she had an awful bad temper but would not do something as terrible as this, that she "just wasn't that kind of person."[33]

As an author, I can't tell you what Detective Kenney was thinking at the time. I have to believe that he now fully understood the paranoid personality that had been described in the ad hoc profile from the Kalamazoo State Hospital. Nothing was Enoch's fault, even when he beat Bernice. Someone was attempting to get rid of him. He accepted no responsibility for his actions. The investigators were dealing with a criminal who did not believe he had done anything wrong.

On October 16, Detective Kenney and Inspector Wood met with Enoch again and, for the first time, got a glimpse of the other side of his personality. Chism was read his rights but refused to sign the waiver this time. Yet he wanted to talk to the officers. After all, this was all just a big misunderstanding.

Inspector Wood opened up the discussion by talking about the Chism family. The mention of Michael Chism made Enoch's personality suddenly change. Rather than being willing to talk, he became sullen and stoic. In Wood's words, "He showed no outward sign that he was remorseful for the anxiety caused his family by his arrest."[34]

Wood sensed that he had hit on something at the mention of Michael and pressed that hard in the interview, asking, "Doesn't it bother you any, Enoch, that your boy is so upset?" Chism jumped, his face flushed with rage. For a moment, he appeared ready to spring and attack Inspector Wood. Detective Kenney intervened and restrained Enoch, who insisted, "Take me back to my cell. I don't want to talk to you anymore!"[35]

On the way back to his cell, at the end of the corridor, Enoch told Kenney that he would like to return and talk to him but did not wish to talk to Inspector Wood again.[36] This incident gave the investigators a taste of what Bernice and the rest of Enoch's family had been facing over the years of abuse. Moreover, they had been given a glimpse of how Enoch Chism manipulated events and people.

* * * *

Motive is not required in Michigan murder trials. While technically not a requirement, John Jereck and the investigators knew that it was something that made a case much stronger. It is hard for jurors to send someone to jail for a crime if there is no motive. Motive provides the context for a crime. It is what makes a crime make sense to a juror.

The motive that the team working the Puyear murder had was thin, and the investigators knew it. Enoch Chism had wanted to purchase the Tasty Cafe. While Paul Puyear would be amiable to selling, Nola would not. She loved her work at the restaurant and did not even consider retirement. Chism pressed her, first through Josie White, then likely on his own.

Nola did something that Enoch could not stand. She said no to him. He could not tolerate that. So Enoch decided to remove Nola from the picture. Then he could purchase the restaurant and bring stability to his marriage. Jereck hoped that this strange chain of thinking was something that a small-town Michigan jury could accept.

While the prosecution felt they had a motive, however sketchy, there was another man in Marshall who had other ideas as to why Enoch may have blown up the Tasty Cafe. That person was Ronald DeGraw. In his mind, this was never about Nola. Enoch was a warped individual, a man not to be underestimated. DeGraw saw a more sinister motive for Enoch: driving Josie White into unemployment or killing her outright.

What the prosecution didn't know was that Josie supported Bernice financially in her last bid to divorce Enoch. DeGraw felt that Enoch sent the bomb to the Tasty Cafe to blow it up and thus deprive Josie of employment and the means to help Bernice if she pressed for divorce again. If the explosion happened to kill Josie, well, so much the better from Enoch's perspective. Addressing the bomb package to Nola shifted suspicion away from Josie, a woman Enoch had already threatened to kill. If Enoch had addressed the package to Josie, the police would have arrested him almost immediately. DeGraw thought the poison pills could have been sent to kill Nola, because her demise would have allowed or forced Paul to either sell or close the Tasty, leaving Josie unemployed. DeGraw felt that Enoch was smart enough to know that the Puyears received their home mail at the restaurant.[37]

DeGraw had no way of knowing what motive the prosecution was going to take to court. John Jereck, at the same time, had no idea what DeGraw was thinking of in terms of motive. Both theories pointed to a man who was devious and cunning, a man who was dangerous to the community, his family, and anyone who even remotely crossed his path.

9

The Long Road to Trial

This case took a long time to go to trial—too long, as it turns out. In researching this, I was surprised and dumbfounded at the reasons. The legal maneuverings only seemed to keep the crime at the forefront in the thoughts of Marshall's citizens.

As the chill of autumn crept across Calhoun County, Enoch petitioned the circuit court to appoint a lawyer for his defense. On October 19, he appeared before Judge Creighton R. Coleman to review his request. Today, such a petition would be resolved quickly. In 1967, it was not so easy.

To understand the context, you must first comprehend that it was only a year earlier that the case of *Miranda v. Arizona* had been resolved, requiring police officers to inform someone of their rights. Four years earlier, the Supreme Court had ruled in *Gideon v. Wainwright* that if someone could not afford a lawyer, the courts would have to provide one. Some states had programs in place as early as the 1920s, and even Michigan had some provisions for providing a public defender, but the reality was that *Gideon v. Wainwright* forced each state to change their perspective.

Michigan law in 1967 in regard to the court appointment of attorneys was somewhat vague and confusing. In Michigan, court-appointed attorneys were generally only provided when defendants had insufficient funds to hire attorneys themselves. With only four years of experience as to *how* these laws were to be applied, each new variation of such a request came with challenges. There were not a lot of precedents for specific situations.

In the case of Enoch Chism, the appointment situation was muddied even more. Enoch was not poor. With two cars, a home, and money in the bank, he could afford an attorney. His initial petition had been sent to Judge Alfred Stuart of the municipal court, who had ruled that Enoch could only have a court-appointed counsel if he could not afford to pay for counsel. Stuart bumped the decision up to Coleman at the circuit court level.[1]

For his part, John Jereck tended to agree with Chism's request. The last thing the prosecutor wanted was for Chism to defend himself or claim that he had insufficient defense. Both of these circumstances might be a basis for appeal of conviction in the future. From what Jereck had seen of Enoch, he did not want him to ever have a chance to be in the community again. He wanted Enoch to have a strong and robust defense so that he would have no leg to stand on in terms of appeal. At the judge's urging, Jereck was asked to meet with the Chism family to see if they would pay for Enoch's counsel. It was an effort bound to fail. Bernice was more than content to keep her dangerous husband right where he was. Coleman held off on making a decision for the time being.[2]

The next day was an annual community event in town, the Marshall High School homecoming game. This year, it was against Coldwater. The annual parade of class floats, replete with the Redskin band, marched down Michigan Avenue. The floats—farm trailers covered with chicken wire and paper flowers—left torn shreds of crepe paper every so often as they lumbered down the street. As Enoch Chism sat in his cell in the jail, the sounds of the band and the crowd would have echoed up to him, acting as a calendar—a reminder of the passage of time.

It appears that Enoch, ever the schemer, concocted a devious way to attempt to beat the system. On October 25, he contacted Bernice and asked her to come visit him in jail along with a lawyer from Ron De-Graw's office. From his jail cell, Enoch signed over all of his property and possessions to his wife as part of their divorce. Using a quitclaim deed, he signed over all he had, in essence becoming indigent and entitled to a court-appointed attorney.[3] His action is reminiscent of the parable of the child who wanted to attend the orphan's picnic so he killed both of his parents.

During my research for this book, Fred Ritchie confided that there was another ploy at work in this incident, a ploy concocted by Bernice. She told investigators that she could get Enoch to confess if she had time with him, and she used this opportunity for him to sign over his property as the vehicle for such a meeting. It was rare for police to allow prisoners to be in the same room with other people, but they opted to do it in this case, in hopes of securing a confession. Bernice, for her part, got Enoch to sign the paperwork and then left the room, leaving the investigators hanging. She had gotten what she wanted—financial freedom from her abusive husband.

Judge Coleman was understandably furious over the ploy. His anger was directed at Attorney DeGraw for executing the action and at Chism for going along with it. He called in Bernice to testify that Enoch had signed over everything to her. He brought in Clayton Anderson of the Marshall Savings and Loan, who assessed the value of the Chism mortgage, property, and bank accounts. The value of the assets was about twenty thousand dollars. Bernice made it clear that she would not spend a cent to do anything to help Enoch.[4]

Coleman was not entirely convinced that the state of Michigan should be paying for Chism's defense. His logic was convincing. Enoch had made himself indigent. That was not the intent of Michigan law in terms of court-appointed attorneys. Judge Coleman deferred his decision again.[5]

A question gnawed at me during the writing of this book. Was Enoch Chism deeply cunning in this ploy, was he simply grasping at straws, or was he being manipulated by Bernice and her attorney? After all, how cunning is a man who attempts to unplug his septic tank with dynamite? Yet this man designed and apparently built a sophisticated mail bomb on his own. There were a lot of layers to Enoch, but as with peeling an onion, there was a stink that came with each new layer.

* * * *

Coleman did appoint two court attorneys to represent Enoch in his preliminary examination on November 16, but they were not to assist him in working on his trial defense. Under Michigan law, the preliminary examination is roughly the equivalent of a grand jury for felony crimes. The prosecution is required to prove that a crime has been committed and that sufficient evidence exists to go to trial. Unlike a grand jury, the preliminary examination is not done before a panel drawn from the community but is presented to a judge. While all of the evidence and witnesses are not produced, the examination does give both sides a taste of what will be brought to trial.

W. Reed Orr and Paul Nicolich drew the short straws to represent Chism and did so vigorously. Judge Stuart was supposed to preside over the preliminary examination, but Orr petitioned that he be disqualified since he had prior experience with Enoch during his arson conviction. As a result, Judge Merele Augustine presided over Chism's preliminary examination.[6]

Reed Orr was already an icon in the legal circles of Calhoun County. Born in 1910 in Pittsburgh, Pennsylvania, Orr had served with distinction in the U.S. Navy in World War II. From 1951 to 1954, he had been elected to the Michigan House of Representatives. A devout Episcopalian, Orr was a Freemason and a member of the VFW, the American Legion, and the Kiwanis. He was a tall, lanky man with a tight-drawn face and a professional presence that commanded respect and attention. His addition to the defense of Chism added weight and credibility. If Orr was heading up the defense team, there would be little doubt that Enoch would get the best defense possible.

There was a limit to what Orr and Nicolich could do. They were only retained to represent Chism at the preliminary examination. Until the issue could be resolved as to who would pay for his defense in the trial, they were to limit their actions to this courtroom event only.

John Jereck brought in a number of witnesses to prove that there were direct links between Enoch and the murder of Nola Puyear. Of the fourteen witnesses who were in court that day, none dealt with the paper-thin motive that Jereck had arrived at. That would have to wait until the trial. The rest of the examination was deferred to November 24.[7]

At the end of the day's court session, Bernice Chism asked the investigators to meet with her. They went to the Chism house. Bernice remembered an incident during the summer that now seemed of potential importance. Enoch had come home from work one day with his hands severely cut, his eyes somewhat blackened, and his stomach cut. When she had asked him what happened, he had said that a machine had exploded at work. Enoch had refused treatment with a doctor and had used salve and some bandages to tend to himself. Bernice could not remember what day this was, and it seemed insignificant at the time.[8]

To the investigators, it wasn't. They checked with Clark Equipment, where Enoch worked, and there was no record of an explosion or of him being injured. In fact, if he had been, he would have been sent to the hospital rather than allowed to go home. To the investigators, this appeared to be a possible dry run with a bomb gone wrong. Enoch hadn't been hurt at work. Perhaps he had been working on a bomb.[9] It was entirely possible that his injuries had been caused from a detonation cap (used to set off dynamite) going off prematurely.

On November 24, Chism's examination came to a conclusion. The most stirring testimony was that of Paul Puyear, who looked at a reconstructed package of the bomb and said that it most certainly looked like the package that had killed his wife. Jereck had saved Paul Puyear to the end, eliciting an emotional confirmation that a crime had indeed been committed. After a short recess, Prosecutor Jereck moved that Enoch be bound over to the circuit court to stand trial.

Attorney Orr answered the motion by saying that the defense conceded that someone had enmity toward the Puyears but that he was not convinced that the evidence pointed to Enoch Chism. The basis of his doubt was that even Paul Puyear had admitted on the stand that he knew no reason for Enoch to want to kill Nola. Orr drove home the point that after knowing the Puyears casually for twenty years, Enoch had never made any threat that would indicate such a rash course of action as premeditated murder. As for the handwriting, Orr pointed out that the reconstructed bomb address lacked any signs of burning or charring. With this and the lack of any motive, there was no reason Chism should be held over for trial.

Judge Augustine felt differently. He approved Jereck's motion.[10] Enoch was going to go to trial. But going to trial and going to trial *quickly* were two different things.

* * * *

Enoch was far from happy at the preliminary ruling. At one point when dealing with Sergeant Ritchie, Chism threatened to kill him, the judge, Detectives Kenney and Steinbacher, and John Jereck. Ritchie was used to boastful threats by prisoners, but not those being held for murder. Ritchie looked at Chism squarely and said, "Face to face, Enoch, I'm not afraid of you." Ritchie understood his prisoner all too well. Enoch would never come at him from the front—that wasn't his style. Enoch would come from behind—that was when Chism was most dangerous. Ritchie made a mental note to never turn his back on Enoch.[11]

Chism, for his part, settled into his life as a prisoner in the Calhoun County Jail. He was a talker and soon frustrated the inmates in cells adjoining his. They asked to be moved. In a row of three cells, Enoch sat in the middle cell, alone. It was a ten-by-six-foot existence. Time passed slowly as he awaited a decision that would allow his case to move to trial.

Enoch had a knack for taking anything he could get his hands on and pocketing it for tinkering in his cell. Prisoners were provided instant coffee and warm water in disposable cups; they stirred in the coffee and drank it up. That wasn't enough for Chism. He managed to get a piece of wire in his cell. Carefully twisting it and inserting it in the side of the cup, Enoch then gently slid it into the power outlet in the cell. Doing this just right did not trip the circuit breaker but heated up the wire, allowing Chism to heat his coffee to a level he wanted.[12] While ingenious and proof of his mechanical/electrical skills, this activity violated the jail rules. At the same time, it demonstrated just how devious Enoch could be.

* * * *

Two things dominated the next year of the Chism case. First was the use of technology to tie the evidence recovered at Enoch's home to the crime scene. Second was the ongoing debate with the court as to whether Chism's defense should be funded by the state. Both of these activities were going to have a bearing on the case.

The pretrial decision as to whether Enoch should have a court-appointed defense attorney took up considerable time. This set of motions went on for fifteen months from the time of his arrest. The heart of the issue was that Enoch had made himself impoverished and, as such, was forcing the state to bear the expense of his murder defense.

There were numerous things that caused this incredible delay. First, Enoch pled the Fifth Amendment as to whether he had made himself indigent. Bernice was subpoenaed several times to come in and produce the documentation that showed that Enoch had money but had signed it over to her. For her part, she didn't want to spend any money to protect the man who had abused her.

Judge Coleman still felt that the state of Michigan should not have to pay for Chism's defense. To hedge his bets, though, he did authorize the state to fund Chism's defense until a superior court could rule on the issue. John Jereck wanted Chism to have a good defense and found himself in an awkward position, emotionally siding with the defense. The matter was bumped up on appeal to the Michigan Court of Appeals, then to the Michigan Supreme Court. The entire process, which started two months after the arrest, led to fifteen months of legal hand-wringing. The final decision was that regardless of how Enoch Chism had become indigent, he was to be afforded the right to state-paid defense.[13]

During that period, the prosecution had not been idle in their efforts to bolster their case. The state police crime lab contacted Prosecutor Jereck and suggested that a new technology be brought to bear on the evidence—neutron activation analysis. Using this technique, material samples could be tested to determine their similarity (at the atomic level) with other samples.

In the Nola Puyear case, this technique could be used to test to see if the marking pencils recovered from Enoch's garage were the ones used on the bomb package. Likewise, the Fisk battery recovered from the home could be tested to see if it was from the same batch of batteries as the one blown up during the crime. Another piece of evidence that could be checked was the masking tape recovered from Enoch's home, to see if it matched the tape found on the bomb.

Neutron activation analysis was expensive, and there were a limited number of laboratories that could perform it. Prosecutor Jereck saw the advantages of this technique quickly. It would solidify his case against Chism for a jury if he could tie evidence recovered from Enoch's home to that recovered at the crime scene.

Reed Orr's primary concern, as raised in court, was that the chain of evidence needed to be maintained. In other words, someone needed to make sure that material unrelated to the crime was not introduced into the process and that the material used in the test was indeed the material sent for testing. John Jereck agreed. He personally traveled to Washington, DC, to ensure that the chain of evidence was maintained during the testing process.[14]

Reed Orr, for his part, wanted the defense team to hire their own expert who would be able to evaluate the test results as well. To do this, he

The marking pencil used to address the bomb package, according to the prosecution's expert witness. (*From the Michigan State Police Files—Nola Puyear Murder Investigation.*)

had to request that the court pay the costs for such an expert, which bled into a long series of pretrial motions that was in play. Orr was exceeding his mandate from the judge to only assist Chism during his appeal to get a court-appointed defender.

For fifteen long months, the wheels of justice slowly churned—just attempting to determine if Enoch deserved a court-appointed attorney. For over a year, Chism sat in jail, standing mute, not giving any interviews. The realization had to set in that his family was not working hard to get him out of jail. Sitting in that cell, biding his time, Chism became more bitter with each passing month.

* * * *

Enoch's defense team was appointed in the summer of 1969. While Jereck hoped to rush into trial as quickly as possible, both Reed Orr and Bert Schulz, who were Enoch's defenders, now turned their attention from appeals to his defense. It took more months, as typical before any trial, to wade through the assorted appeals. These were the types of motions made before any murder trial, attempts to get evidence suppressed or excluded and so on.

The summer of 1969 changed the world around Marshall, Michigan. Woodstock took place, surprising a nation. In the late summer, a hippie named Charles Manson ignited a wave of terror that gripped Los Angeles. Across the state, in Ann Arbor, a serial killer named John Norman Collins, the "Co-Ed Killer," had finally been arrested. A small country named Vietnam was getting more press as local boys from Calhoun County were sent off to its jungles. The Nola Puyear murder no longer seemed as sensational. In some respects, it had become old news.

On July 14, 1969, just a few days before Neil Armstrong walked on the moon, Bernice Chism filed for divorce from Enoch. Her filing was simple. She claimed that there was no community property to divide, since Enoch had signed all of his possessions over to her back in 1967. Reed Orr replied, "He [Enoch] in October of 1967 put in the plaintiff's sole name, his interest in real estate and personal property accumulated by the parties during their married life, this transfer was not in a nature of settlement of the property rights of the parties in and said property." He added, "The transfer was made on the assurance by the plaintiff that she would use the defendant's share of said property for his benefit and she refused and neglected to do so."[15]

Suddenly, Enoch's attempt to shelter his property had been turned against him now that Bernice was going to bring an end to their marriage. Judge Ronald Ryan did not see matters the way that Enoch did. There was a downside to his signing over his property rights to his wife, and only while in jail did he realize it.

Time passed slowly for Enoch in the jail. The seasons were measured by the sounds from outside, such as the screams that reached Marshall from the ride goers at the Calhoun County Fair. Echoes of sounds from the homecoming parade and then the Christmas parade bounced off of the jail walls to remind him that the world continued on without him. Worse, being imprisoned, he could not coerce Bernice to stop her divorce filing. Inside of his cell, the only true way he could measure the passage of each month was when a barber came in and cut his hair. All Enoch had for entertainment was some well-worn paperback books and time on his hands.

The monotony was shattered on November 16, 1969, when three inmates in the adjoining cell block overpowered one of the guards and escaped. Enoch never saw them—his cell faced nothing but a wall in the corridor. But he could hear their cries and those of the guard.[16]

The news of the jailbreak stunned the community, and more than a few people feared that the most well-known prisoner in the jail, Chism, might be on the list of those who had escaped. But there had been no attempt to spring Enoch. While the prisoners were caught over the next three days, Chism bided his time in his small cell.

10

"Did Enoch Chism, In Fact, Do It?"

The trial of Enoch Chism was a sensation in Calhoun County for a couple reasons. First, with all of the delays thanks to Chism's legal and financial machinations, the crime still stung the community like a throbbing headache that simply would not go away. Second, murder trials in the county were rare at the time, and a bombing murder was unique in local history.

Chism had aged considerably during his almost two and a half years of incarceration. His hair had grayed, and he had lost weight in jail. While he wore a nice black suit for the proceeding, he had taken to wearing eyeglasses. He was forty-six years old by the time the trial started. At first glance, he did not appear as a cold-blooded killer. He could have passed for any businessman if seen out of the context of the courtroom.

In the passage of time, there had been only one other murder in Calhoun County—that of M. C. Knight. On October 3, 1969, Wesley Brown had entered Knight's pool hall in Battle Creek and joined in some backroom gambling. In a dispute over winnings in a dice game, Brown had shot Knight, who languished for nineteen days before he died. Brown had been arrested and tried and was convicted of second-degree murder the week before the Chism trial began, despite being arrested almost two years after Chism had been. While Brown's prosecution for murder had been swift, Chism's had dragged on for years because of the issue of a court-appointed attorney.

The man charged with putting Enoch Chism behind bars was Prosecutor John Jereck. Born in 1936, he was a graduate of the University of Detroit and the Detroit College of Law. Jereck was admitted to the bar in 1964, a mere three years before Nola Puyear's murder. The 1964 elections were good for the Democratic Party in Michigan, and when the job of prosecutor came up, Jereck's name was floated simply because he had been in the paper recently for passing the bar. Jereck said to me, "I told

Enoch Chism as he
appeared in court.
(*From the Chism
Defense Files.*)

them I wasn't a Democrat, but they insisted on me running for them.
I figured that their campaigning would be good advertising for me."[1]
At the time, the job of prosecutor in Calhoun County was a part-time
job. John Jereck was looking forward to practicing family law more than
thinking of being a prosecutor.

Jereck didn't campaign much, assuming that he would not get the job
since he wasn't a Democrat. Much to his surprise, when the elections
were finished, he woke up as the youngest prosecutor in the history of
Calhoun County. The Puyear killing was to be his first first-degree murder trial, and Chism proved to be an adversary looking to give the young
prosecutor a run for his money.[2]

The weekend before the trial, Jereck was visited at his home by Detectives Kenney and Steinbacher and Deputy Fred Ritchie. Jereck's courtroom style was laid-back, but when his blood was up, he could be very aggressive. The purpose of the meeting was to instill that sense of urgency in the young prosecutor. As Ritchie later recalled, "We went to the house before the trial and talked to him like a Dutch uncle. In other trials, he could come across very nonchalant, and we went to tell him what he was up against. We said, 'John, you have to do your best on this. You only have one shot at this with this guy.' This guy was dangerous.'" The officers who had apprehended Enoch and had been threatened by him knew they were dealing with someone who would kill again if given the chance. They also pressed Jereck to put Michael Chism on the stand. They all felt that Michael knew more than he had let on. Jereck took their encouragement to go after Chism to heart but refused to put Michael on the stand. He had other plans.[3]

Defending Enoch was the stately and seasoned W. Reed Orr. He had led Chism's defense during his preliminary examination. Orr was known as a lawyer's lawyer, a cool, levelheaded man who did thorough research in mounting a defense.

Chism's "second-chair" defense was a young attorney from Saginaw, Michigan, Bert Schulz. Like Jereck, the tall, gregarious Schulz was facing his first murder trial in the Chism case. He had initially heard of the crime while cramming for his bar exam after his graduation from the Wayne State University School of Law. He shared a hotel room with another young lawyer-to-be, Roger Mathews. In August of 1967, Mathews came in and said, "You won't believe this. There was a bombing in my hometown." Schulz had taken a job with the Sullivan, Hamilton, and Ryan law firm in Battle Creek. Schulz had defended a handful of felony cases, mostly breaking and entering and armed robberies, but nothing on the scale of the Chism trial in terms of publicity and scope. Now, Bert Schulz found himself defending the very bomber he had heard about over two years before.[4]

* * * *

The January of 1970 was one of the coldest in a half decade. Temperatures rarely poked into the double digits, and the word *windchill* marked the weather forecasts. The high temperature on the day that jury selection for Enoch Chism's trial started—Tuesday, January 20, 1970—was ten degrees, with a windchill of five degrees below zero.

Jury selection began 886 days after Nola Puyear opened the bomb wrapped in brown paper in the Tasty Cafe and was blown apart by the explosion. Judge Creighton R. Coleman presided over the affair, the most widely publicized trial that the county had ever witnessed up to that time. Coleman realized quickly that the trial was unlike any other in the history of Calhoun County when he received requests from local news crews to set up their cameras in his courtroom. Coleman responded by banning camera crews or any media with cameras from the court. This was the first time such a media ban had been imposed in the county.[5]

The circuit court sat in the county seat in Marshall, a mere five blocks from the scene of the crime. For the locals with time on their hands, the trial was destined to be an exciting form of entertainment, a way to break the monotony of the gray skies of the Michigan winter. For many, it was a chance for them to look into the eyes of the killer who terrorized their community.

Selecting an impartial jury in the county was going to be tricky. News coverage by newspapers, radio, and television had possibly tainted the pool of prospective jurors. Calhoun County was big, but its communities were close-knit, and it would be hard to find someone who had not heard of the case or was not associated in some way with either the plaintiff or the defendant. Also, based on the pretrial filings, the trial was going to involve the presentation of scientific evidence. While commonplace now, the presentation of such material was new in 1969 and presented a challenge to the acceptance of many jurors, out of fear that they might not be able to mentally digest the complicated material.

Coleman took the precaution of querying each juror individually about their previous knowledge of the case or their potential associations with anyone involved with the trial. This approach of individually questioning jurors was done so that their answers would not be cross-contaminated by those of other potential jurors. Sometimes a potential juror might blurt out, "Yes, I know the defendant, and he's a crook," inadvertently tainting the other potential jurors' knowledge of the case. This new approach that Coleman implemented prevented such contamination of the juror pool.

This was the first time this method had been employed in a trial in Michigan, though the approach was widely accepted as a practice in other states. Once Judge Coleman was done, Chism's defense team of Reed Orr and Bert Schulz had twenty preemptory dismissals at their disposal, and Jereck had fifteen. The large jury pool that was called for the trial was whittled down during the ten hours of preliminary examinations. Ten jurors were dismissed because of their admitted knowledge of the case, one of the witnesses, or the defendant. Orr exercised seventeen of his twenty dismissals, while Jereck used eight of his fifteen.[6]

In the end, eight men and four women served as jurors for the case, with two men as alternates. All were between the ages of twenty and fifty, and all were white.[7] Only two of the jurors were from Marshall. It was hard to find anyone in the tiny town who did not know someone involved in the case or had not heard about it.

* * * *

On the first day of the trial, January 20, 1970, the courtroom was packed with nearly two hundred observers. In the audience was a nervous Bernice Chism. Detective Kenney's wife, Anita, had been asked by the investigators to sit with her to offer comfort and support through the trial. During breaks for lunch, the two of them dined with each other.[8]

I spoke with several people who sat with Bernice during the trial. The investigators into the Puyear murder never said it, but she was almost as much of a victim of Enoch as Nola was. Nola was no longer able to be tormented by Enoch Chism. Bernice would not truly be free of him unless he was convicted and locked away.

Prosecutor Jereck spoke first to lay the foundation of the case. He recounted the events that led up to the death of Nola Puyear on a day two and a half years earlier. He described her last utterance as "Oh!" just as the bomb went off. Nola was not just killed, he told the jury; her death was even more grim: "I believe the experts say, (she died) of evisceration." He described it as the disembowelment of the body. It set a dark tone for the kind of person who would commit such a crime.

With the skill of a novelist, he crafted the story of the killing and presented how the investigators had come to realize that Enoch Chism was the murderer. Jereck laid out how the evidence had been gathered at the crime scene and had been tested. He told the jury he would prove that it was Enoch Chism's handwriting on the bomb and on the poison pills sent to Nola Puyear. Jereck also told them that he would show scientifically that the components of the bomb had come from Enoch's home.

As he wrapped up his opening argument, Jereck brought the story of Nola's death into the context of the law for the jury: "The very act of sending a package through the U.S. Mail displays premeditated murder. (As such) it is necessary for you to find the defendant guilty of first degree murder."[9]

The lanky Reed Orr then rose from his seat to give the jury their first glimpse of Enoch Chism's defense: "It is conceded that the facts will permit no conclusion other than that whoever murdered Nola Puyear did so willfully and deliberately; whoever mailed this bomb to Mrs. Puyear in August of 1967 did premeditate his or her act, and did mail it with the obvious intent of killing her. Under these circumstances, the killing was murder in the first degree as defined by our legislature. Tragically, the receipt of the bomb package through the mail, and the attempt to open it, cost Mrs. Puyear her life. The defense in this case does not question these points and indeed the defense admits them. The only question in this case to be decided by you as the jury is: Did Enoch Chism, in fact, do it?"[10]

Orr contended that some of the fragments of wrapping that the police gathered at the murder scene might not have even come from the bomb itself. Orr further promised that the defense team would bring in their own battery of scientific experts who would refute the testimony that the prosecution was bound to present.

Orr's portrayal of Chism was that of a man who was at the wrong place at the wrong time. Enoch wasn't a killer. In fact, he had cooperated with the authorities at every opportunity during the investigation—even granting them permission to search his home and willfully submitting handwriting exemplars. All throughout the investigation, Orr contended, Enoch had been "stating at the time he had nothing to hide."[11]

It was then that Orr laid out his own theory to cast doubt on Chism's guilt. He told the jury that there may have been more than one suspect in the bombing murder. "The one person who gained financially was also the man who handed her the bomb," he said.[12] Orr had planted the seed that perhaps the killer was none other than Nola's husband, Paul.

He concluded, "The proofs will show that Enoch Chism did not gain anything. We will try our best to stick to the issue of who did it."[13]

The witnesses who were brought in during the opening of the trial described the bombing of the Tasty Cafe on the morning of August 18, 1967. Donald Page, who had been in the restaurant when the package exploded, told the jury, "I thought that the stove that he (Mr. Puyear) was at blew up. It knocked me to the floor. I got up and that place was in shambles." He and Paul Puyear rushed outside. They then turned back to look for Nola: "Mr. Puyear was hysterical. He kept calling her name. He was moving too fast—I couldn't get a hold of him."[14] Other witnesses included Herold Reuss and others who arrived at the Tasty that day, describing the grisly images they had been exposed to at the scene of the murder.

Dr. Phillip Glotfelty testified that he had declared Nola dead at the scene. "From the neck to hips she was totally blown apart," he reported. He later described the painstaking details of recovering metallic fragments from her body, identifying them as evidence.[15]

Jereck introduced eight photographs of the bombing into evidence, showing the wrecked shambles of the Tasty Cafe. Two of the photographs showed the decimated body of Nola Puyear. Orr objected, claiming that showing the photographs to the court would be "highly prejudicial to the jury." Judge Coleman felt differently and overruled the defense.[16] The jury was, for a few moments, put in the Tasty Cafe on the day of the bombing. They were being told of the tang of gunpowder in the air; they were shown the horrific effects of the bomb on the victim. Enoch Chism sat at the defense's table, silent, seemingly unmoved by the horrors of Nola's demise.

* * * *

The second and third days of the trial were dominated by Paul Puyear's testimony. Puyear had left Marshall to move to California to be near his son. He had sold the Tasty Cafe to Thomas Guy, who had reopened the restaurant over a year ago. Gone were the scars of the bombing. The Tasty had been renamed, but it was a struggle to develop a new crop of regulars. While Marshall had erased the evidence of the crime on its main street, the memories still stung in the backs of most citizens' minds. All that remained was that justice had to be dealt to the person who did it. While Marshall had put the crime behind it, the memories and emotional scars were still carried by Paul Puyear in the court.

Jereck handled Puyear carefully, with a skill that one might expect from a more experienced prosecutor. The grandfatherly, white-haired Puyear described the delivery of the package to the Tasty, "At the time I had it in my hand, something was said more or less in a joking way," he said about shaking the package and hearing a rattle inside, "like there was something loose in there." His eyes teared up as he recounted the explosion and the death of his wife.[17]

The prosecutor entered into evidence the reconstructed wrapper of the bomb, complete with the word remnant "OOKS" on it. Did this look like the package wrapper Paul Puyear had seen? Yes, Puyear responded that it did.[18]

Reed Orr was faced with planting the seed of doubt with the jury. That meant he had the unenviable task of a vigorous cross-examination of Paul Puyear. First, he went after his identification of the package: "May I ask, this LOOKS like the wrapper on the package?" Agitated, Paul responded bluntly, "That IS the wrapper."[19] This opening set the stage for their contentious discussion.

There are questions that will never be answered in this case, at least in my mind. Orr had access, through discovery, to all of the investigative reports of the crime. He had to have been intimately aware of the magnitude of Paul Puyear's infidelities. This must have added to the tension in the court. Would Orr bring up Puyear's affairs to damage his credibility as a witness? Or better yet, would he use them to make the jurors wonder if a jilted former lover might have killed Paul's wife, as opposed to Enoch Chism?

Orr drilled on the topic of money—namely, the money that Paul Puyear had received as a result of his wife's death. Paul revealed that he had control of the couple's joint bank account bearing $43,000, as well as Nola's half of the value of the Tasty Cafe, which had been sold for $18,000. Their home and other investment properties were worth a combined $26,500. This included his now-abandoned trailer in Barryton and the land it sat on.

There was more. His son had sold a life insurance policy to Nola that had netted $20,000. Nola's much-exaggerated share of property from her brother's death had been a piece of property in Arkansas worth another $16,000 after past due taxes and legal fees. Paul said that he had turned over the control of the land to his son, John.[20]

Orr did not come out and ask the question that loomed over the jury and the packed courtroom—did Paul Puyear kill his wife? He didn't have to. The sum of money that had come under Paul's control might seem paltry today, but by 1967 standards, it was worth the modern equivalent of over $650,000. People had been killed for much less.

Jereck did not want the issue of Paul's potential involvement to sit fertile in the minds of the jurors. On reexamination, he had only one question: "Mr. Puyear, I must ask you this question: Did you kill your wife?" "No sir," Paul replied sternly, with conviction.[21] In one question, Jereck hoped he had derailed Orr's implications that Paul Puyear might be involved with the death of his wife.

* * * *

Having established the particulars of the crime itself, Prosecutor Jereck began the task of putting the proverbial noose around the neck of Enoch Chism. To do that, on the fourth day of the trial, he called three witnesses: Sergeant Fred Ritchie, Josie White, and Sene Buckner.

Motive was the weak link in John Jereck's case, and he knew it. He wasn't required to prove motive legally. At the same time, he knew that if it didn't provide any motive at all, that would cause doubt in the minds of some of the jurors. The young prosecutor opted to tackle the problem head-on. If the jurors were going to want to know why Enoch had killed Nola, he would tell them, regardless of how flimsy the reason seemed on the surface.

Sergeant Ritchie was the first to hit on the motive. He testified that when Enoch had been taken into custody, he had admitted that he had been interested in purchasing a restaurant like the one the Puyears owned.[22]

The slender Sene Buckner took the stand and related to the jury her story of the mysterious meeting that took place at the rear of the Tasty Cafe about six weeks before Nola's murder. She had seen Enoch Chism and had overheard only the confrontational tone of the meeting. Mrs. Puyear's discussion with Chism was "unpleasant" and "disagreeable."[23]

After the encounter, "Nola poured a cup of coffee and sat down at the counter with it. She was disturbed. Her hands was shaking."[24]

Reed Orr did not let the matter pass. He pressed Sene for details about the meeting. Could she remember how far away the conversation took place? She estimated that it was forty feet. Could she remember any details of what Mr. Chism was wearing? All Sene could remember was that "he was neat, it wasn't work clothes."[25]

Jereck pushed on to further link Nola and Enoch. Enoch's mother-in-law, Josie White, took the stand and told the jury how Enoch had developed a strong desire to purchase a restaurant in 1967. He had asked her if the Puyears would be interest in selling the Tasty. She had told him, "No, I don't think so." Enoch had taken her on a search for a restaurant and had even asked her if she wanted to work for him once he purchased one.

Josie related a story of having dinner with Enoch and the family about a week before he was arrested. He had "looked a little funny" when the subject of Nola's death had come up. She recounted that "he acted a little shaky," that his hands were visibly shaking after the discussion of Nola's death.[26] At one point in that discussion, Enoch had said, "I don't think they'll find whoever did that. It must have been some child."[27]

Having put Enoch and Nola together, Jereck wanted to paint a more insidious picture of Chism. His next evidence was the mysterious poison pills that had been sent to Nola. Orr was not about to let this go without debate, arguing that these pills were not evidence related to the murder of Nola Puyear. Jereck parried and countered that he would prove in his expert testimony that the pills were tied to previous attempts to kill Nola. Judge Coleman allowed the pills to be entered into evidence. What was not discussed was that these pills represented a second package of pills sent to Nola. The first package, along with the handwriting on it, had been discarded before the bombing. Much like the "Atomic Shocking Book" that had been recovered at the restaurant, while the packages of pills pointed to an extended wave of terror on Nola, neither could be linked to Chism or the bomb package.

Jean Reed, the beautician who Nola had shown the pills to, took the stand and testified that Nola had received them with a note telling her they were for her nerves. Mrs. Reed testified that she had put some of the substance in the pills on her tongue and that "they were bitter, and burned."[28]

Charles Quick, a toxicologist for the Michigan Public Health Department's crime detection laboratory, was called to the stand to testify that the capsules were filled with sodium hydroxide (lye) chemically identical to the household brand Drano. The pills were so caustic that they had eaten through the brown paper envelope they had been placed in while in police custody. Jereck showed the jury the holes the lye had burned in the evidence envelope. Quick told the jury and packed courtroom that if the pills had been consumed, the lye would have eaten through the victim's stomach lining and wall, resulting in a slow, agonizing death.[29]

Throughout the presentation of evidence, a pale Enoch Chism sat passively, displaying no emotion whatsoever.[30] If Jereck was getting to Chism, the latter wasn't revealing it—at least not in front of the jury. When Fred Ritchie encountered Enoch on his way back to his cell, Chism once more assured him that he was going to kill him and the other officers involved with the case.[31] Enoch's persona in the courtroom did not mirror his inner fires of hatred and violence.

* * * *

Court reconvened again on Tuesday January 27, another biting cold day in Marshall. Prosecutor Jereck's strategy was to move to the strength of his case—the physical evidence. While motive was useful in the minds of the jurors, it meant nothing if he could not convince them that Enoch Chism had sent the bomb.

To do this, he called several of the investigators to the stand to establish the chain of evidence. Myron P. Wood and Robert Kenney told the jury of the evidence recovered in the remains of the Tasty Cafe and at the Chism home. Each told about the pieces of evidence that were recovered and about how they were preserved and tracked.

Jereck chose to start his examination of the physical evidence with some of the most complicated material and testing—the neutron activation analysis (NAA). His expert witness was C. Michael Hoffman of the Michigan Department of Treasury. Hoffman had written for numerous professional journals on radioactive analysis as part of crime scene investigation. He had overseen the testing of the samples from the Puyear case at the U.S. Naval Research Laboratory.[32]

The real problem with NAA was that it was highly complicated and difficult to understand, especially for small-town jurors. From a 1970s perspective, it sounded like science fiction. The samples recovered from Enoch's home and from the crime scene, as well as some control samples, were irradiated for a half hour in a pool-type atomic reactor. The samples were then measured for the gamma radiation given off, using a sodium iodide detector. In measuring the radiation given off by the activation of the neutrons, it was possible to compare materials at the atomic level. The results were presented in complicated tables of numbers and graphs.[33] Jereck faced a real risk that the jurors would become lost in the myriad of details associated with the testing and not understand the results in terms of real-world implications.

Hoffman's testimony initially started out buried in the details, but Jereck skillfully managed to keep it in the context of the evidence. After a half day of testimony, Jereck was able to hit the key points for the jurors. The battery parts recovered from the body of Nola Puyear were virtually identical to those of the Fisk C-cell battery recovered from Chism's nightstand. The masking tape sample recovered from Enoch's workbench was also tested and was found to be the same tape as the fragments the detectives had recovered from the bomb package. In contemporary times, there are many manufacturers of masking tape, and it comes in all sorts of colors and widths. In 1967, however, only the 3M company made this type of tape, and it came in rolls of three sizes. Chemically, according to Hoffman, the samples tested were not just the same 3M tape but appeared so similar that it was likely they came from the same manufacturing batch. With each batch, very faint and subtle differences surfaced at the atomic level, but the tape at the Chism home and that on the bomb wrapper were incredibly close. The same held true of the plain brown wrapping paper, which was chemically almost identical to that recovered from Enoch's home.

The testing of the red marking pencils was another matter altogether. The investigators had recovered one pencil from the shower in the Chism garage; one from Clark Equipment, where Enoch worked and claimed he got the pencil found in his home; and samples from the crime scene. The test also used a control sample. The pencils from Chism's home and work tested much closer than the control to the one used on the bomb package. Hoffman felt comfortable saying not just that the recovered pencils were manufactured from the same batch but that one of them was definitely used to address the package. For the moment, the scientific evidence squarely pointed to Enoch as the man who sent the bomb to Nola.

There was one sample, however, where the NAA testing had failed the prosecution: the hair found stuck under the masking tape recovered from the crime scene. Hair samples had been taken from the entire Chism family, but the NAA analysis showed that no one among them had contributed the hair. If the hair had not come from the bomber while wrapping the package, who had it come from?[34]

Bert Schulz, an attorney for the defense, had been waiting like a hawk ready to pounce on its prey. His role in the trial was to attack and dismantle the scientific evidence that the prosecution presented in front of the jury—an unenviable and complicated task. Schulz was prepared, though, and didn't flinch at the job ahead of him. He spent a half day tearing apart the testimony of Hoffman. As a witness, Hoffman didn't recant his testimony. What Hoffman did more than anything was to define the limitations of NAA testing. Yes, it was widely accepted, but the results were subject to the quality of the testing facilities and the skills of those interpreting the results. "(NAA) is only as good as the operator and the equipment used," Hoffman conceded.[35] While these points did not alter his own analysis, their concession laid the foundation for the defense.[36] If anything, it gave Jereck a taste of what was to come from the defense team.

The time had come to pull out the big guns for the prosecution. Jereck called James Dibowski, his handwriting expert, to the stand. Enoch's handwriting was what put him at the crime scene, even though he physically was not there that day. Dibowski's credentials were impressive. He had been a postal inspector since 1950 and had analyzed "more than a quarter of a million handwriting samples" in his career.[37]

Jereck and Dibowski came prepared. They had enlarged photographs of the packaging for the pills and of the reconstructed bomb wrapper, along with seven other samples of Enoch Chism's handwriting. The defense attempted to keep the enlargements out of the trial, since they were not the actual evidence but simply photographs of it and were selected samples of Chism's handwriting. Judge Coleman did not side with Orr, though; Dibowski's displays were permitted.[38]

Dibowski's testimony was a half day long, and while handwriting analysis can be a tedious and boring subject, the careful questioning by Prosecutor Jereck managed to make it interesting. There were a string of conclusions that Dibowski presented to the jurors: the addressing and writing on the pills matched that of the bomb package, and the samples of Enoch Chism's handwriting he had analyzed—specifically the boat registration, his employment records from Clark Equipment, his driver's license application, his signatures and writing on forty-five cancelled checks, and the handwriting from the brown notebook his wife turned in—were all written by the same hand. His summary conclusion drove home the point: "It is my opinion that the person who addressed people's exhibits 13 and 14 [the package wrappers for the bomb and pills] was the same person who wrote seven samples of Chism's now and specimen handwriting."[39]

There was a sticky issue that still had to be dealt with by the prosecution—the sample of handwriting that Enoch had provided on August 28 to the police. That sample was one that Dibowski had used, earlier in the investigation, to exclude Chism as a suspect. Jereck knew this would be a sticking point, and to counter it, he called up the investigators to testify that Chism had broken the pencil during the sample and was visibly nervous as he scrawled his name. It seemed to them that Enoch was altering his writing deliberately to deceive them. To support Dibowski's work, Jereck called Sergeant Fred Ritchie and postal inspector Myron Wood to the stand. They testified that Enoch had been sweaty and nervous when providing the sample and had seemed to be attempting to alter his handwriting.

Bert Schulz led the effort to chisel away at Dibowski's testimony, but to little avail. Schulz asked if there were parts of the handwriting samples that were inconsistent with each other? Dibowski said that there were, adding that this was not unusual and that, in the case of Enoch Chism's handwriting samples, there were more consistencies than exceptions.[40] If Schulz was looking to generate doubt about the handwriting analysis, Dibowski had given him very little to go on.

John Jereck had several other witnesses, including Captain Wallace Van Stratt, called to further validate the handwriting samples that Chism provided; and Betty Kedo, who testified that Enoch's signature on his driver's license application was made in her presence. Jereck still had one more trump card to play, though there were some risks in it. He considered calling Chism's daughter, Sharon Norton, to the stand.

In Jereck's meetings with Sharon during the investigation into her father, she had said that she felt the sample of the handwriting in the *Marshall Evening Chronicle* was from her father's hand. But Enoch Chism was a manipulative and threatening figure. What if he had gotten to Sharon in the long months leading up to trial? What if his mere presence in the courtroom was enough to sway her testimony. Jereck decided to take the risk and call her to the stand.

Years later, in my conversations with John Jereck about his decision to put Sharon Norton on the stand, he said it was a great gamble. The prosecutor and investigators had come to know Enoch Chism far too well during the investigation and the long road to trial. Jereck said, "We knew he wasn't above attempting to intimidate witnesses, especially with his family. Given his history of abuse, it was a real roll of the dice to put her on the stand. In the end though, I could tell in the faces of the jury that her testimony, more than any other, had gotten to them."[41]

Twenty-three-year-old Sharon Norton took the stand as one of the last of the prosecution witnesses. She was the only member of the Chism family who had been called to testify for the prosecution. Jereck asked her if her father had ever spoken about opening a restaurant. She replied, "He was very interested in having a restaurant and he wanted to go into the business himself." Sharon added that Enoch had asked her if she thought the Puyears would sell the Tasty Cafe. She had told him "No. I didn't think so because that was her [Nola's] main interest in life."[42]

Jereck then asked Sharon if she was familiar with her father's handwriting, and she replied she had seen it "practically every day of my life as long as I lived at home." Jereck then deftly pointed to the enlarged photograph of the bomb package. Did that look like Enoch's handwriting? "It looks like my father's," she said. When showed the sample from the packaging for the lye-laced pills, she replied, "I see what looks like my father's handwriting."[43] Enoch had not gotten to his daughter before the trial, or if he had, he had not been able to influence her.

Orr pointed out that Sharon was not a handwriting expert, a point that was conceded. From John Jereck's point of view, the damage had been done. Enoch Chism had been condemned by his own daughter.

One observer in the court watched as Jereck passed by Chism at the defense table. He saw Enoch silently mouth the words "I will kill you" in the direction of the prosecutor.[44] Jereck had struck home with Enoch, and he had struck hard.

After thirty-three witnesses and sixty-four pieces of evidence, the time had come for the defense to attempt to sway the jurors away from thinking of Enoch as a killer. And their best witness to that was prepared to take the stand—Enoch Chism himself.

11

"Murder Is Not the Product of a Normal Mind"

I was surprised that the defense team put Enoch on the stand. Much of that surprise is based on the belief that he might have done more damage to his case than good. The questions that the defense crafted for him, though, were carefully constructed—a testimony to the skills of both Orr and Schulz. They didn't open many cracks for the prosecution to exploit on cross-examination.

The morning of January 28, 1970, was the first day of the trial when the air outside of the courthouse showed any sign of getting warmer—peaking at almost twenty degrees. The Bogar Theatre announced a new movie for the weekend, the dinosaur classic *The Valley of the Gwangi*, starring Richard Carlson. For members of a community that had been huddled up to avoid the bone-chilling cold, the new movie was going to offer someplace to go, if only to get out of their houses.

The courtroom was packed with two hundred spectators that day, including twenty students from Marshall High School who were attending as part of their government class. All were in for a rare treat. Not only were they being allowed to sit in on a murder trial, but after long months of being quiet, Enoch Chism was going to take the stand and offer his own version of events.

Chism sat on the witness stand while Reed Orr served him up questions, hoping to shatter the image that the prosecution had painted of him. "Now I ask you point blank . . . I show you the people's exhibit 13 (the bomb wrapper). Is that your handwriting?" "No sir, it is not," Enoch replied in a low, almost monotone voice. Orr showed him the wrapper and pills sent to Nola Puyear and asked, "Is that your handwriting there?" "No sir," Enoch responded, "it is not my handwriting."[1] The questioning continued:

"Mr. Chism, did you ever make a bomb of any kind?"

"No sir, I did not."

"Did you ever mail a bomb to Mrs. Puyear?"

"No sir."

"Mr. Chism, did you kill Mrs. Puyear?"

"No sir, I did not."[2]

Enoch described his job at Clark Equipment and told the jury he used the red marking pencils all the time to mark defects. "Usually when I went home I'd drop a pencil in my pocket," Enoch said. He almost always emptied his pockets before he showered and went into the house. That was why the police had found the marking pencils in his garage shower.

Enoch then laid out his whereabouts and alibi for August 16, 1967—the day that the bomb had been dropped into the mail. Enoch said he had left work at noon because he had asked to be assigned to a later work shift so that he could spend time working at home and in the yard. Chism said he had stopped at a restaurant to have a cup of coffee after leaving work. He then spent the rest of the day making a trip to the dump with a trash can and planting shrubbery. His son, Michael, had gone to the dump with him.[3]

Enoch claimed that he knew the Puyears "by name and by sight" and had spoken to them from time to time. He had gone fishing once with Paul Puyear and Hollie White, Enoch's former father-in-law. That was the extent of their relationship and interaction.

He even admitted that he had spoken to Nola Puyear once, but the occasion was perfectly innocent. She had asked him to bring some wax paper to the restaurant, and he was working at Kellogg at the time and could easily fulfill her request. That had been sometime in 1965 or '66.[4]

When Orr asked him about his interest in purchasing a restaurant, Enoch said that it was true he wanted to own a small business. He had sent letters to companies in Chicago and Youngstown, Ohio, asking for information. He had even met with two men from Youngstown to discuss having a restaurant in Marshall—something they recommended against given the number of tiny cafes already operating there. In stark contrast to his emotionless demeanor during the trial up to that point, Enoch seemed almost excited when talking about the restaurant business. "As a matter of fact," he said, "I went so far as to go pick out the lot and everything in Kalamazoo, but the other party (he was working with) lost interest."[5] In contrast to what he had told Sergeant Ritchie at the time of his arrest, Enoch now openly admitted that he had talked to his mother-in-law, Josie White, about working for him. In regard to any desire to purchase the Tasty Cafe, Chism added, "But as far as buying it or anything, I never did try to buy it."[6]

Enoch could explain the Fisk battery found in the house: "I have quite a few articles that use batteries. Flashlights, cameras, time recorders, and Michael's pinball machine."[7] As for the roll of masking tape, he said, "I was doing some painting in the bathroom, and used masking tape around the baseboards."[8] These explanations sounded simple enough. Surely everyone had a battery or two in their house or owned masking tape.

Chism said that he was familiar with dynamite but did not have the experience to make a bomb. Orr asked him if he ever put a battery in a bomb? "No sir," Chism responded, "I did not."[9]

Orr attempted to blunt the veiled motive testimony that Sene Buckner had given the court. Under the defense attorney's prompting, Enoch claimed he didn't know Sene Buckner. "It is not true that I was in the Tasty Cafe," he said, adding, "I never had a 'heated conversation' with Nola Puyear."[10]

After two and a half hours, Enoch's testimony was over. Orr had kept it limited to only a few key points—mostly aimed at refuting the witnesses presented by the prosecution. The longer that Chism talked on the stand, the more he was open to cross-examination. Putting him on the stand in the first place was a risk for the defense, and Orr did what he could to mitigate that risk.

Now it was John Jereck's turn with Enoch. He had only met with the accused a few times prior to the trial, but now he could go after him on the points Orr had raised. Jereck squared off with Enoch by hitting him first on the dynamite issue. He knew that in the eyes of the jury, putting dynamite in Chism's hands was critical.

Jereck prodded Enoch on how he had used the explosives and where he had obtained them. Enoch admitted to purchasing about three sticks of dynamite from Kendall Hardware in Battle Creek. His purpose was to dynamite his dry well. A coworker at Clark Equipment had suggested it. The first attempts to dynamite the well had failed. Enoch had gone off three days later to purchase six more sticks. He had set off the explosives in the presence of his son, Michael. "I blew my dry well to pieces," he admitted. When Jereck asked him where he had learned to use the dynamite, Enoch said that he had asked the employees at Kendall Hardware how to detonate it. According to Enoch, he was unaware that dynamite could be set off by means beyond a lit fuse.[11]

John Jereck held a few cards close to his chest if he needed them. He had heard that Enoch had learned to work with dynamite back in Arkansas, where he had used it to blow up tree stumps when working as part of a road construction crew. Also, Enoch had stumbled into a trap with the dynamite. Not only had he admitted that he had it, but he had also created doubt as to where the rest of the dynamite was. Surely he hadn't used all six sticks to blast his septic system, had he?[12]

Anticipating that the defense would possibly challenge the handwriting samples that Enoch provided, Jereck asked Chism if he had written and printed the twenty-one samples provided. He said that he had. When Jereck then asked if Enoch had given the police permission to search his property, the usually emotionless Chism reacted unexpectedly in a terse tone. "Yes," he said, "I authorized the officers present to search my house, but not the whole state of Michigan."[13]

Jereck went after Enoch's refutation that he had been in the Tasty Cafe and had an argument with Nola, an argument that Sene Buckner had allegedly witnessed. Under grilling by Jereck, Enoch said he had never seen Sene before her testimony. "Do you have any idea," Jereck asked, "why she would say that she had seen you at the Tasty Cafe?" "I have no idea,"[14] Enoch countered. By not having an excuse, he seemed to actually solidify Sene's testimony.

At this point, Jereck stopped. Enoch's word was already refuted in many cases by multiple witnesses and with scientific evidence. There was not to be any grand moment where the defendant was going to break on the stand.

In researching the trial, a part of me wondered why John Jereck didn't try to set off Enoch on the stand, especially given his known temper. This curiosity is the product of my watching far too many television shows about trials and not dealing with the realities of a trial before. I learned that Jereck's approach to the trial was more about strategy and getting things in the minds of the jurors than raw emotions. Jereck didn't have to set Enoch off to win the trial—plain and simple.

The dapper young Bert Schulz stepped up for the defense next, going after the scientific evidence that had been presented in court. He called the defense team's own expert, Dr. Don Gordas from the University of Michigan. Gordas opened by stating the facilities for conducting NAA at the University of Michigan were "at least 15 to 18 times as accurate" as the facilities used at the U.S. Naval Research Laboratory, where the prosecution had tested the evidence.[15]

Dr. Gordas contested the findings on the masking tape first. He claimed that he had tested fifteen different samples of tape, including the sample taken from Enoch's home, and had not found any that seemed to match the tape recovered at the murder scene.[16]

Gordas's test of the marking pencils did not yield nearly the results that the defense had hoped for. He merely said that the results were not identical. His conclusion was that the pencil recovered from the Chism home might not be the one used on the package.[17]

Dr. Gordas added that he could not conclude that the Fisk battery was the type pulled from Nola Puyear's remains. In essence, Dr. Gordas had essentially refuted all of the NAA evidence that had been presented by the prosecution. Any conclusions drawn in jury deliberation were going to be a matter of who the jury believed more in terms of professional witnesses.

Schulz next called Dr. David Boswell, a local physician, to the stand. One of the more damaging pieces of testimony in the case had been delivered by Sergeant Fred Ritchie and Inspector Myron P. Wood about Enoch's August 28 sample of handwriting. Dr. Boswell had treated Enoch that day at Oaklawn Hospital for vomiting and extreme stomach pains. He had diagnosed him, with a cursory examination, as potentially having a kidney infection. Certainly, Schulz got the witness to say, that would explain why he had appeared sweaty and nervous.

John Jereck was prepared for this testimony, though. Under cross-examination, he pressed Dr. Boswell on his diagnosis. Boswell had only spent a few minutes with Chism and had never confirmed his cursory diagnosis. When Jereck pressed him further, Boswell agreed that the symptoms that Enoch had displayed could have come from nervousness or

extreme anxiety—symptoms that Chism's own medical history showed
he suffered. Also, Enoch had not gone to the doctor until late in the
evening, after he had given his writing sample.[18] Jereck clearly planted
it in the jurors' minds that Enoch's anxiety—nervousness that the police
were finally onto him—had probably made him sick. When Dr. Boswell
took his seat, the defense rested.

My research demonstrated one thing clearly: Enoch Chism got a vigorous defense from his court-appointed attorneys. They had not, much
to my surprise, shared information on Paul Puyear's infidelities and
sexual escapades. In 1967, lawyers were more discreet. Besides, as one
lawyer who practiced then told me, Orr and Schulz weren't about to do
work for the police. Their job was to create doubt about Chism, not to
drag Paul Puyear through the mud to do it.

* * * *

Closing arguments don't allow for new evidence to be presented in court.
They are a last chance to summarize the facts, as each side sees them,
for the jury. For young John Jereck, the prosecution's closing argument
was his last chance to attempt to cement the case that Enoch Chism had
brutally murdered Nola Puyear.

Jereck opened bluntly, "Enoch Chism is, in fact, the man who made
and sent the bomb with the premeditated intent of taking her (Nola's)
life."[19] He then turned to his strongest evidence that had not been rebut-
ted during the trail—the handwriting evidence. Two handwriting experts, James Dibowski of the U.S. Postal Service and Captain Wallace
Van Stratt, had both identified Enoch Chism's handwriting not just on
the reconstructed bomb package but on the package of poison pills sent
to Nola. They had given their testimonials "without reservation."[20]

Jereck then did something unexpected—he admitted the weakness
in his case. "The motive for the killing was a very flimsy excuse," he
said in reference to the concept that Enoch had killed Nola to purchase
the Tasty Cafe. "Often times in murder cases, murder is not the product
of a normal mind. A normal mind does not produce murder," Jereck
explained.[21] He continued, "Enoch Chism didn't have the guts to negoti-
ate about buying the restaurant with Nola Puyear face-to-face. But what
makes people do these things, only they know."[22]

Turning to the evidence, Jereck conceded that the proofs he had presented were "circumstantial and consistent in the accusation against Chism." Chism had "most likely" mailed the bomb on August 16. By his own admission, Enoch had left work early—a peculiar act on his part. "At that time he decided to change shifts so that he could work at home. That was the morning on which Enoch Chism mailed the package," Jereck sternly contended for the jury.[23]

At Enoch's contention that he was sick on August 28, the day he gave his writing sample, Jereck offered a different perspective: "If he was feeling as he said he was, why did he go down to the Sheriff's Department?"[24] In coping with Bert Schulz's masterful rebutting of the testimony from the prosecution's NAA expert, Jereck simply downplayed it: "I think you're going to have to weigh the merit of these expert testimonies. You have to end up agreeing with Mr. Hoffman's testimony."[25] John Jereck took his seat and turned over the floor to Chism's defense team.

Reed Orr led off with an attempt to repair any damage that Jereck had done. "The fact that he (Chism) might have done it is not the issue," he declared. Just because Enoch might have done the crime was not the same as having done it. Orr simply dismissed the prosecution: "This case has not proved beyond a reasonable doubt that Enoch Chism did this horrible deed."[26]

Orr attempted to slip Enoch's head out of the noose that the handwriting analysis had formed. Dibowski had said that sickness could alter the handwriting of someone providing a sample. Hadn't the defense proven that Enoch Chism was indeed sick the day he had given the police his sample? Dibowski's testimony was not so easily shaken. Pointing to the exhibits of the addresses on the bomb package and the package of pills, Orr hoped that the jury would form their own opinion: "Careful examination by you of these two exhibits will raise doubts in your mind to this (Dibowski's) opinion."[27]

The NAA analysis was still contested by the defense. Orr hoped that the contest was enough to raise reasonable doubt with the jury. He claimed that the prosecution had failed to prove that the items they had tested were indeed tied directly to their client.

The image that Reed Orr tried to paint of Enoch Chism was that of a man who had tried to be helpful to the police but had somehow been misidentified as the murderer. "He had nothing to hide," Orr claimed.

Enoch had even granted them consent to search his home. "A guilty man," Orr pointed out, "would probably have said, 'I want an attorney before I say anything.'"[28]

The motive for the crime still hung in the air in the cramped courtroom, and Orr did not let it go. Hitting the lack of motive might be enough to get at least one juror to feel that there was reasonable doubt of Chism's guilt. "There's no evidence to show that Enoch Chism ever talked to Paul or Nola, or that Nola ever talked to Mr. Chism concerning an attempt to purchase the restaurant," Orr argued. He labeled Jereck's motive as "somewhat fantastic."[29]

So who did kill Nola Puyear? Orr tactfully deflected suspicion away from Enoch to someone else. "If anyone had a motive," he said, "it was her husband Paul who gained substantially from her death."[30]

In their closing argument, the prosecution had insinuated that Enoch was mentally unstable. Orr latched onto this insinuation like a dog with a bone. "There is not one scintilla of evidence that Enoch Chism has a sick and diseased mind," he argued. If the prosecution had believed that, he said, they should have called in doctors and submitted their testimony.[31]

As Orr finished, Judge Coleman gave the jury extensive instructions as to the definitions of circumstantial evidence, reasonable doubt, first-degree murder, and acquittal. He also provided them with guidelines for accepting expert testimony. As a final piece of his instructions, he told the jury that they had only two choices in their finding, given the nature of the case: guilty of murder in the first degree or not guilty.[32] At 11:30 a.m., the jury was taken out of the packed courtroom to begin their deliberations.

* * * *

Jury deliberations can go a long time, especially if there is some indecision among the jurors regarding the guilt of the defendant. The members of the jury asked for lunch and were escorted out to the Fireside Inn at the edge of town, where the county had reserved a private room for them to dine in. After a secluded meal, they returned to the courthouse in Marshall to continue their work.

The afternoon dragged on for all parties involved. Given that January

30 was a Friday, most at the packed courthouse thought it likely that deliberation would continue on through the weekend. For their part, the jurors were methodically going over the evidence. There were no holdouts or debates; they simply wanted to be thorough in their decision.[33]

What did the jury consider? One juror later reported to me, "Ultimately it was the handwriting evidence. The defense had not put up any real rebuttal to the experts. It didn't require an expert to see it was the same handwriting." The NAA analysis did not sway them one way or another. The same juror explained, Chism "had all of the components to build the bomb in his home—and the handwriting was obviously his."[34]

The defense had wanted to refute the prosecution's witnesses on the handwriting but were hampered by two things. First, the county had not granted them funds to secure expert testimony that would say that the handwriting was not Chism's. Also, the experts they could get for free were not entirely sure that it wasn't his handwriting. Putting them on the stand might actually damage their case more than help it.[35]

Everyone was surprised when word was sent to Judge Coleman at 5:00 p.m. that the jury had reached a verdict. Chism, for his part, was nervous, wringing his hands and muttering in a low voice as the jury was brought in.[36] The courtroom shuffled to silence as jury foreman Darrell VanVleet of Battle Creek rose to say, "We find the defendant guilty as charged."[37]

Enoch Chism, the man who had only displayed veiled emotions during the trail, exploded: "Oh no!" Some of the jurors were visibly shaken by the outburst. For a moment, Enoch remained in his seat, visibly quaking in his chair. As Judge Coleman thanked the jurors, Chism rose from his seat quickly and started for the bench, shouting at Coleman as he took two large steps: "I am not guilty of this crime!" Bert Schulz grabbed one of Enoch's arms to hold him back, but to no avail. The six deputy sheriffs in the room converged on Enoch and grappled with him as he struggled, yelling out, "They sent my son to South America so he couldn't testify. He's the only witness I have."[38] Bert Schulz and Reed Orr tried to help restrain their client as he continued his rant: "I'm not guilty of this crime. I didn't kill no one. No, sir, I didn't kill no one. You are lying!"[39]

Judge Coleman was concerned. Speaking down from the bench to the deputies, he said, "I think we should take this prisoner from the courtroom." The deputies took their charge under control and forcibly removed him, taking him across the enclosed elevated bridge back to his maximum security cell in the county jail.[40]

The courtroom eruptions were not over. As the audience began to leave, another voice erupted, that of Ruby Bagwell, Enoch's sister from Battle Creek. Her venom was directed at Bernice Chism. "You got what you wanted!" she called out.[41] Bernice, for her part, broke out in tears at the announcement of the verdict. When asked why, she replied that it was "because of all the tension that had built up over nearly two and a half years." Her only parting comment to the press was, "I hope to build a new life now."[42] A sheriff's deputy escorted her from the crowd and to her car. Bernice drove home to C Drive North—this time alone.

Enoch's outburst regarding his son was peculiar on several levels. It was true that Michael had gone with three other teenagers from the Emmett Street Missionary Church to do some volunteer work in Haiti. While he had been gone for two weeks, he had returned a week before, on Friday, January 23.

For John Jereck's part, he had not felt that Michael had any testimony that was material to the prosecution's case. Likewise, Orr and Schulz had not felt that Michael could have exonerated Enoch or provided him with the alibi that he so desperately needed.

Enoch had tried to carefully craft an alibi in his arson arrest, only to have it unravel. Was he planning on using his own son to prove he didn't send the bomb? Michael could only testify for his father's time after Enoch came home from work that day, and even then, there may have been gaps. What kind of a person sucks his children into a murder plot, even as an alibi?

* * * *

On February 5, 1970, Enoch Chism was brought back into the court-room of Judge Coleman for his sentencing. The crowd that had filled the seats of the room during the trial were gone; only ten onlookers were present. Marshall had moved on. Enoch was already being written out of the town's history.

Chism himself appeared different. Gone was the conservative suit and tie he had worn during the trial. The pale man stood before the judge wearing his jail denims. When asked if he had anything to say, Enoch remained calm and resolute—in contrast to his explosion at the end of the trial. He only commented, "I'd like to say that I didn't commit this crime and there has been a terrible mistake."[43]

Coleman passed sentence quickly. Enoch was sentenced to the custody of the Michigan Department of Corrections "for the period of your natural life."[44] That night, he met with Bernice.

Before he was escorted from the courtroom, Enoch posed another question to the court: "May I have an attorney for an appeal?" Judge Coleman agreed.[45] Enoch was allowed to meet with his sister Ruby for a few minutes and then was put in an unmarked sheriff's car. The reason given for his rapid transfer was "security concerns," even though he had been "a model prisoner most of the time."[46]

* * * *

A few months after Chism's conviction, Ronald DeGraw received the reward from the *Detroit News* for the tip he provided as part of their Secret Witness program. He gave the money to his secretarial staff—in particular, to Shirley Lawcock, whose boat title had proven instrumental in Chism's arrest. The reward from the U.S. Postal Service never came.[47]

12
The Appeal

With Enoch Chism's conviction, Marshall felt as if a burden had been lifted off its shoulders. The community was fully prepared to put this blemish on its reputation and image behind it. Justice had been served. No one spoke about how the community had allowed this evil to fester in the first place, how no one had helped Bernice or how they had ignored the signs in Chism that pointed to his mental and violence issues. That was all in the past, where it could be buried and ignored. All that mattered was that life went on. Enoch Chism had been cut from the community like a cancer. The murder and events around it were swept under the rug. But, like virulent cancer, Chism was not prepared to let the community that had sent him to prison rest easy.

An appeal of Chism's verdict was inevitable. First-degree murders were rare in Calhoun County at that time, and even on the day of the trial, Chism's defense attorneys were talking about their appeal options. Enoch was taken to the state prison in Jackson, Michigan, for a period, then was transferred to the prison in Marquette, Michigan.

His attorneys felt that two elements formed the basis for appeal. The first involved the evidence—specifically, the handwriting samples that Bernice had given the police on October 12. On that day, she had given them Enoch's brown notebook and a copious number of canceled checks, all laden with Enoch's handwriting. Their contention was that she did not have the right to turn over Enoch's property. The police had conducted their search, which Chism had given permission for, on the day of his arrest. Enoch, via his lawyers, contended that Bernice did not have permission to turn over his property after the initial search.

The second contention that the appeal was based on was that Enoch had been denied a speedy trial. The appeal on this point was centered around the fact that Enoch had sat in jail for nearly two years, without bail, and without representation for fifteen months of his incarceration. On this front, the facts were fairly clear. Judge Coleman had claimed that

Enoch was not entitled to public defense. He gave Enoch representation during this period, but only for appealing the judge's decision—not to prepare his defense. The Michigan courts had taken a long time to reverse the opinion of Judge Coleman. Only in August of 1969 did a final ruling come down from the Michigan Supreme Court, according to which Enoch was granted defense for the crime he was accused of. By the time all of the pretrial motions were complete, Enoch's trial did not start until January 1970. Carefully omitted from the appeal was the fact that Chism's own actions had caused Judge Coleman to contest his claim of being indigent.[1]

The appeal based on the handwriting evidence was rejected out of hand. Several deciding factors drove the court's opinion. The checks and notebooks had been seen by the officers during the search on October 11 but had not physically been taken into custody at that time. While Chism's defense attorneys claimed that they had been picked up during a search on October 12, the reality was that it was not a search. In fact, it was a visit by the officers to ask for the information. While the defense claimed that Enoch had not given them permission to take the materials in a separate search, the courts felt differently. The officer's visit was seen as a follow-up visit, common in such cases.[2]

The argument that Bernice Chism did not have the right to turn over her husband's handwriting to the officers also melted in the hot light of examination. The home was jointly owned by them; in fact, Enoch had signed it over to her in a quitclaim deed, making her the technical owner of the house. Also, the checks were from a joint account, giving Bernice as much legal ownership of them as Enoch had. It seemed that the investigators' actions were perfectly within legal limits. Still, the defense team validated that the Supreme Court had never ruled on the issue of a wife releasing evidence against her husband, so in their mind, there was a potential angle that could be explored.[3]

On the argument that Enoch had been denied a speedy trial, the Michigan Court of Appeals did not grant the motion for appeal. In their thinking, Enoch had been partially responsible for the delay that took place and was not entitled to claim that he had been denied a speedy trial.

Chism was undeterred. His defense attorneys appealed the case to the Michigan Supreme Court, a common course of action. The court upheld the lower court's rulings. For four years of appeals through the Michigan court system, it appeared that Enoch Chism was going to remain in jail for the rest of his life.

* * * *

Technology changes constantly, and such was the case with neutron activation analysis. By 1980, the technique was fading out. Court rulings at the state and federal level demonstrated that NAA was flawed as a means of validating evidence. The technique itself worked. What made it difficult to present in court was the fact that it was subject to the skills and competencies of the tester. Prosecutors no longer wanted to use it, and after the Supreme Court tossed out NAA evidence on that basis in a case, it faded from use.

* * * *

While in jail, Enoch Chism was not entirely idle. At Christmas every year he was in jail, he sent a card to Prosecutor John Jereck, the investigators tied to the crime (Kenney and Steinbacher from the state police), and several jurors. He sent cards to Judge Coleman and to his attorneys. Some of the Christmas cards were simply signed "Enoch Chism." Some jurors received messages from Chism, saying that he knew that the jury had met after the trial and had decided he was innocent. At least one juror received a note indicating that *the juror* should be in prison, not Enoch. Chism's defense attorney, Bert Schulz, did not see these cards as threats. To him, it was simply his former client maintaining contact with him. For the jurors and for the investigators tied to the crime, it was obviously a veiled threat, a reminder that he had not forgotten them and that he knew where they lived.[4]

When I interviewed John Jereck, he had been involved with eight murder trials during his tenure as the Calhoun County prosecutor. I asked him how many of his convicted criminals had written him from jail? The answer: only Enoch Chism. There is no way to interpret Enoch's sending of the cards as anything short of an attempt to intimidate the officers and prosecutor who had put him away. What was about to unfold with his case made matters even more disturbing.

Bernice's final divorce from Enoch was granted while he was in jail, on April 13, 1970.[5] With her ex-husband in jail, Bernice had to have felt safe at last. After all, unless he escaped, there was no chance of her ever seeing him again except on her terms. Was there?

* * * *

Having exhausted the Michigan court system for appeals, Enoch turned to the federal system. This time, he found assistance from an unlikely source, the American Civil Liberties Union (ACLU). William S. Easton of Marquette and Joel M. Shere of Detroit took up the Chism case in the federal system. The Federal District Court of Western Michigan reviewed the case and considered it very differently than the state courts. While they found no merit to Chism's claims that Bernice had given his handwriting evidence inappropriately, they instead focused on the question of his Sixth Amendment right to a speedy trial.

The need for a speedy trial is based on the concept that, over time, witnesses can have failing memory or may die altogether, disallowing their testimony, or that critical evidence will be lost. Bert Schulz, looking back at the case, didn't feel that a lack of a speedy trial necessarily hurt Enoch, because none of these things seemed to be a result of the delay. "In some respects," Schulz said, "the delay in getting him to trial could have helped us in the case. It might have generated some sympathy for Enoch—his having spent so long waiting in jail to go to trial."[6]

The ACLU crafted their appeal to the federal court very carefully. They pointed to the motive in the case and said, in essence, that for fifteen months, Enoch had not had defense counsel working on his defense. While the prosecution had enjoyed quick access to the witnesses, over a year had passed before Enoch's court-appointed lawyers began to question witnesses.[7]

In looking at similar cases, the measure applied was whether this deficiency gave an unfair advantage to the prosecution. In the Chism case, they deemed it did. In April 1975, federal judge Ralph Freeman reversed the Michigan court ruling and honored a writ of habeas corpus to have Enoch freed from jail. In a relatively standard move, he delayed that order to give the state time to appeal to the district court of appeals.

In the years since the trial, John Jereck had returned to private practice. The new Calhoun County prosecutor, John J. Rae, found himself reeling. One of the most notorious murderers in county history was being given his freedom. Rae and the state's deputy attorney general, Mrs. Jan Ryan Baugh, ushered the appeal to the Sixth District Court of Appeals in Cincinnati. At risk was nothing less than the thought of turning a murderer loose on the streets. Even more disturbing was when the U.S. district court upheld the lower court's ruling.

There was one avenue left: appeal to the U.S. Supreme Court. Rae and the state of Michigan sent the case up in hopes of keeping Chism in jail. On April 20, 1976, the Supreme Court refused to take up the case—in essence, upholding the lower court's ruling. Within twenty-five days, Chism was ordered to be released from prison.[8] Rae was downtrodden at the results, saying, "It is sickening that Chism is being released. I don't think that we can do anything further. The county and state did everything we could. I'm terribly, terribly disappointed with the outcome. What more can I say but that it's tragic."[9]

* * * *

The former jurors of the Chism case had mixed reactions to his sudden release, especially in light of the fact that he had been sending them his strange Christmas cards while in prison. One juror commented, "It's too bad he had to be released on a technicality. It now seems like such a waste of time going through with the trial. What is bad is the fact of innocence or guilt was not an issue with his being let go." Another juror said, "I think it's a big disappointment. We (jurors) did in our best judgment what we thought we should have done in convicting him. Now after several years he's being released." Another added, "The delay (in bringing Chism to trial) did not alter the fact that he was guilty. If the delay had any effect on his innocence, then the court action is fine. But the delay did not change the facts in the case. The delay, as we saw it, was the effort of his attorneys and Chism himself."[10]

Another juror summed up his sentiments by saying, "If some injustice had been done, his release should set it straight. But we feel he committed the act and in convicting him felt that justice had been done." There was at least one voice of dissent, that of a juror who said, "There may have been a long time in getting Mr. Chism to trial, but I think a lot of the delay was part of the means to keep him from getting a speedy trial. I wonder where the injustice is . . . for Chism or for the others involved."[11]

While Enoch could not be retried for the same crime, that did not mean that the wheels of justice were done with him. The U.S. district attorney ordered the evidence sent to him so that he might consider trying Chism for the crime of sending a bomb through the mail. While far from the justice that Nola Puyear deserved, the prospect of such a trial was something that Prosecutor Rae clung to. The district attorney's decision, however, was that the same reason used to grant Enoch his appeal would be used again for his defense in such a case.

Enoch Chism had entered jail in October of 1967. The issue of his eligibility for a court-appointed attorney ate away at fifteen months of his life. His own attorneys assigned to his defense spent nine months filing delays and attempts to exclude evidence. Following his conviction in January of 1970, he had been in jail another six years. In total, Enoch had spent just over nine years in jail for the murder of Nola Puyear. He was fifty-two years old.

On April 30, 1976, Chism was released from the Jackson State Prison. His brother Lonnie picked him up in a white-over-gray Buick. The Calhoun County police had the car followed. Their biggest concern was that Enoch would seek to return to the Marshall area.[12] They were right to be afraid.

13

A Shadow Returns to a Peaceful Community

The good people of Marshall went about their lives in 1976 oblivious to
the thought that Enoch Chism was now circulating among them. The U.S.
Bicentennial was the big news for the country. The events of 1967 were
long ago, pushed back in the townspeople's minds. But for some people,
those closest to the case, the release of Enoch Chism was a curse—the
worst kind of curse law enforcement could conceive. In their minds, this
was not just a miscarriage of justice; it now put them and their loved ones
at risk.

After being convicted of murder in a pastoral county like Calhoun, having been reviled and lambasted by the press for the better part of two
years, one would think that Enoch Chism would have gone anywhere
else to live. To go back to the same mid-Michigan county that labeled
him a wife beater, an arsonist, a bomber, a madman, and a murderer did
not make sense. He was a social pariah. Why wouldn't he go anywhere
else, where he could blend in, where his past could be eluded? The answer to that question was locked away in the dark recesses of Enoch's
mind. Regardless of his logic, Enoch moved to Battle Creek, Michigan,
twenty minutes from the scene of his crime.

For the men who had put him behind bars, Chism's return to the
area was greeted with frustration and fear. They were frustrated that the
legal system had failed—that it had put a diabolical killer back where he
might commit crimes again. Despite their dedicated investigative work,
this notorious bomber was loose again. They saw his annual Christmas
cards from jail as a reminder that he had not forgotten them and that he
knew where they lived.

The fear they felt also came from another source. When the guards
went through Chism's cell in Jackson State Prison, where he was last

held, they found a list—a hit list. The names on the list included state troopers Lohrstorfer and Boland, who had been involved with his arrest. The judge, jurors, and John Jereck were also named on the list. So were Detectives Kenney and Steinbacher. The state police were only informed that the list had been found a few days after Chism's release. Whatever else Enoch had been doing in jail for those years, he seemed to have been planning his revenge.[1]

For the officers, this meant that some began carrying guns in their off-hours. Some of the men made a point of starting the family cars when their wives or kids went to drive. Their fear was that if Chism wanted to extract revenge on the men who put him away, he might think a bomb would just do the trick.[2] From most accounts, the family members were not aware of the protection that their spouses or fathers were providing them. The fear was contained to a handful of men dedicated to protecting their loved ones.

Fred Ritchie had retired from the sheriff's department by 1976 and was stunned at the news of Chism's release. He had good reason to be concerned: on two occasions, Chism had threatened to kill him. Ritchie told me in an interview, "I set a record for getting the fastest concealed gun carry permit in the state of Michigan. I got a call from John Olsen, who told me that Enoch was going to be released from jail in the morning. He asked if I had my CCW [carry concealed weapon] up to date, and I told him it had expired. If Chism was getting out, I knew I needed to have a gun. He [Olsen] told me how to walk it thru. I got my prints done and hand-carried the permit to Lansing, and they walked it through to get it." By the afternoon, Fred Ritchie was armed.[3]

Ronald DeGraw received a phone call from the state police the day that Enoch was released. The call came with a warning—both he and Judge Coleman were "targeted" by Enoch for retribution. The police said they could not guarantee twenty-four-hour protection but would step up patrols in his neighborhood. There wasn't a great deal that he could do to protect himself. If Enoch wanted to get DeGraw, he could rig a bomb to DeGraw's mailbox, his garage door, his car. There was no way for De-Graw to fully protect himself. DeGraw suggested sending his wife and children away but realized the futility of that effort. How long could they be away from their home before it was safe?[4]

With the surfacing of the list from his former jail cell, the police began a surveillance of Enoch. This was not as much a formal surveillance as the act of a brotherhood of officers and law enforcement protecting their own. For weeks at a time, they kept tabs on Enoch, but there seemed to be no sign of him fulfilling his veiled threats. Then, suddenly, they lost track of Enoch.[5]

* * * *

Bernice had managed to do what she had said she would at the end of the trial—she had started her life anew. She had met Stewart Ferguson, the owner of a well-respected construction company, and remarried. She had put Enoch behind her and moved on.

On June 16, 1976, just a few weeks after the police lost tabs of Enoch and three months after he was released from jail, a fire was reported at the Ferguson-Fruin Construction Company's warehouse in Battle Creek. The building was shared with the Battle Creek Urban League, Crown Courtright Paper Company, and Jack Pearl's Sport Center for storage. Ferguson-Fruin Construction stored lumber there.[6]

The fire started at the center of the building, with no apparent ignition source. While the fire was eventually contained and extinguished, firemen reported seeing blue-tinged flames, hinting at an accelerant. As the state fire marshal came in, they measured the areas of deepest charring and determined that the fire started near one of the interior doors, near a column.[7]

There had been no witnesses. At Crown Courtright, there were two signs found that none of the employees had seen the night before—one reading "Joe of Wis. The Rat" and another reading "US Army." No one understood the strange references.[8]

The media smelled a story even before investigators did. Was it possible that Enoch Chism had been behind the arson? Stewart Ferguson spoke with Captain James Newburn of the Battle Creek Fire Department to see if something could be done to keep the media from getting any information about the incident. Captain Newburn assured him that his department had not said anything to the newspapers or TV.

The captain obviously sensed there might be a reason for this request. He pressed his suspicion—was it possible that Enoch had been involved? Stewart stated that he didn't think his wife's former husband had committed the crime. They had not heard from Enoch since his divorce had been finalized. There had been no harassment or threats of any nature. Bernice had heard, from family ties, that Enoch may have been out of the city at the time of the arson.[9]

To this day, the crime remains unsolved. Enoch Chism and one other man, an arsonist who was confined to his ward at the Battle Creek Veteran's Hospital the night of the crime, are the only two listed suspects. Others involved with Enoch's murder trial firmly believe that the only person who might have had a reason to set fire to the warehouse was Enoch Chism.[10]

* * * *

A few months after Enoch's release, John Jereck went to his mailbox as he did every day. Waiting for him was a book-size package wrapped in plain brown wrapping paper. The address on it was a scrawl, scribbled hastily, and wasn't any handwriting that he recognized. There was no return address on the package. For the man who put Enoch Chism away, the package had an eerie resemblance to the one that had killed Nola Puyear.

Jereck reached out to Detective Kenney to ask him what to do. There was still no bomb squad in western Michigan to check out the package. Kenney told Jereck that he should carefully put the package in his car and drive it to the state police post in Battle Creek. Suddenly, every pothole and crack in the road became a hair-raising bump, as John Jereck made the slow trip.

When he arrived, Detective Kenney met him. Kenney daintily pulled the package out of the car and put it on the trunk. He examined it slowly and methodically. Using a razor blade, he cut the brown paper wrapping and removed it with the skill of a surgeon, making sure that the paper was not somehow rigged. All of this occurred in the parking lot of the state police post.

Kenney had unwrapped two packages of cigars, a gift from one of the divorce clients John Jereck had serviced. He and Kenney let go long sighs of relief that the package wasn't a bomb. At the same time, Enoch Chism was terrorizing them just by being on the streets.[11]

Bert Schulz came home one day and found a mailing tube, unmarked, wedged into his screen door. Before the Chism trial, he would have simply picked it up and opened it. But an unmarked package sitting there had new meaning after the trial. With a snow shovel, he carried the tube out into the yard. Using a tree for cover, he cut through the tube with an ax. When he went to check it out, the smell of mint wafted in the air. Some well-meaning sales person had put a sample tube of toothpaste in his door. It was a subtle reminder of how Enoch Chism had changed the community.[12]

Fred Ritchie firmly believed that Enoch was attempting to scare or intimidate the officers who had apprehended him. He told me in an interview, "After he quit the force, Steinbacher bought a bar. A month or so after Chism was released, someone had climbed up on the roof of his bar and had torn down all of his TV antennas. That was classic Chism— strike at you when you weren't around." Ritchie continued,

"I had a fearful night around the same time. I saw a car pull into my driveway with its lights off at night. It just sat there parked in the dark. Well, I figured it was him [Chism], so I got my gun and headed out at it. Whoever it was backed out the driveway and drove away with the lights off. I called the department, but there wasn't anything that they could do about it."[13]

* * * *

Just over a year after his release, Enoch had moved to nearby Albion, Michigan. Somehow he met and fell in with another former convict, James Coleman of Toledo. Coleman had a standing warrant out for jail escape from Genesee County. The two of them devised a scheme to rob three people. One was "a disabled man, Enoch Chism's brother's son-in-law."[14] The man was identified as being wheelchair bound. The other two people were men both of the schemers knew, Ralph Sheldon and David Warner. The plan was to commit armed robbery of the three men using weapons that Coleman had secured.

What Chism and Coleman didn't know was that the state police had been tipped off to the planned robbery. Working with the Albion Police Department, they had managed to secure audiotapes of the men plotting their crime. On June 29, 1977, the police moved in, apprehending

Enoch at Dan's Dairy Bar. He was taken back to the Calhoun County Jail, a facility where he had spent over two years awaiting his last trial.

The charges leveled at the two men were conspiracy to commit armed and unarmed robbery. Assistant prosecuting attorney Roger Caswell appeared before the court and asked for high bail for the men, thirty thousand dollars for each of the two charges per man. In the case of Enoch, he said he was asking for so much "considering his prior criminal record." He only was able to reference the 1965 arson conviction, though, something the court simply could not ignore. But the judge did not take that recommendation. He set Chism's bail at forty thousand dollars.[15] Having made bail, Chism was released.

Enoch had been suffering from ailments since his release from jail. As it turns out, he had developed cancer. The pains of the disease forced him to check into Leila Hospital in Battle Creek. While still awaiting trial, Enoch Chism passed away on January 15, 1979. Rumors circulated that he had a brain tumor at the time of his death. His survivors included his son and daughter, his six living sisters, and four brothers. Bernice was not listed.[16]

With Enoch's death, the investigators and prosecutors involved in the Nola Puyear case could relax a little. The long dark shadow that Enoch had cast over them disappeared. But the memories of the fear remained.

Epilogue

You would think that this crime would be etched in the history of Marshall. Quite the opposite is true. The baby boomers remember the murder, but their memories are often a jumble of inaccuracies and misconceptions. The generations that followed simply don't know about the crime. It was not a subject that ever came up, and when it did, the discussion was always short.

When you talk to the people of Marshall about the death of Nola Puyear, they more often than not don't talk about the victim—they talk about her killer. It is as if Nola is almost lost behind the image of the bomber who terrified the entire community.

Certain other things emerge, things that make no sense when you know the facts of the case. Many people say that Enoch learned to use explosives in the army, but he was not in the army, nor was that ever misreported in the newspapers. How this little fragment of collective memory got stuck in the minds of Marshallites is unknown. The strength of the community grapevine in Marshall, the gossip spun out of the beauty parlors and barber shops, seems to have more weight than reality.

Some in Marshall don't want to talk about the crime, even today. Nola's violent death and the probing investigation seemed to open up the seamy underbelly of the quiet little town. One woman who was contacted during the writing of this book said, "Polite people don't want to talk about what happened. That crime doesn't represent Marshall." Oddly enough, gossiping about the events seems exempt to this attitude. The whispered stories of infidelities were both indecent and tantalizing and were not a secret in town. After Enoch's conviction, the dark secrets were all carefully tucked away. Marshall wanted to embrace its quaintness and did so.

Throughout his trial, there was no editorial about Chism or the murder. Even after his sentencing, nothing appeared in the *Marshall Evening Chronicle* until his 1977 arrest. While that story was front-page news, there was a sense that the people of the town didn't want to hear about the crime or the criminal any more. There was a desire to return to the days before August of 1967, and in some ways, Marshall did just that. Perhaps that was how the community dealt with the inner guilt of having suspected their friends and neighbors of being murderers.

On Michigan Avenue, across from the Marshall Post Office, the building where the Tasty Cafe once was housed still remains, now used as a dance studio. Except for the older folks, people walking by don't know the story of what happened there and how the web of intrigue consumed the entire town.

Part of what helps fuel this self-deception is that, on the surface, so little has changed. Win Schuler's still remains as an icon of fine dining for the state. The aroma of Louie's Bakery is seductive and alluring. A new high school has been built, and in a fit of political correctness gone wild, the Marshall High School Redskins changed their name to the Redhawks, but their football games still dominate the autumn Friday nights. During Saturday nights in the summer, teenagers still "cruise the gut" on the main street, looping around the brightly lit Brooks fountain. To view Michigan Avenue today compared to 1967, all that seems to have changed is the style of the automobiles lining the street.

The Calhoun County Fair no longer has harness racing but still stands iconic as the event marking the end of summer. Every spring, around Memorial Day, the Brooks fountain is once more filled with water, and its colorful lights are replaced. After Labor Day, in an act that marks time like the removal of a page on a calendar, the fountain is drained for the season—just as it has been done for decades. The modern Christmas parade is almost indistinguishable from parades run a half century earlier. Marshall has managed to envelop itself in its traditions and well-groomed past—a past in which the events of August of 1967 simply don't need to be included. Marshallites don't want to remember that for a few horrific months, the community turned in on itself in search of a killer. Many don't like the reminder that the murder that took place could have been averted if only someone, anyone, had taken a stand. Such memories are best pushed back to the recesses of history. As the lady said, "Polite people don't want to talk about what happened."

Yet the legacy of the crime remains. Despite its dainty and highly protected image, the people of Marshall still lock their doors at night.

Author's Afterword

"Aren't you just reopening old wounds?" That question and variants of it dogged me during the writing of this book, accompanied by the admonition "We don't want Marshall thought of in *that* light." At the book's conclusion, my response remains the same as it has always been: this is a historical book dealing with the most infamous murder that took place in Marshall. The self-appointed stewards of Marshall's history often huff away at such a comment. There's a reason for that: Marshall's gene pool is relatively shallow. There are people there who either were part of the story or have relatives who were. I must admit, though, that a lot of people I talked to who are new to the town or of young generations are sincerely interested in the crime, and for that I am thankful. Everyone should know more about their local history—good, bad, and ugly.

At the start of my research on this book, I reached out to John Puyear. John still lives in Marshall. He was reluctant to talk to me, and I don't blame him. "You probably know more about what happened than I do," he said.

I also reached out to the Chisms—Bernice Ferguson, Sharon Norton, and Mike Chism. This was a matter of professional courtesy, to let them know that the book was coming out and to give them a chance to respond to questions. In many respects, they could have filled in the gaps about events and Enoch. I respect the fact that Sharon and Mike did not respond. I will not speculate why. I acknowledge that they have been through enough.

Bernice did reach out to me. At first, she greeted me with righteous indignation that the book was being written. "No one will care about this book," she said. I disagreed. She then told me, "Nobody knows the twenty-five years of hell I went through living with that man." That is hard to debate. I reminded her that this was her chance to set mat-

179

ters straight, to tell her side of events. Otherwise, readers would be left to draw their own conclusions and may never know why she married Enoch in the first place or if there was a turning point that led to his slide from reality.

Her response was to ask me how much money I would be willing to pay her to answer my questions: "How can I make money off of this?" As a professional author, I could not bring myself to submit a money offer. Whatever her secrets are, Bernice is welcome to keep them.

In many respects, the surviving Chism family members were almost as much victims of Enoch as Nola Puyear was. Almost. I would go so far as to say that Bernice may owe her life to Nola. Enoch was a time bomb with a short fuse. If he had not killed Nola, he most certainly would have killed someone—most likely someone in his family. Clearly, Bernice was his target of choice for unleashing his anger. In respect to Sharon Norton, her testimony carried a great deal of weight with the jury. For her to take the stand against her father had to be emotionally releasing. I prefer to think of it that way, regardless of what she may feel.

I replaced the names of many people in the book. I wish I could have protected Paul Puyear as well, but it was not possible. My reason for using this convention, made popular by true crime author Ann Rule, was simple. I did not want someone confronting me with the line "You said my grandfather was cheating on my grandmother and was a pervert—he was a good man!" I have, wherever possible, protected people's identities. Unfortunately, it was impossible to do this with the individuals who were closest to the case. Rest assured that I know the true names behind the replacements, these are not fictional people.

In working on this book, I had my own "secret witness," a source who provided me firsthand accounts of some events and glimpses into the personalities of those associated with the case. My own source, at least for now, must remain anonymous.

One of the questions posed to me often is whether I believe the motive for the crime as presented in court—that Nola was killed because she would not sell the restaurant to Enoch. My answer is no, not completely. I have the advantage of reviewing Enoch's psychiatric evaluations and the stories of the officers who intervened in his rages on his family. I don't entirely subscribe to the motive. I think things were much simpler. In my mind, Enoch didn't kill Nola because she wouldn't sell the Tasty Cafe; he killed her because she was a woman and she said no to him. Strong-willed stubborn women from Arkansas infuriated Enoch. Then again, that's just my theory.

What are we to make of Enoch's outburst at the end of his trial, his claim that his son, Michael, could have exonerated him? In my interview with Bert Schulz, one of Enoch's defense attorneys, I raised this question. He responded, "Frankly I have no recollection of this issue. I must assume, given Orr's proven thoroughness, that had such an issue proven to be viable, we would have followed through." I asked Fred Ritchie if he thought Michael could have helped his father, and Ritchie summed up his thinking on the matter succinctly: "In my opinion, his son could have done just the opposite. I always suspected that his son was there when he [Enoch] put it [the bomb] together and mailed it. He might not have known what it was at the time, but I thought he was in the know. I suggested to John Jereck that he put the kid on the stand. He wanted to concentrate on the daughter and the wife." The police files show that Michael was unable to tell the investigators anything of value, though one report says there is a feeling that the boy may know more than he was letting on. As Bernice put it to me in our one conversation, "My son was only thirteen or fourteen at the time, and I did what I could to shield him from this." Time has a way of obscuring details, and so we may never know how Michael's testimony might have affected the trial's outcome.

Was there any lasting impact of the murder? Marshall did change, as much as pundits refuse to admit it. People living there always wanted to feel comfort in the thought that these kinds of crimes did not happen in Marshall. That changed. Before the murder, people there didn't think twice about the arrival of a package that they didn't order. Afterward, such unexpected packages were viewed as potential bombs.

There is also the thought that even the best of citizens living at the time had to contemplate who in their tight little community might have done the crime. To put it bluntly, some people in Marshall ratted on each other. Only one, the secret witness, steered the authorities in the right direction. Others simply let their paranoia and suspicions get the better of them.

Finally, there is an unspoken collective feeling of guilt. The Chism family was facing random nightmares every night, and the community knew about it. As one person told me, "We all knew that Chism beat his wife." Where were the church groups or individual citizens intervening to help? In the 1960s, domestic violence was glossed over by most people; it was considered part of someone's private life. Anyone stepping in to help Bernice may have been enough to prevent Nola's murder. If Enoch had been given a harsher sentence for his arson, that, too, might have saved Nola Puyear. Some people in Marshall may yet need to come to grips with their quiet complacency.

Many of the key players are no longer with us. Detectives Kenney and Steinbacher are sadly gone now, though Fred Ritchie is still with us. Don Damon is alive still and remembers the address of every stop on his route to this day. Bert Schulz is an assistant city attorney in Battle Creek, where he is in charge of criminal prosecutions. John Jereck, the young prosecutor who rolled the dice during the trial, is still alive and practicing law as well. Herold Reuss is still with us and remembers vividly the images of Nola the day she died. The secret witness, Ron DeGraw, is still alive as well, no longer having to check that a piece of tape is unbroken on the hood of his car before he starts it. Some of the jurors are alive and living in the area, though none talk openly about the case—as if there is still a hint of fear about it. Even though he is dead and buried, Enoch Chism still has the capability to cause a ripple of fear among people associated with the case. Perhaps that terror is his only real legacy.

Cast of Characters

*Names changed by author

Bernice Louise (White) Chism—wife of Enoch Chism and daughter of Josie and Hollie White; later Bernice Ferguson

Bert Schulz—defense lawyer for Enoch Chism during his trial

Bobby Lewis—a five-year-old whose birthday party was in Marshall the day of the murder

Boyd Simmons—city editor for the *Detroit News* and head of the Secret Witness program

Bruce Norton—husband of Sharon Norton

Bruce O'Leary—Marshall's fire chief at the time of the bombing

Carl Chism—Enoch Chism's brother who owned the house that Enoch attempted to burn down

Clarence Schier—director of the Kalamazoo State Hospital

C. Michael Hoffman—Michigan Treasury Department expert in neutron activation analysis

Columbus Chism—Enoch Chism's father

Creighton R. Coleman—justice presiding over the *People v. Enoch Chism* trial

Darrell Beattie—acting chief of the Marshall Police Department at the time of the murder

Dave Hart*—Battle Creek resident having an affair with Sene Buckner

David Avery*—former owner of the restaurant that became the Tasty Cafe and friend of Paul Puyear

Deborah "Bettie" Lipton*—Barryton resident who was having an affair with Paul Puyear at the time of the murder

Denise Reish—Marshall resident who witnessed Nola receiving a disturbing phone call

Donald Bennett—investigator with the Michigan State Police Crime Laboratory

Donald Damon—postal delivery person who delivered the bomb to the Tasty Cafe

Donald Page—truck driver who was a customer at the Tasty Cafe the day of the bombing

Donna Sharp—wife of Oscar Sharp and visitor to Paul Puyear's trailer in Barryton

Ed Bowman—customer at the Tasty Cafe the day of the bombing

Ed Carroll—Marshall Fire Department captain who found the oil can that led to Enoch Chism's arson conviction; father of John Carroll

Elliott Court—owner of the Court Funeral Home

Emily Judith Martin*—Battle Creek resident and former mistress of Paul Puyear

Enoch Dalton Chism—husband of Bernice Chism and son-in-law to Hollie and Josie White; convicted of the murder of Nola Puyear

Eve Jones*—Barryton resident and former mistress of Paul Puyear

Felix "Fritz" Hoffman*—Marshall resident and close friend of Paul Puyear who visited Puyear's trailer in Barryton; allegedly had an affair with Eve Jones

Fred Ritchie—sergeant of the Calhoun County Sheriff's Department assigned to the case on the first day

Gertrude Westhaven*—Barryton resident and former mistress of Paul Puyear

Helen Hazen—nurse who Nola Puyear showed the poison pills to; worked at the Mi-Lady's Beauty Shop

Herold Reuss—assistant police chief of Marshall at the time of the murder (later chief)

Hollie White—husband of Josie White, Enoch Chism's father-in-law, and a friend of Paul Puyear; allegedly had an affair with Gertrude Westhaven

Jack O'Grady—friend and lover of Paul Puyeur.

James Coleman—convict arrested with Enoch Chism for planning armed robbery

James Dibowski—director of the post office laboratories from Cincinnati, Ohio, and handwriting expert for the postal service

James Herman—neighbor to the Chisms

James Tompert—Enoch Chism's attorney for his arson trial

Jane Marie Morton*—Barryton resident and former mistress of Paul Puyear

Janet Embury—employee of the Tasty Cafe

Jean Reed—individual who tasted the poison pills sent to Nola Puyear

John Carroll—officer of the Marshall Police Department and son of Captain Ed Carroll of the Marshall Fire Department

John Jereck—prosecutor in the Nola Puyear murder trial

John Lohrstorfer—sergeant, Michigan State Police

John Puyear—son of Nola and Paul Puyear

Josie White—employee at the Tasty Cafe and mother of Bernice Chism

Joyce "Ludie" Chism—Enoch Chism's mother

Judge Ralph Freeman—judge who ruled in favor of Enoch Chism's release

Keith Flowers*—friend of Paul Puyear

Legland Whittaker—officer of the Marshall Police Department

Leroy Steinbacher—detective with the Michigan State Police and one of the principal investigators working the case

Lewis "Louie" Shellenberger—owner of the Marshall ambulance service

L. Harold Caviness—doctor treating Enoch Chism for his mental issues

LuLu Simmons*—Marshall resident and former mistress of Paul Puyear and Oscar Sharp

Marg Warsop—Marshall resident and longtime friend of Nola Puyear

Mark Puyear—brother of Paul Puyear

Matthew J. Reinhard—postal inspector from Michigan assigned to the case

Michael Chism—son of Bernice and Enoch Chism

Minor Myers—postal inspector from Kalamazoo assigned to the case

Mrs. Ruth Bruce—woman who performed her own handwriting analysis on the package of pills sent to Nola Puyear

Myron P. Wood—postal inspector from Detroit assigned to the case

Nancy Church—co-owner of the Mi-Lady's Beauty Shop in Marshall

Neil Finley—Enoch Chism's parole officer

Nola Puyear—victim of the bombing, co-owner of the Tasty Cafe, and wife of Paul Puyear

Orville Chism—Enoch Chism's brother in Detroit

Oscar Sharp—bisexual friend and lover of Paul Puyear and regular
    visitor to Puyear's trailer in Barryton.

Paul Nicolich—defense lawyer for Enoch Chism during his preliminary
    examination

Paul Puyear—husband of Nola and co-owner of the Tasty Cafe

Phillip Gloifelty—assistant medical examiner of Calhoun County

Richard Lockwood—customer at the Tasty Cafe the day of the bombing

Robert Kenney—detective with the Michigan State Police and one of
    the principal investigators working the case

Ronald DeGraw—attorney in Marshall at the firm of Schroeder,
    DeGraw, and Mathews, next door to the Tasty Cafe; represented
    Bernice Chism in her divorce efforts from Enoch Chism and was the
    "secret witness" who turned in Enoch

Ronald Ryan—judge for Enoch Chism's arson trial

Ruby Bagwell—Battle Creek resident and sister of Enoch Chism

Sharon (Chism) Norton—daughter of Bernice and Enoch Chism

Shirley Lawcock—Ronald DeGraw's secretary who purchased a
    boat from Enoch Chism and supplied the boat title with Chism's
    handwriting, a turning point in the investigation

Thomas Guy—man who purchased the Tasty Cafe from Paul Puyear

Tom and Karen Swalwell—young couple living next to the Tasty Cafe
    who were friends of the Puyears

Velma Halter*—Barryton resident and former mistress of Paul Puyear

Violet "Sene" Buckner—friend of the Puyear family and regular at the
    Tasty Cafe

Wallace Van Stratt—captain, Michigan State Police, a handwriting
    expert

Wayne Mills—Nola Puyear's brother who died just prior to her murder,
    leaving her a modest inheritance

Whitman Chism—Enoch Chism's brother in Toledo

W. Reed Orr—lead defense counsel for Enoch Chism

Notes for Book Clubs

True crime fans love a good crime story and love sharing their own theories about the crime and the characters. These are some questions book club readers may want to consider. Any book clubs desiring to have the author call in for their meetings should contact the author at bpardoe870@aol.com.

The author has presented three theories as to the motive of Enoch Chism. The first, utilized by the prosecution, is that Enoch desired to purchase the Tasty Cafe and that Nola had refused him. The second, forwarded by Ron DeGraw, is that Enoch desired to kill or force Josie White into unemployment. The third, presented by the author, is that Enoch had an issue with any woman who refused him. Which motive do you think is most plausible? Why?

How important was the motive in this case? Do you feel that the prosecution made a case for Enoch's motive? Were you convinced? Why?

Was it possible that Enoch Chism was set up? Could it be that he was a patsy, framed for the crime? Who would have a motive to do this? How could it have been done?

Small towns are tiny universes on their own. How did the small-town community of Marshall possibly contribute to the crime? How did this community possibly delay the arrest?

Paul Puyear's large number of affairs were a distraction for the investigators. Or were they? Are any of the men or women he slept with potential

candidates for the murderer? What motive would they have for committing the crime?

Watch the Alfred Hitchcock thriller *Shadow of a Doubt*. What kind of
parallels can you draw between that film and the incidents in this book
or between the communities represented in each?

Enoch Chism's outburst at his conviction implied that Michael Chism
may have been able to exonerate him. While his lawyers and the prosecution did not believe this, in what way might Michael have been able
to assist his father's case? How might he have potentially hurt it?

Domestic violence laws are dramatically different now than in 1967.
How might this case play out differently if it were to happen today?

Discuss the appeal of living in a small town? In what ways is Marshall a
special place? Have you ever been to a town like this? Describe the similarities that all such small towns have? Do you think it is more desirable
to live in a small or large town? What is the appeal of small-town life?

What do you make of the defense's position that the only person who
profited from the death of Nola Puyear was her husband, Paul? Is it possible that Paul was responsible for her death? What are the pros and cons
to that line of thinking?

The beauty parlor played an important role in 1967 society. Has that
changed? Has social networking replaced the role of such institutions?

Enoch Chism was a killer whose anger festered for some time in the
community. Would it be possible today for such a murderer to remain
at large?

Did the delay in getting Enoch to trial hurt his case? How? Did it help
him in some ways?

The release of Enoch Chism from jail was stunning to the community.
Was it right for the courts to release him? Should they have tried him

again, using federal laws as the basis for a new trial? Why do you think he moved back to the area? What are your views of the ACLU as a result of this decision to release Chism?

How might modern investigative techniques and technologies have changed the investigation and resolution of this case? For example, what role could DNA have played?

Arkansas was the home of both the Chisms and the Puyears. Do you think this is only a coincidence? Is it possible that there was a relationship between Enoch and Nola that the police never uncovered?

Notes

Note on Sources

The majority of the sources for this book come from the police files related to the Nola Puyear case as drawn from the Michigan State Police Archives. Because multiple jurisdictions were involved in the investigation, there are multiple references to case numbers. In all instances, the sources are referring to MSP 46-1941-67 (5.7) or File 1.1 (5.7), Postal Inspectors File Case 373-47933-E, Calhoun County Reports File 1892–67.

Prologue

1. "Pavilion Repainting," *Marshall Evening Chronicle,* August 18, 1967.
2. Michigan State Police Archives, Nola Puyear Murder, August 18, 1967, p. 2.
3. "$3000 Reward Posted by *News* in Mail Murder," *Detroit News,* September 20, 1967.
4. Michigan State Police Archives, Nola Puyear Murder, August 18, 1967.
5. "Probe Continues in Bomb Slaying," *Battle Creek Enquirer and News,* August 21, 1967.
6. Michigan State Police Archives, Nola Puyear Murder, Memorandum of Interview, Paul Puyear, by M. P. Wood, Postal Inspector, August 22, 1967.
7. "$3000 Reward Posted by *News* in Mail Murder."
8. "Bombing Called Murder by Prosecutor Jereck," *Battle Creek Enquirer and News,* August 19, 1967.
9. Ronald DeGraw, in discussions with author, April 2011.
10. "Bombing Called Murder by Prosecutor Jereck."
11. "$3000 Reward Posted by *News* in Mail Murder."
12. "Bombing Called Murder by Prosecutor Jereck."
13. "Numerous Witnesses Called in Examination of Enoch Chism," *Marshall Evening Chronicle,* November 17, 1967; Michigan State Police Complaint, August 18, 1967, p. 2.

14. "Mrs. Nola Puyear Loses Life in Restaurant Blast," *Marshall Evening Chronicle,* August 18, 1967; Michigan State Police Complaint Report, 46–2942–67.

15. Michigan State Police Archives, Nola Puyear Murder, Detroit State Police Post, Statement of Donald Page, August 18, 1967, pp. 1–2.

16. Ronald DeGraw, in discussion with author, April 2011.

17. Don Damon, in discussion with author, February 2011.

Chapter 1

1. Richard Carver, *A History of Marshall* (Virginia Beach: Donning,1993), 30.

2. Ibid. 433–501; Mabel Cooper Skjelver, *Nineteenth Century Homes of Marshall Michigan* (Marshall, MI, Marshall Historical Society, 1978), 1–19.

3. "Bombing Called Murder by Prosecutor Jereck," *Battle Creek Enquirer and News,* August 19, 1967.

4. "Mrs. Nola Puyear Loses Life in Restaurant Blast," *Marshall Evening Chronicle,* August 18, 1967.

5. "Witness Relates Grim Tale of Fatal Marshall Bombing," *Battle Creek Enquirer and News,* August 20, 1967.

6. "Mystery Explosion," *Battle Creek Enquirer and News,* August 18, 1967.

7. Herold Reuss, in discussions with author, 2010.

8. Ibid.

9. Lewis Shellenberger, in discussions with author, January 30, 2010. Several individuals claimed they were the first to arrive on the scene. My account, pieced together from interviews, presents the most likely order of arrival.

10. Michigan State Police Archives, Nola Puyear Murder, Detroit State Police Post, Calhoun County Complaint Report, August 22, 1967.

11. Don Damon, in discussion with author, February 2011. This is the account that Damon provided the author. A discussion with Dr. Bob Heidenreich yielded a version that did not match Damon's completely.

12. Fred Ritchie, in discussion with author, February 2011.

13. John Carroll, in discussion with author, March 2011.

14. "Bombing Called Murder by Prosecutor Jereck."

15. Don Damon, in discussion with author, February 2011.

16. Author's recollection of events.

17. http://www.oaklawnhospital.org/history.

18. "Mrs. Nola Puyear Loses Life in Restaurant Blast."

19. Michigan State Police Archives, Nola Puyear Murder, Memorandum of Interview, Dr. A. E. Humphrey, by M. P. Wood, Postal Inspector, August 28, 1967.

20. Herold Reuss, in discussions with author, February 1, 2010.

21. Calhoun County Sheriff's Office, Desk Log, August 18, 1967.

22. Herold Reuss, in discussions with author, February 2010.

Chapter 2

1. Kenny family members, discussions with author, February 12, 2010.

2. Michigan State Police Archives, Nola Puyear Murder, August 18, 1967, p. 1.

3. Ibid., p. 3.

4. Ibid., pp. 3–4.

5. Ibid., p. 3.

6. Ibid., p. 4.

7. Reminiscences of author regarding Elliott Court.

8. Michigan State Police Archives, Nola Puyear Murder, August 18, 1967, pp. 4–5.

9. Ibid.

10. Fred Ritchie, in discussions with author, February 2011.

11. Michigan State Police Archives, Nola Puyear Murder, August 18, 1967, pp. 1–3.

12. Ibid., p. 2.

13. Michigan State Police Archives, Nola Puyear Murder, Police Department, City of Marshall, Report by Herold Reuss, August 18, 1967.

14. Michigan State Police Archives, Nola Puyear Murder, Calhoun County Sheriff's Complaint Report, Interview with Josie White, August 23, 1967, p. 1; Postal Service Case File, Memorandum, Results of Interview—Josie White, September 6, 1967.

15. Ibid.

16. Michigan State Police Archives, Nola Puyear Murder, August 18, 1967, p. 2.

17. Ibid.

18. Michigan State Police Archives, Nola Puyear Murder, Notes from D. Sergeant Thorne and Detective Carchow, August 18, 1967, p. 1.

19. Ibid., pp. 1–2.

20. Sidney Fine, *Violence in the Model City: The Cavanagh Administration, Race Relations, and the Detroit Riot of 1967* (Ann Arbor: University of Michigan Press, 1989), 165.

21. Michigan State Police Archives, Nola Puyear Murder, Memorandum of interview, Persons Interviewed: Paul Puyear and John Puyear, by M. P. Wood, Postal Inspector, August 28, 1967, p. 3.

22. Michigan State Police Archives, Nola Puyear Murder, Postal Inspector Case File, Interviews in Arkansas, by M. P. Wood and M. L. Myers, August 20, 1967, p. 3.

23. Michigan State Police Archives, Nola Puyear Murder, Notes from D. Sergeant Thorne and Detective Carchow, August 18, 1967, p. 2.

24. Karen Swalwell, in discussions with author, March 2011.

25. "Bombing Called Murder by Prosecutor Jereck," *Battle Creek Enquirer and News*, August 19, 1967.

26. Michigan State Police Archives, Nola Puyear Murder, Additional Complaint Report 46–1941–67, File 1.1 (5.7), August 18, 1967, p. 6.

27. Marshall Postal Museum staff, in discussion with author, August 8, 2010.

28. Donald Damon, in discussions with author, February 2011.

29. Editorial, *Marshall Evening Chronicle,* August 19, 1967, 4.

Chapter 3

1. "Postal Officers Are Irked over Practical Joke," *Marshall Evening Chronicle,* September 14, 1967, 5.

2. "This Package Was Fishy," *Battle Creek Enquirer and News,* August 20, 1967.

3. Michigan State Police Archives, Nola Puyear Murder, Memorandum, Interview Conducted by John Jereck, Calhoun County Prosecutor, Dictated by M. P. Wood, Postal Inspector, August 23, 1967.

4. Michigan State Police Archives, Nola Puyear Murder, Report on Harrisburg, Arkansas, and Interviews, by M. P. Wood, August 20, 1967, p. 1.

5. Michigan State Police Archives, Nola Puyear Murder, Memorandum of Interview, Paul Puyear (by telephone), by M. L. Myers, Postal Inspector, September 11, 1967.

6. Ibid.

7. Michigan State Police Archives, Nola Puyear Murder, Report on Harrisburg, Arkansas, and Interviews, by M. P. Wood, August 20, 1967, p. 4.

8. Michigan State Police Archives, Nola Puyear Murder, Memorandum of Interview, Paul Puyear (by telephone), by M. L. Myers, Postal Inspector, September 11, 1967.

9. Ibid.

10. Ibid.

11. Michigan State Police Archives, Nola Puyear Murder, Memorandum of Interview, Keith Flowers, by K. Wiltenen, and M. J. Reinhard, Postal Inspector, August 23, 1967.

12. Michigan State Police Archives, Nola Puyear Murder, Memorandum, Interview Conducted by John Jereck, Calhoun County Prosecutor, Dictated by M. P. Wood, Postal Inspector, August 23, 1967.

13. Michigan State Police Archives, Nola Puyear Murder, Report by Sergeant Erland Wittanen, August 23, 1967.

14. Michigan State Police Archives, Nola Puyear Murder, Memorandum, Interview Conducted by John Jereck, Calhoun County Prosecutor, Dictated by M. P. Wood, Postal Inspector, August 23, 1967.

15. Michigan State Police Archives, Nola Puyear Murder, Memorandum of Interview, Paul and John Puyear, by Leroy Steinbacher, M. L. Myers, and M. P. Wood, September 1, 1967.

16. Michigan State Police Archives, Nola Puyear Murder, Memorandum of Interview, Paul and John Puyear, by Detective Robert Kenney and M. P. Wood, Postal Inspector, August 31, 1967, p. 2.

17. Ibid., p. 3.

18. Michigan State Police Archives, Nola Puyear Murder, Memorandum of Interview, Deborah Lipton, by M. P. Wood, August 29, 1967, pp. 1–2.

19. Ibid.

20. Ibid., p. 4.

21. Ibid., p. 5.

22. Michigan State Police Archives, Nola Puyear Murder, Memorandum of Interview, Bob Avery, by M. L. Myers, August 18, 1967.

23. Michigan State Police Archives, Nola Puyear Murder, Memorandum of Interview, Paul Puyear, by M. L. Myers, M. J. Reinhard, and M. P. Wood, Postal Inspectors, and J. R. Dibowski, Director, ID Lab, p. 2.

24. Michigan State Police Archives, Nola Puyear Murder, Interview of Josie White, by M. L. Myers and M. P. Wood, September 6, 1967.

25. Marshall Police Department, Arrest Report, Emily Judith Martin, January 15, 1966.

26. Michigan State Police Archives, Nola Puyear Murder, Memorandum, Interview Conducted by John Jereck, Calhoun County Prosecutor, Dictated by M. P. Wood, Postal Inspector, August 23, 1967.

27. Michigan State Police Archives, Nola Puyear Murder, Interview of Emily Judith Martin, by Leroy Steinbacher, September 6, 1967.

28. Michigan State Police Archives, Nola Puyear Murder, Calhoun County Sheriff's Complaint Report, Interview of Robert Gore, September 8, 1967, p. 1.

29. Michigan State Police Archives, Nola Puyear Murder, Memorandum of Interview, Paul and John Puyear, by M. L. Myers, M. P. Wood, and Leroy Steinbacher, September 1, 1967, p. 2.

30. Michigan State Police Archives, Nola Puyear Murder, Memorandum, Persons Interviewed: Paul Puyear and John Puyear, by M. P. Wood, August 28, 1967, p. 3.

31. Michigan State Police Archives, Nola Puyear Murder, Memorandum of Interview, Paul Puyear, by M. L. Myers, M. J. Reinhard, and M. P. Wood, Postal Inspectors, and J. R. Dibowski, Director, ID Lab, p. 2.

32. Michigan State Police Archives, Nola Puyear Murder, Memorandum of Interview, Deborah Lipton, by M. P. Wood, August 29, 1967, p. 3.

33. Michigan State Police Archives, Nola Puyear Murder, Memorandum of Interview, Hollie White, by Robert Groot and M. L. Myers, August 23, 1967.

34. Michigan State Police Archives, Nola Puyear Murder, Memorandum, Interview Conducted by John Jereck, Calhoun County Prosecutor, Dictated by M. P. Wood, Postal Inspector, August 23, 1967.

35. Michigan State Police Archives, Nola Puyear Murder, Report, by Leroy Steinbacher, August 24, 1967, p. 1.

36. Michigan State Police Archives, Nola Puyear Murder, Calhoun County Sheriff's Additional Complaint Report, Interview of Felix Hoffman, by Fred Ritchie, August 23, 1967, p. 2.

37. Michigan State Police Archives, Nola Puyear Murder, Memorandum of Interview, Deborah Lipton, by M. P. Wood, August 29, 1967, p. 2.

38. Michigan State Police Archives, Nola Puyear Murder, Memorandum of Interview, Harry King, by M. P. Wood, September 22, 1967, p. 1.

39. Michigan State Police Archives, Nola Puyear Murder, Memorandum of Interview, Deborah Lipton, by M. P. Wood, August 29, 1967, p. 2.

40. Michigan State Police Archives, Nola Puyear Murder, Memorandum of Interview, Jack O'Grady, by Robert Kenney and M. L. Myers, Postal Inspector, August 23, 1967.

41. Michigan State Police Archives, Nola Puyear Murder, Memorandum of Interview, Paul Puyear (by telephone), by M. L. Myers, Postal Inspector, September 11, 1967.

42. Michigan State Police Archives, Nola Puyear Murder, Memorandum of Interview, Paul Puyear, by M. P. Wood, M. J. Reinhard, Detective Fred Ritchie, and Detective Leroy Steinbacher, September 14, 1967.

43. Ibid.

44. Michigan State Police Archives, Nola Puyear Murder, Memorandum of Interview, Paul Puyear (by telephone), by M. L. Myers, Postal Inspector, September 11, 1967.

45. Michigan State Police Archives, Nola Puyear Murder, Memorandum of Interview, Paul Puyear, by M. P. Wood, M. J. Reinhard, Detective Fred Ritchie, and Detective Leroy Steinbacher, September 14, 1967.

46. Michigan State Police Archives, Nola Puyear Murder, Interview with John Puyear, by Detectives Steinbacher and Kenney, August 21, 1967.

47. Michigan State Police Archives, Nola Puyear Murder, Memorandum of Interview, John Paul Puyear, by Robert Kenny and M. P. Wood, Postal Inspector, August 24, 1964.

48. Michigan State Police Archives, Nola Puyear Murder, Calhoun County Sheriff's Complaint Report, Search of Puyear Home, August 23, 1967.

49. Fred Ritchie, in discussions with author, February and May 2011.

50. Michigan State Police Archives, Nola Puyear Murder, Report by Sergeant Erland Wittanen, August 23, 1967.

51. Michigan State Police Archives, Nola Puyear Murder, Memorandum, Interview Conducted by John Jereck, Calhoun County Prosecutor, Dictated by M. P. Wood, Postal Inspector, August 23, 1967.

52. Michigan State Police Archives, Nola Puyear Murder, Search Results, Puyear Residence and Cabin, by Detective Robert Kenney, August 19, 1967, p. 3.

53. "Bombing Victim Funeral Rites Held This A.M.," *Marshall Evening Chronicle*, August 21, 1967.

54. Michigan State Police Archives, Nola Puyear Murder, Report, by Trooper Edward Wendry, Jonesville Post, August 22, 1967, pp. 1–5.

55. Michigan State Police Archives, Nola Puyear Murder, Calhoun County Sheriff's Complaint Report, Interview by Fred Ritchie and Leroy Steinbacher, September 12, 1967.

56. Michigan State Police Archives, Nola Puyear Murder, Memorandum of Interview, Enoch Chism, by Detective Leroy Steinbacher, Fred Ritchie, and M. P. Wood, Postal Inspector, August 28, 1967; "Chism Trial Enters Fourth Day: 'She Looked Up and Said Oh!' Before the Package Exploded, Witness Testifies at Trial," *Marshall Evening Chronicle*, January 23, 1970, 1, 8.

57. "Reward Offered in Puyear Bomb Case," *Marshall Evening Chronicle*, September 7, 1967.

58. Michigan State Police Archives, Nola Puyear Murder, Memorandum of Interview, by Detective Don Bennett, August 21, 1967, pp. 1–2.

59. Michigan State Police Archives, Nola Puyear Murder, Memorandum, Interview Conducted by John Jereck, Calhoun County Prosecutor, Dictated by M. P. Wood, Postal Inspector, August 23, 1967.

60. Michigan State Police Archives, Nola Puyear Murder, Memorandum of Interview, Nancy Church, by M. L. Myers and M. P. Wood, September 11, 1967.

61. Michigan State Police Archives, Nola Puyear Murder, Interview of Josie White, by M. L. Myers and M. P. Wood, Postal Inspectors, September 6, 1967.

62. Michigan State Police Archives, Nola Puyear Murder, Memorandum of Interview, Violet (Sene) Buckner, by M. P. Wood and M. L. Myers, Postal Inspectors, and Detectives Robert Kenney and Leroy Steinbacher, September 7, 1967.

63. Michigan State Police Archives, Nola Puyear Murder, Interview of Mrs. Violet Sene Buckner, by M. L. Myers and M. P. Wood, Postal Inspectors, September 7, 1967.

64. Michigan State Police Archives, Nola Puyear Murder, Report, by Robert Kenney, August 24, 1967.

65. Michigan State Police Archives, Nola Puyear Murder, Interview with Charles Quick and Curtis Fluker, Michigan State Public Health Lab, Criminal Division, by M. J. Reinhard, Postal Inspector, September 5, 1967.

66. Michigan State Police Archives, Nola Puyear Murder, Report, by Robert Kenney and Leroy Steinbacher, September 7, 1967, p. 1.

67. Michigan State Police Archives, Nola Puyear Murder, Memorandum of Interview, Denise Reish, by M. L. Myer, August 31, 1967.

68. Michigan State Police Archives, Nola Puyear Murder, Interview of Denise Reish, by M. P. Wood and M. J. Reinhard, Postal Inspectors, September 6, 1967.

69. Michigan State Police Archives, Nola Puyear Murder, Interview with Bruce Buckner, by Leroy Steinbacher, August 28, 1967.

70. Michigan State Police Archives, Nola Puyear Murder, Interview by Leroy Steinbacher and M. P. Wood, September 11, 1967.

71. Michigan State Police Archives, Nola Puyear Murder, Calhoun County Sheriff's Complaint Report, Interview by Fred Ritchie and Leroy Steinbacher, September 12, 1967; Postal Service, Memorandum of Interview, Josie White, September 6, 1967.

72. Michigan State Police Archives, Nola Puyear Murder, Memorandum of Interview, Paul Puyear, by M. P. Wood, September 1, 1967, p. 2.

73. Michigan State Police Archives, Nola Puyear Murder, Memorandum of Interview, Mrs. Joseph Warsop, by Postal Inspectors M. L. Myers and M. J. Reinhard, August 22, 1967.

74. Michigan State Police Archives, Nola Puyear Murder, Offense Report, Hutchins Cafe, Mrs. Phyllis Myers, August 18, 1967.

75. Michigan State Police Archives, Nola Puyear Murder, Interview of Mrs. Violet Sene Buckner, by M. L. Myers and M. P. Wood, Postal Inspectors, September 7, 1967.

76. Michigan State Police Archives, Nola Puyear Murder, Interview of Margaret Warsop, by M. P. Wood, Postal Inspector, and Robert Kenney, September 7, 1967.

77. Michigan State Police Archives, Nola Puyear Murder, Lie Detector Results, Paul and John Puyear, by Robert Kenney and M. P. Wood, Postal Inspector, September 6, 1967.

Chapter 4

1. Michigan State Police Archives, Nola Puyear Murder, Interview of Dr. Clarence M. Schier, Kalamazoo State Hospital, by Detective R. Kenney, August 29, 1967, p. 1.

2. Ibid.

3. Ibid., p. 2.

4. Defense Files, Notes from *Detroit News* Clippings.

5. William Beeson, "Open This Package and Die," *Inside Detective Magazine,* March 1968, 25.

6. Ibid.

7. Ibid.

8. Marshall Postal Museum staff, in discussion with author, May 2010.

9. "$2000 Reward Offered in Puyear Bomb Case," *Marshall Evening Chronicle,* September 7, 1967, 1.

10. Michigan State Police Archives, Nola Puyear Murder, Report filed by Leroy Steinbacher, August 8, 1967.

11. Michigan State Police Archives, Nola Puyear Murder, Report filed by Robert Kenney, September 14, 1967.

12. Michigan State Police Archives, Nola Puyear Murder, Report filed by Leroy Steinbacher, September 12, 1967.

13. Michigan State Police Archives, Nola Puyear Murder, Results of Interview, Mr. Richard Galloway, by M. P. Wood and Myron Myers, September 8, 1967.

14. Paul Gainor, "Writing Studied in the Hunt for Killer," *Detroit News,* September 14, 1967.

15. Ibid.

16. James Stewart-Gordon, "Secret Witness in the War on Crime," *Rotarian,* November 1971, 25.

17. Robert M. D'Arcy, "*News* Secret Witnesses Help Nab 5 Suspects," *Detroit News,* September 24, 1967.

18. Report by Robert Kenney, September 21, 1967, News Release.

19. Michigan State Police Archives, Nola Puyear Murder, Interview with Margaret Warsop, by Detective Robert Kenney, October 4, 1967, p. 2.

20. Michigan State Police Archives, Nola Puyear Murder, Personality Assessment from the Handwriting—from the Pill Parcel in the *Enquirer* and in *News,* September 21, 1967.

21. Ronald DeGraw, in discussions with author, April 2011; Shirley Lawcock, in discussion with author, March 2011; Report Filed by M. P. Wood. Interviewing Officers, Fred Ritchie and M. P. Wood.

22. The name of the secret witness in this case, DeGraw, is being revealed for the first time in this book.

Chapter 5

1. Fred Ritchie, in discussions with author, March 2011.

2. Confidential source, in discussion with author, April 2011.

3. Herold Reuss, in discussions with author, February 2011.

4. Defense Files, Enoch Chism v. People of Michigan.

5. John Carroll, in discussions with author, March 2011.

6. State of Michigan, Circuit Court for the County of Calhoun, People of the State of Michigan v. Enoch Chism, Docket No. 21-447, Finding, pp. 1–3.

7. Ibid.

8. State of Michigan, Circuit Court for the County of Calhoun, People of the State of Michigan v. Enoch Chism, Docket No. 21-447, Motion to Excuse Defendant, pp. 1–2.

9. State of Michigan, Circuit Court for the County of Calhoun, People of the State of Michigan v. Enoch Chism, Docket No. 21-447, Finding, pp. 3–4.

10. Ibid., p. 4.

11. State of Michigan, Circuit Court for the County of Calhoun, People of the State of Michigan v. Enoch Chism, Docket No. 21-447, Notice of Alibi, pp. 1–2.

12. State of Michigan, Circuit Court for the County of Calhoun, People of the

State of Michigan v. Enoch Chism, Docket No. 21-447, Transcript of Sentence, April 5, 1966, pp. 2–4.

13. Ibid., p. 4.

14. Herold Reuss and Fred Ritchie, in discussions with author, February 2011.

15. Calhoun County Sheriff's Office, Duty Log, May 21, 1965; Defense Files, Enoch Chism v. People of Michigan; Fred Ritchie, in discussion with author, April 2011.

16. Calhoun County Sheriff's Office, Duty Log, August 24, 1965; Defense Files, Enoch Chism v. People of Michigan.

17. Michigan State Police Archives, Nola Puyear Murder, Calhoun County Sheriff's Report, Interview with Neil Finley, Probation Officer for Enoch Chism, by Sergeant Fred Ritchie, October 6, 1967, p. 1

18. Ibid.

19. Ibid.

20. Ibid, p. 3.

21. Ibid. The file lists Enoch's dismissal date as July 30, 1967, but the report is laid out chronologically. Given that he took on other full-time jobs after July 30, 1966, it is logical that this is merely a typo.

22. Michigan State Police Archives, Nola Puyear Murder, Calhoun County Sheriff's Report, Interview with Neil Finley, Probation Officer for Enoch Chism, by Sergeant Fred Ritchie, October 5, 1967, p. 2.

Chapter 6

1. Chism's employment application, Clark Equipment. Genealogist Jean Armstrong constructed the Chism family tree.

2. Defense Files, Enoch Chism v. People of Michigan, Report of L. Harold Caviness, May 25, 1965, p. 1.

3. Calhoun County Circuit Court, Divorce Filing, Bernice L. Chism v. Enoch D. Chism, May 26, 1965.

4. Defense Files, Enoch Chism v. People of Michigan, Report of L. Harold Caviness, May 25, 1965, p. 1.

5. These comments were obtained by the author through several interviews, many impromptu, with individuals who claimed to have known Chism. One person approached me at a book signing in Battle Creek for my book *Lost Eagles* and commented, "I worked with Enoch and found him to be disturbed." She did not provide her name, but her comments were in line with other comments people contributed.

6. Michigan State Police Archives, Nola Puyear Murder, Report, by Detectives Steinbacher and Kenney, October 11, 1967, pp. 1–2.

7. Defense Files, Enoch Chism v. People of Michigan, Report of L. Harold Caviness, May 25, 1965, p. 1.

8. Ibid.

9. Michigan State Police Archives, Nola Puyear Murder, Calhoun County Sheriff's Report, Interview with Josie White, by Sergeant Dean and Postal Inspector Myers, October 11, 1967.

10. Ibid.

11. Michigan State Police Archives, Nola Puyear Murder, Interview with Ronald DeGraw, by M. P. Wood, Detective Robert Kenney, and M. W. Hammond, October 17, 1967, p. 1.

12. Ibid.

13. Calhoun County Circuit Court, Divorce Filing, Bernice L. Chism v. Enoch D. Chism, May 26, 1965; Preliminary Injunction, August 25, 1965, pp. 1–2.

14. Ibid.

15. Ibid.

16. Ibid.

17. Defense Files, Enoch Chism v. People of Michigan, Report of L. Harold Caviness, Admission and Treatment, May 12, 1965, p. 1.

18. Ibid., p. 2.

19. Defense Files, Enoch Chism v. People of Michigan, Report of Doctor Karl Kadlub, Admission and Treatment, May 25, 1965, p. 2.

20. Ibid.

21. Defense Files, Enoch Chism v. People of Michigan, Report of L. Harold Caviness, Admission and Treatment, May 21, 1965, p. 3.

22. Ibid.

23. Defense Files, Enoch Chism vs. People of Michigan, Report of L. Harold Caviness, Admission and Treatment, May–June, 1965, p. 4.

24. Defense Files, Enoch Chism v. People of Michigan, Report of L. Harold Caviness, Admission and Treatment, June–July, 1965, p. 6.

25. Ibid., p. 7.

26. Ibid.

27. Calhoun County Circuit Court, Divorce Filing, Bernice L. Chism v. Enoch D. Chism, May 26, 1965; Preliminary Injunction, August 25, 1965, pp. 1–2.

28. Michigan State Police Archives, Nola Puyear Murder, Calhoun County Sheriff's Report, Interview with Neil Finley, Probation Officer for Enoch Chism, by Sergeant Fred Ritchie, October 5, 1967, p. 1.

29. Ibid.

30. Fred Ritchie, in discussions with author, April 2011.

31. Michigan State Police Archives, Nola Puyear Murder, Calhoun County Sheriff's Report, Interview with Neil Finley, Probation Officer for Enoch Chism, by Sergeant Fred Ritchie, October 5, 1967, p. 2. The file lists Enoch's dismissal date as July 30, 1967, but the report is laid out chronologically. Given that he took on other full-time jobs after July 30, 1966, it is logical that this is merely a typo.

32. Ibid., p. 3.

Chapter 7

1. Michigan State Police Archives, Nola Puyear Murder, Calhoun County Sheriff's Report, Chain of Evidence Discussion with Betty Kedo and Ellen Palmer, by Sergeant Fred Ritchie, October 2, 1967.

2. Michigan State Police Archives, Nola Puyear Murder, Interviews with Charloe Gill, k and James Herman, by Detectives Kenney and Steinbacher, October 4, 1967, p. 1.

3. Ibid.

4. Michigan State Police Archives, Nola Puyear Murder, Report, by Detectives Kenney and Steinbacher and Postal Inspector M. P. Wood, September 27, 1967.

5. Michigan State Police Archives, Nola Puyear Murder, Interview with Ronald DeGraw, by M. P. Wood, Detective Robert Kenney, and M. W. Hammond, October 17, 1967, p. 1.

6. Ronald DeGraw, in discussions with author, April 2011.

7. Michigan State Police Archives, Nola Puyear Murder, Interview with Ronald DeGraw, by M. P. Wood, Detective Robert Kenney, and M. W. Hammond, October 17, 1967, p. 2.

8. Ibid.

9. Ronald DeGraw, in discussions with author, April 2011.

10. Michigan State Police Archives, Nola Puyear Murder, Conference Report, by Detective Kenney and Sergeant Ritchie, October 3, 1967.

11. John Lohrstorfer, in discussions with author, 2009.

12. Michigan State Police Archives, Nola Puyear Murder, Conference Report, by Detectives Kenney and Steinbacher, October 10, 1967.

13. Michigan State Police Archives, Nola Puyear Murder, Calhoun County Sheriff's Complaint Report, Arrest of Enoch Chism, by Sergeant Ritchie and Detective Steinbacher, October 11, 1967.

14. John Lohrstorfer, in discussions with author, 2009.

15. Ibid.

16. Michigan State Police Archives, Nola Puyear Murder, Calhoun County Sheriff's Complaint Report, Arrest of Enoch Chism, by Sergeant Ritchie and Detective Steinbacher, October 11, 1967.

17. Michigan State Police Archives, Nola Puyear Murder, Investigation on 10–11–67, by Detectives Steinbacher and Kenney and Sergeant Ritchie, October 12, 1967.

18. Ibid.

19. Ibid.

20. Ibid.

21. Michigan State Police Archives, Nola Puyear Murder, Arrest of Enoch Chism, WALM Morning News Script.

22. *Marshall Evening Chronicle,* October 11, 1967, 1.

23. "Examination of Enoch D. Chism Scheduled for 9:30 am," *Marshall Evening Chronicle*, October 12, 1967, 1.

24. Michigan State Police Archives, Nola Puyear Murder, Interview of Paul Puyear, by Detective Kenney, October 16, 1967.

Chapter 8

1. Michigan State Police Archives, Nola Puyear Murder, Interview with Enoch Chism, by Detectives Steinbacher and Kenney, October 11, 1967, p. 1.

2. Michigan State Police Archives, Nola Puyear Murder, Mrs. Enoch Chism Interview, by Detective Leroy Steinbacher, October 12, 1967, p. 1.

3. Ibid., pp. 1–2.

4. Michigan State Police Archives, Nola Puyear Murder, Calhoun County Sheriff's Additional Complaint Report, by Sergeant Ritchie, October 11, 1967, p. 3.

5. Fred Ritchie, in discussions with author, February 2011.

6. Michigan State Police Archives, Nola Puyear Murder, Mrs. Enoch Chism Interview, by Detective Leroy Steinbacher, October 12, 1967, pp. 1–2; Michigan State Police Archives, Nola Puyear Murder, Calhoun County Sheriff's Additional Complaint Report, by Sergeant Ritchie, October 11, 1967, p. 2.

7. Michigan State Police Archives, Nola Puyear Murder, Mrs. Enoch Chism Interview, by Detective Leroy Steinbacher, October 12, 1967, p. 2.

8. Ibid.; Michigan State Police Archives, Nola Puyear Murder, Calhoun County Sheriff's Additional Complaint Report, by Sergeant Ritchie, October 11, 1967, p. 3.

9. Ibid.

10. Michigan State Police Archives, Nola Puyear Murder, Photography Report, by Detective Groop, October 11, 1967, pp. 1–3.

11. John Jereck, in discussions with author, 2010.

12. Michigan State Police Archives, Nola Puyear Murder, Photography Report, by Detective Groop, October 11, 1967, pp. 1–3.

13. Ibid.

14. John Jereck, in discussions with author, 2010.

15. Michigan State Police Archives, Nola Puyear Murder, Photography Report, by Detective Groop, October 11, 1967, pp. 1–3.

16. Michigan State Police Archives, Nola Puyear Murder, Interview with Enoch Chism, by Detectives Steinbacher and Kenney, October 11, 1967, p. 2.

17. Michigan State Police Archives, Nola Puyear Murder, Calhoun County Sheriff's Additional Complaint Report, by Sergeant Ritchie, October 11, 1967, pp. 2–3.

18. Ibid., p. 3.

19. Michigan State Police Archives, Nola Puyear Murder, Calhoun County Sheriff's Additional Complaint Report, Interview with Josie White, by Sergeant Dean and Inspector Myers, October 11, 1967, p. 1.

20. Ibid.

21. Ibid.

22. Ibid., pp. 1–2.

23. Ibid., p. 2.

24. Ibid.

25. Michigan State Police Archives, Nola Puyear Murder, Calhoun County Sheriff's Additional Complaint Report, by Sergeant Ritchie and Detective Steinbacher, October 17, 1967, p. 1.

26. Michigan State Police Archives, Nola Puyear Murder, Calhoun County Sheriff's Additional Complaint Report, by Sergeant Ritchie and Detective Steinbacher, October 12, 1967, p. 1.

27. Ibid.

28. Michigan State Police Archives, Nola Puyear Murder, Report, by Kenney and Steinbacher, August 18, 1968.

29. Ibid.

30. Michigan State Police Archives, Nola Puyear Murder, Calhoun County Sheriff's Additional Complaint Report, Interview with Enoch Chism, by Sergeant Ritchie and Detective Kenney, October 13, 1967, pp. 1–2.

31. Ibid.

32. Ibid.

33. Ibid.

34. Michigan State Police Archives, Nola Puyear Murder, Memorandum of Interview, Enoch Chism, by M. P. Wood and Detective Robert Kenney, October 16, 1967.

35. Ibid.

36. Ibid.

37. Ronald DeGraw, in discussions with author, April 2011.

Chapter 9

1. Michigan State Police Archives, Nola Puyear Murder, Memorandum of Interview, Enoch Chism, by M. P. Wood and Detective Robert Kenney, October 16, 1967.

2. "Judge Coleman Reserves His Decision on Appointment of Counsel of Enoch D. Chism," *Marshall Evening Chronicle,* October 19, 1967, 1.

3. John Jereck, in discussions with author, 2010.

4. "Judge Coleman Reserves His Decision on Appointment of Counsel," 1.

5. "Chism Signs Property Over to His Wife," *Marshall Evening Chronicle,* October 25, 1967, 1.

6. Ibid., 8.

7. "Numerous Witnesses Called in Examination of Enoch Chism," *Marshall Evening Chronicle,* November 17, 1968, 1.

8. Michigan State Police Archives, Nola Puyear Murder, Michigan State Police Complaint Report, Examination of Enoch Chism, by Detectives Kenney and Steinbacher, November 17, 1967, p. 1.

9. Ibid., p. 2.

10. "Chism Bound Over to County Circuit Court," *Marshall Evening Chronicle,* November 24, 1967, 1.

11. Fred Ritchie, in discussions with author, February 2011.

12. Confidential source, in discussion with author, December 3, 2010.

13. Stan Kaufman, "Chism Wins Battle for His Freedom," *Battle Creek Enquirer and News,* April 20, 1976. The trial transcripts for the Chism case have been lost. The author was forced to reconstruct the pretrial and posttrial motions through newspaper articles and the scant few court records that remain.

14. Michigan State Police Archives, Nola Puyear Murder, Report of Hearing on Neutron Activation Analysis, by Detective Kenney, December 1, 1967.

15. Calhoun County, Divorce Filing, Bernice Chism v. Enoch Chism, July 14, 1969.

16. "Mail Bomb Suspect Waits and Waits for Trial," *Detroit News,* November 23, 1969, 11B.

Chapter 10

1. John Jereck, in discussions with author, 2010.

2. Ibid.

3. Fred Ritchie, in discussions with author, March 2010.

4. Bert Schulz, in discussions with author, March 2010.

5. Defense Files, Enoch Chism v. People of Michigan, Court Order, by Creighton Coleman, January 20, 1970.

6. "In Chism Trial, Judge Explains New Method of Jury Selection," *Marshall Evening Chronicle,* January 23, 1969, 1, 7.

7. Ibid.

8. Kenney family members, in discussions with author, 2009.

9. "In Chism Trial, Judge Explains New Method of Jury Selection," 1.

10. Ibid.; Defense Files, Enoch Chism v. People of Michigan, Script of Opening Statement by W. Reed Orr.

11. Ibid.

12. Ibid.

13. "In Chism Trial, Judge Explains New Method of Jury Selection," 7.

14. Ibid.

15. Ibid.

16. Ibid. Almost all of the official photographs associated with the crime scene have been lost, along with the trial transcripts for this case.

17. "Chism Trial Enters Fourth Day: 'She Looked Up and Said Oh!' Before the Package Exploded, Witness Testifies at Trial," *Marshall Evening Chronicle,* January 23, 1970, 1.

18. Ibid.

19. Ibid., 7.

20. Ibid.

21. Ibid., 1.

22. "Chism May Have Been Interested in Cafe, Prosecution Contends," *Marshall Evening Chronicle*, January 23, 1970, 1.

23. "Chism Victim Had 'Unpleasant' Talk, Witness Reports," *Battle Creek Enquirer and News*, January 24, 1970, 1.

24. Ibid.

25. "Chism May Have Been Interested in Cafe," 8.

26. "Chism, Victim Had 'Unpleasant' Talk," 1.

27. "Chism May Have Been Interested in Cafe," 1.

28. "Chism Trial Enters Fourth Day," 1.

29. "Chism, Victim Had 'Unpleasant' Talk," 2.

30. Ibid.

31. Fred Ritchie, in discussion with author, March 2010.

32. Defense Files, C. Michael Hoffman, Credentials as a Professional Witness.

33. "Chism's Handwriting Identified," *Battle Creek Enquirer and News*, January 27, 1970, 1.

34. Ibid.; "Prosecution Slated to Close Case against Chism Today," *Marshall Evening Chronicle*, January 28, 1970, 1.

35. "Prosecution Slated to Close Case against Chism," 1.

36. "Prosecution Calls First Expert Witness to Testify in Trial," *Marshall Evening Chronicle*, January 27, 1970, 1.

37. "Chism's Handwriting Identified," 1.

38. Ibid.

39. Ibid.

40. "Prosecution Slated to Close Case against Chism," 1.

41. John Jereck, in discussions with author, 2010.

42. "Prosecution Calls First Expert Witness to Testify," 8.

43. Ibid.; "Daughter Identifies Chism's Writing," *Battle Creek Enquirer and News*, January 27, 1970, 1.

44. Confidential source, in discussion with author, May 2010, July 2010. In discussions with author, John Jereck, July 2010, said that he was unaware that Enoch was threatening him. There is also no report of anyone in the jury seeing Enoch mouth that threat.

Chapter 11

1. "Chism Takes Stand and Denies Connection with Making Bomb," *Marshall Evening Chronicle*, January 29, 1970, 1; Defense Files, Enoch Chism v. People of Michigan, Proposed Questions of Mr. Chism.

2. Ibid.

3. Ibid.

4. Ibid.

5. Ibid.

6. "Chism Case Goes to Jury," *Battle Creek Enquirer and News,* January 29, 1970, 1.

7. "Chism Takes Stand and Denies Connection," 7.

8. "Chism Case Goes to Jury," 1.

9. Ibid.

10. "Chism Takes Stand and Denies Connection," 7.

11. Ibid.

12. John Jereck, in discussions with author, 2010. Jereck admitted that he knew of Enoch's experience using dynamite but that the sources for that were not entirely reliable. The count of the missing dynamite was never brought out in the trial.

13. "Chism Case Goes to Jury," 1.

14. Ibid.

15. "Experts Disagree in Trial," *Battle Creek Enquirer and News,* January 28, 1970, 2.

16. Ibid.

17. "Chism Takes Stand and Denies Connection," 7.

18. Ibid.

19. "Fate of Enoch D. Chism Now in Hands of Calhoun Jury," *Marshall Evening Chronicle,* January 30, 1970, 1.

20. Ibid.

21. Ibid.

22. Ibid.

23. Ibid.

24. Ibid.

25. Ibid., 7.

26. Ibid.

27. Ibid.

28. Ibid.

29. Ibid.

30. Ibid.

31. "Chism Deemed Certain to Appeal First Degree Murder Conviction," *Battle Creek Enquirer and News,* January 31, 1970, 1.

32. "Chism Found Guilty by Jury," *Marshall Evening Chronicle,* January 31, 1970, 1–2.

33. Two jurors, in discussion with author, July 2010. Both have asked to not have their names printed in this book.

34. Juror, in discussion with author.

35. Defense Files, Enoch Chism v. People of Michigan.

36. "Chism Deemed Certain to Appeal," 1.
37. Ibid.
38. "Chism Found Guilty by Jury," 1–2.
39. "Chism Deemed Certain to Appeal," 1.
40. Ibid.
41. Ibid.
42. Ibid.
43. "Chism Gets Mandatory Life Sentence; Taken to Prison," *Battle Creek Enquirer and News,* February 5, 1970, 1.
44. Ibid.
45. Ibid.
46. Ibid.
47. Ronald DeGraw, in discussions with author, April 2011; Shirley Lawcock, in discussion with author, March 2011.

Chapter 12

1. Court Filings, Nos. 75-1989, 75-1990, Enoch D. Chism, Petitioner v. Theodore Koehler, April 18, 1975.
2. Ibid.
3. Ibid.; Defense Files, Enoch Chism v. People of Michigan, Appeals Folder.
4. John Jereck, in discussions with author, 2010; two jurors, July 2010; and Bert Schulz, in discussions with author, March 2011; "Jurors Have Mixed Reaction to Chism's Impending Release," *Battle Creek Enquirer and News,* April 30, 1976, in Defense Files, Enoch Chism v. People of Michigan.
5. Calhoun County, Divorce Filing, Bernice Chism v. Enoch Chism, July 14, 1969.
6. Bert Schulz, in discussion with author, March 2011.
7. Court Filings, Nos. 75-1989, 75-1990, Enoch D. Chism, Petitioner v. Theodore Koehler, April 18, 1975; "Rae Participates in Chism Hearing," *Battle Creek Enquirer and News,* date unknown, in Defense Files, Enoch Chism v. People of Michigan.
8. "Chism Wins Battle for His Freedom," *Battle Creek Enquirer and News,* April 20, 1976, 2.
9. Ibid.
10. "Jurors Have Mixed Reaction to Chism's Impending Release."
11. Ibid.
12. Michigan State Police Archives, Nola Puyear Murder, Telefax—Nola Puyear Case File, April 30, 1976.

Chapter 13

1. John Lohrstorfer, in discussions with author, 2009.
2. Ibid.
3. Fred Ritchie, in discussions with author, March 2011.
4. Ronald DeGraw, in discussions with author, April 2011.
5. John Lohrstorfer, in discussions with author, 2009; John Jereck, in discussion with author, July 2010.
6. Battle Creek Fire Department, FM-18A Fire Incident Report, by Captain James S. Newburn.
7. Ibid.
8. Ibid.
9. Ibid.
10. Ibid.; John Jereck, in discussions with author, 2010.
11. John Jereck, in discussions with author, 2010.
12. Bert Schulz, in discussions with author, March 2011.
13. Fred Ritchie, in discussions with author, March 2011.
14. Calhoun County Circuit Court Records, Court Filing, Arrest of Enoch Chism, June 29, 1977.
15. "Freed Convict Enoch Chism Back in County Custody for Robbery," *Marshall Evening Chronicle,* June 29, 1977, 1.
16. Albion Public Library, Obituary File, Enoch Chism, January 18, 1979.

About the Author

Blaine Pardoe was raised outside of Battle Creek, Michigan, and earned his bachelor's and master's degrees from Central Michigan University. He is the author of over fifty books on a variety of subjects, from science fiction novels to best-selling works on business management. He is best known as a historian, authoring several highly received books, including *Terror of the Autumn Skies: The True Story of Frank Luke, America's Rogue Ace of World War I* and *The Cruise of the Sea Eagle: The Amazing True Story of Imperial Germany's Gentleman Pirate.* This is his second book dealing with Michigan history, the first being the widely acclaimed *Lost Eagles: One Man's Mission to Find Missing Airmen in Two World Wars.*

Blaine lives in Virginia, outside of Washington, DC. During his "day job," he works for Ernst & Young LLP as an associate director. He has a wife, Cyndi; a son, Alexander; a daughter, Victoria; and a grandson, Trenton. The rest of his family still lives in and around Calhoun County, Michigan.

Secret Witness is his first true crime book. He is currently working on a book about the Daisy Zick murder in 1963. He can be reached at bpardoe870@aol.com or via his website: www.blainepardoe.com.

Printed and bound by CPI Group (UK) Ltd, Croydon, CR0 4YY

13/04/2025

14656529-0001